NEW DEFENCE STRATE

Also by Philip Webber

CRISIS OVER CRUISE: A Plain Guide to the New Weapons
  (*with Graeme Wilkinson and Barry Rubin*)
LONDON AFTER THE BOMB: What a Nuclear Attack Really Means
  (*with Owen Greene, Barry Rubin, Neil Turok and Graeme Wilkinson*)

and contributions to:

THE MILITARISATION OF SPACE
(*edited by Stephen Kirby and Gordon Robson*)
SOMETHING IN THE WIND: Politics after Chernobyl
(*edited by Louis Mackay and Mark Thompson*)

New Defence Strategies for the 1990s

From Confrontation to Coexistence

Philip Webber

MACMILLAN

First published 1990

Published by
MACMILLAN ACADEMIC AND PROFESSIONAL LTD
Houndmills, Basingstoke, Hampshire RG21 2XS
and London
Companies and representatives
throughout the world

Printed in Great Britain by WBC Ltd., Bridgend

British Library Cataloguing in Publication Data
Webber, Philip
New defence strategies for the 1990s: from confrontation
to coexistence.
1. Western Europe. Military policies
I. Title
355'.0335'4
ISBN 0–333–53596–0 (hardcover)
ISBN 0–333–53597–9 (paperback)

To Halina and Matthew

Contents

List of Figures

List of Tables

List of Boxes

Acknowledgements

I thank Hugh Beach, Paul Eavis, Richard Erskine, Owen Greene, Shaun Gregory, Patrick Litherland, Bjørn Møller, Jane Shilling and Halina Webber for reading part or all of the text at various stages of drafting and for helpful editorial or technical suggestions and comments. Some (anonymous) publishers' reader's comments also helped me to develop some of my arguments, I thank them too.

Special thanks to Jane Shilling for guiding me through the literary jungle to my eventual destination.

I thank all those associated with the book's production, particularly Elizabeth Black, Belinda Dutton and Keith Povey.

I gratefully acknowledge Hunting Engineering for provision of a photograph of the JP233 weapons system and MLRS International Corporation for photographs of the Multiple-Launch Rocket System and the Army Tactical Missile System (ATACMS).

Philip Webber

List of Abbreviations

ABM	anti-ballistic missile
ACM	advanced cruise missile
ALARM	air-launched anti-radiation (radar) missile
ATACMS	attack missile system
ATI	advanced technology international
AWACS	Airborne Warning and Command System
C3I	command, control, communications and intelligence
CDI	conventional defence(improvements)
CDII	conventional defence improvements initiative
CENTAG	Central Army Group
CFE	Conventional Armed Forces in Europe
CNAD	Conference of NATO Armaments Directors
CND	Campaign for Nuclear Disarmament
DEFCON	Defence Condition (US alert state)
DIA	Defence Intelligence Agency
DOBS	dispersed operating bases
DPC	Defence Planning Committee (NATO)
DRG	Defence Research Group
EFA	European Fighter Aircraft
EMP	electromagnetic pulse
EPG	European production group
ESECS	European security study
ET	emerging technology
EUCOM	European High Command
FEBA	forward edge of the battle area
FLOT	front line of own troops
FOFA	follow-on forces attack
GIUK	Greenland–Iceland–UK
HARM	homing anti-radiation (radar) missile
ICBM	intercontinental ballistics missile
IDEA	International Defense Electronics Association
IEPG	Independent European Production Group

IFF	identification friend or foe
IISS	International Institute for Strategic Studies
INF	Intermediate Nuclear Forces
JSTARS	Joint Surveillance Target Attack Radar System
JTACMS	Joint Tactical Missile System
LADS	low altitude dispenser system
LERTCON	alert condition (NATO)
MDTT	Martin Marietta, Diehl, Thomson-CSF and Thorn EMI (consortium)
MIFF	Mine Flach Flach (anti-tank mine)
MLRS	multiple-launch rocket system
MOBS	main operating bases
MSOW	modular stand-off weapon
MUSA/MUSPA	Multi-splitter active (fragmentation mine)
NAPR	National Armament Planning Review
NIAG	NATO Industrial Advisory Group
NORTHAG	Northern Army Group
OMG	operational manoeuvre group
PAPS	Periodic Armaments Planning System
PGM	precision-guided missile
POMCUS	pre-positioned matériel configured to unit sets
SACEUR	Supreme Allied Commander European Forces
SADARM	'Sense and Destroy Armour' Munition
SAID	Strategic Arms Initiative for Disposal
SAL	State of the Art Limited
SAS	Study Group on Alternative Security Policy
SDI	Strategic Defence Initiative
SDIO	Strategic Defence Initiative Office
SIPRI	Stockholm International Peace Research Institute
SLCM	Sea-launched cruise missile
SOUTHAG	Southern Army Group
SRAM	short-range attack missile
SRINF	shorter-range intermediate forces
STABO	start bahn bombe (airfield attack munition)
START	Strategic Arms Reduction Treaty
STOL	short take-off and landing
TASM	tactical air-to-surface missile

TGW	terminally guided warhead
TMSA	Technical Marketing Society of America
VHSIC	very high-speed integrated circuits
VSTOL	vertical/short take-off and landing
WEU	Western European Union

Si Pacem Vis, Para Bellum
If you want peace prepare for war
(Vegetius – 4th century AD)
An inappropriate saying from the first millennium

Introduction

The twenty-three member countries of NATO and the Warsaw Pact spend around $600 000 000 000 (600 billion) a year in a huge concentration of military power in and around Europe. This is slightly more than *one million dollars a minute*. And the spending is not just money. The cost is valuable resources and human creative effort. It is the efforts of some 40 per cent of scientists and engineers. Large amounts of rare and precious materials. It diverts effort and money from other domestic needs and urgent global problems.

But what is all this effort for? With the thaw in East–West relations and a succession of revolutionary changes in Eastern Europe, is this effort really necessary to keep Europe from war? Or could it be the *cause* of war in Europe?

Leading politicians and authorities are now accepting that the Cold War is over.[1] International relations between the two superpower blocs, NATO and the Warsaw Pact, are now in a state of unprecedented flux characterised by new uncertainties, challenges and opportunities.

The astonishing speed and momentum of change in the former eastern bloc states, Poland, Hungary, Czechoslovakia, East Germany and Romania, calls into question the very notion of an eastern bloc itself. National identities and differences are now very much more important.

New East–West talks are in progress, discussing cuts in conventional and nuclear arms. New economic and social pressures combining with the superpowers' increasingly limited ability to influence world affairs are forcing both to seriously reconsider their fundamental strategies.

In this book I argue that NATO and the Warsaw Pact have a historic opportunity to stabilise their potentially disastrous confrontation in Europe and to reduce military spending drastically. However, to get the arms race under control and to assure lasting security, arms cuts resulting from the new arms talks will not be sufficient. Such an achievement will require both East and West to adopt significantly new thinking about some perennial security problems.

This book explains why new thinking is needed in defence, and introduces and argues the case for a complete practical package of military reforms and restructuring together with the associated political

1

adjustments needed for the new idea to gain acceptance. The new idea is 'defensive deterrence'.

WHY ARMS CONTROL IS NOT ENOUGH

There are two new major arms reduction negotiations in progress:

1. The START talks (STrategic nuclear Arms Reduction Talks) are aimed at reducing the numbers of strategic nuclear weapons deployed by the USSR and USA worldwide by about 30 per cent.
2. The CFE (Conventional Forces in Europe) negotiations have the goal of eliminating 'the capability for launching surprise attack and for initiating large-scale offensive action' and eliminating 'disparity [in numbers of forces] prejudicial for stability and security'.[2]

While success in these talks would be a major advance, major threats to security and stability would still remain.

The START Talks

START cuts would still leave the USA and Soviet Union with over 6000 long-range nuclear warheads each. Many more thousands of additional warheads on shorter-range missiles and bombs, not covered by these talks, would still remain. French, British, Chinese and strategic nuclear warheads possessed by other countries are also not covered.

Yet only 1000 nuclear warheads could devastate civilisation in the Northern Hemisphere and probably initiate severe global cooling – the so-called 'nuclear winter'.[3] To reduce just the US and Soviet strategic nuclear warheads to these levels, ignoring for the moment all the other warheads, would require *eight* consecutive START cuts without the build-up in the meantime of any other systems.

The sheer amount of nuclear reductions needed illustrates how far the nuclear arms race has progressed – if 'progressed' is the right word – beyond the numbers of weapons to assure mutual destruction.

It should also not be forgotten that very large stocks of deadly chemical weapons, sometimes called 'the poor man's nuclear bomb', are held by nineteen or more countries, many in the developing world.

The CFE Talks

The agreed Mandate for the CFE talks excludes nuclear weapons (the talks also do not consider naval forces, but these are the subject of some other negotiations in Stockholm).[4] Some nuclear systems are covered, via the back door as it were, in that some of the conventional weapons systems subject to negotiation are 'dual-capable' (for example, planes or artillery which can fire nuclear weapons). The Pact and many nations in NATO would have preferred to include short-range nuclear systems in the CFE talks too, but moves to have nuclear weapons included in the Mandate were successfully resisted, chiefly by Western Europe's three nuclear powers, France, the UK and the USA.

Omission of nuclear systems from the CFE talks is a fundamental flaw, because it undermines the goal expressed in the CFE Mandate of eliminating the 'capacity for surprise attack . . . large-scale offensive action' and force disparities 'prejudicial to stability and security'. These are fine goals, but as I argue in Chapter 1, it is hard to conceive of systems which are more destabilising and capable of surprise attack than many of the shorter-range nuclear weapons deployed in Europe. Longer-range strategic nuclear weapons are specifically *designed* to be capable of 'large-scale' 'offensive' action. A mere ten warheads of the larger sizes in the US, French, UK or Soviet arsenals have a combined firepower of 10Mt, equivalent to 10 million tons of TNT high explosive, a destructive power greater than the total expended by all combatants in the five years of the Second World War.

Turning to purely conventional arms, which *are* covered in the CFE talks, the major NATO emphasis is upon achieving very major cuts in Warsaw Pact forces to bring them down to NATO force numbers. Initially, relatively small cuts to NATO forces are envisaged. However cuts in forces are not the same thing as removing a surprise-attack capability or a capability for launching large-scale 'offensive' action. The military of both NATO and the Warsaw Pact insist that an offensive capability is absolutely vital as part of a defensive strategy. Neither NATO nor the Warsaw Pact are going to negotiate away all their tanks and strike aircraft. Even if they did, 'offensive' action could still be achieved with infantry, as in the World War of 1914–18.

A second-stage CFE agreement could mean cuts of up to 50 per cent in NATO and Warsaw Pact forces. Only at this stage could appreciable expenditure be saved by NATO countries. But if cuts occur and NATO and Warsaw Pact forces remain broadly similar to the forces which exist now, stability could actually be decreased. NATO could argue that with half the present forces they could not cover the long front line, and that manoeuvrable Soviet divisions could break through and outflank their forward defensive lines. To underline this fear, both NATO and the Pact would still possess some 10 000 tanks each, over twice the 3–4000 that were deployed by Hitler in the Eastern front and which reached the very gates of Moscow fighting much larger Soviet forces.

Box I.1   Flaws in the INF Agreement

The INF agreement covers the destruction of 2695 nuclear launch systems east and west – about 8 per cent of a world total of about 37 000 nuclear-capable launch systems. However, none of the 3995 warheads carried on these systems have to be destroyed. The warheads are removed and may be re-used in other nuclear weapons.
    The USA, the UK, France and West Germany have already discussed new designs of air- and sea-launched missiles specifically intended for deployment and to 'compensate' for (that is, to reduce the military impact of) the INF removals.
    The US Department of Defense Report to Congress for Fiscal Year 1989 refers to these Western missile developments as 'force adjustments' necessary after the INF Treaty to maintain a 'full range of [nuclear] flexible response options'.[5]

DEFENSIVE DETERRENCE

This book argues the case for defensive deterrence in three sections. Part I argues that an alternative security policy is urgently required which is not reliant upon large numbers of nuclear weapons. Part II discusses the present resources and management of NATO, and in the process looks at some of the powerful national, bureaucratic and industrial forces which strongly influence NATO decision-making. Part III, Chapters 4 and 5, examines whether NATO could in fact stand up to hostile Warsaw Pact conventional attack and describes the phenomenon of threat exaggeration. In Chapters 6 and 7, I propose a detailed reorganisation and financing of NATO's current military resources in a reformed military strategy of defensive deterrence. Finally, Part IV discusses the political changes necessary for such change to come about and presents an agenda for military reform towards AD 2000.

I acknowledge that forces capable of retaliation (including nuclear weapons) have a deterrent capability, but the intention in defensive deterrence is to remove forces likely to be perceived as highly offensive or those designed to be used first in a conflict. This implies the removal of particularly destabilising nuclear weapons capable of incorporation in nuclear war-fighting strategies.

A major element of the military reforms proposed in defensive deterrence concerns conventional arms. The possibilities of more defensive tactics and new, cheaper, precision-guided weapons, combined with military reforms, open up a great opportunity to reduce military budgets whilst increasing security. This can be achieved by reductions in offensive forces such as strike aircraft and tanks to pay for large numbers of cheaper and more defensively effective anti-tank and anti-aircraft weapons together with other defensive measures. This addresses the classic arguments that nuclear weapons are so much cheaper than conventional forces, and that better conventional forces inevitably mean larger, unaffordable defence budgets. To give one pertinent example, one all-weather strike aircraft such as the Panavia Tornado or the US F–15E costs around $42 million and its pilot and navigator cost an additional $8 million to train; there are further costs tied up in highly trained ground crew and maintenance. One missile, such as the US Hawk, capable of shooting the Tornado down, costs $500 000 – a cost ratio of 1:100 with the $50 million aircraft.[6]

This type of cost difference between weapons systems is typical. In general the direction of military technical innovation in modern weaponry is moving in the direction of the tactical (shorter-range) superiority of small, cheap precision-guided warheads over complex, expensive weapons platforms such as large surface vessels, major aircraft and main battle tanks. In short, the pendulum of offence and defence is swinging towards the superiority – in cost-effectiveness – of defence over offence. These new economic and technical realities will be increasingly felt over the next five to ten years, which also represents a realistic timetable for arms control reduction and reform measures to be brought about.

Defensive deterrence is, however, much more than a military reform concept. If adopted, the concept of defensive deterrence would create a rational framework for the creation of stable postures and strategies for nuclear and conventional forces in Europe. Such a framework is important and necessary because reductions in forces, whilst desirable and necessary, are no guarantee of greater security. Even if East and West achieve a perfect balance of forces this is no guarantee of stability. To use an analogy, if two gunfighters are each holding two guns to the other's head, a 50 per cent force level reduction (to one gun each) is no great advance. It would be much more effective to make a structural change to the confrontation. Rather than just cutting the numbers of guns it would be far more effective to holster the guns in some safe, mutually acceptable way, whilst perhaps obtaining a bullet-proof vest. In defensive deterrence, a mutual defensive superiority of forces could be created to build a stable balance.

Apart from providing a safe and rational framework for arms reductions, defensive deterrence could also complement arms control in other ways. Historically, military technical innovation has accidentally or deliberately bypassed many of the goals of arms control. The innovation of several warheads per launch rocket bypassed the first strategic arms limitation treaty SALT–1. The next, SALT–2, was bypassed by cruise missiles. The most recent, the INF agreement, is likely to be bypassed by proposals for new longer-range air- and sea-launched weapons to be deployed in Europe. Defensive deterrence would be an example of a technical and strategic innovation assisting and complementing the arms control process in a way which would help to prevent the bypassing of a treaty.

The art of successful negotiation to a stable balance of forces demands that a position be found which is seen to be of benefit to all negotiating parties and which increases their common security. Alternative defence concepts create such a focal point of potential consensus because they identify a convergence of security concerns between East and West, between NATO and the Western Peace Movement and between the political Left and Right.

A similar idea to defensive deterrence, 'non-provocative defence' has now been embraced by several major political parties in Western Europe, including the Social Democratic Parties in Denmark and the Federal Republic of Germany and the Labour Party in the UK.

In the Eastern Bloc, a unilateral two-year programme of reductions in Soviet forces in East Germany, Czechoslovakia and Hungary was announced by Mikhail Gorbachev in his speech to the United Nations Assembly in December 1988. Substantial reductions of East German, Polish and Czech forces are also in progress. Most of these reductions are in just those weapons which NATO says it finds most threatening: tanks, artillery and bridge-laying equipment. The concept of non-provocative defence was instrumental in supporting these initial reductions and restructuring of Warsaw Pact forces.

These changes, however, are only initial steps towards the possible adoption of defensive deterrence. If East–West relations are to improve genuinely and lastingly, restructuring of the conventional forces of East and West is required. Nuclear removals are needed. The levels of forces need to be drastically reduced below their current levels.

ECONOMIC AND ENVIRONMENTAL SECURITY

There is a growing realisation that the nations of NATO and the Warsaw Pact have spent too much upon military might and not enough in maintaining economic and environmental security. Economic security has two aspects: domestic and international. On the domestic side, money is required for health and social spending programmes. Spending is needed on infrastructure, industry, education and research to rebuild the US, Soviet and European economies to make them competitive with new economic giants such as Japan. It is an irony that Japan, thwarted in its goal of world domination by military force in the Second World War, has, to a large extent, achieved it by economic means.

In the international arena, with the rise of the importance of economic competition, the USA is reassessing its world priorities. From 1992 the single European Act will turn the EC into a more integrated economic entity more able to compete with the USA. Potential US–European economic conflict and increased European–Soviet cooperation may overshadow the former priority of the US–European military alliance. Longer-term problems are massive Third World debt and huge resource inequalities between the more developed countries and the developing countries which are building the causes of future wars which may not be contained by pure military might.

Turning to the environment, the scale of human activity has grown with the size of the human population and the technological revolution to a point where it is now very significant in relation to the size and resources of the planet as a whole. Now, the destruction of vast areas of the few remaining rain-forests threatens the air we all breathe. Atmospheric pollutants produced by car exhausts, aerosols and fires are punching large holes in the protective ozone layer. Global warming – the greenhouse effect – threatens to devastate farming and to drown ports and major centres of population as the polar ice caps melt and the sea level rises. These problems demand global solutions and global cooperation. A sustainable programme of global development addressing major demographic, economic, and domestic problems in the developing countries could be paid for by the diversion of a relatively small fraction of the money currently spent upon arms (this issue is addressed at greater length in Part III of this book).

THE CHANGING INTERNATIONAL ENVIRONMENT

The most vital factor which makes change thinkable is a new perception of East–West relations, much of which has been fostered by new thinking backed up by concrete changes in the Soviet Union. The Gorbachev leadership is demonstrably different from the Brezhnev era which preceded it. The Brezhnev leadership was reliably unimaginative and predictable; it posed no challenge to Western policies based upon nuclear deterrence and 'containment' of the 'Soviet threat'. Gorbachev has challenged all these perceptions and has launched sweeping reforms in the Soviet Union based on *perestroika* (reconstruction), *glasnost* (openness) and democratisation. If these reforms are carried through successfully they will radically alter the Soviet economy, its society and its relations with foreign powers.

In his speech to the United Nations Assembly in December 1988,[7] Mikhail Gorbachev presented an analysis of startling vision and scope for any world leader let alone a leader of one of the world's most powerful nations. Gorbachev argued that nuclear and chemical weapons were simply too dangerous, that the world was now too interconnected, interdependent and vulnerable in so many ways for nuclear or chemical war to achieve *any* political goal. If this is the case, Clausewitz's famous maxim that war is the extension of politics by 'other means' no longer holds. The 'other' military means are no longer effective for political gain, only for mutual destruction. The only 'means' left are political: concerted international action for change and greater international security.

In my view this analysis presented by Gorbachev is more representative of the reality of our current world situation than that presented, or at least publicly admitted, by many NATO leaders. NATO collective decision-making prefers to maintain the nuclear *status quo*, arguing that change may be more dangerous than the admitted problems of current strategies. Whatever the truth of the situation, change demands that *both* NATO and the Warsaw Pact must act to reform their military confrontation in Europe and in the process bring widespread benefits for East–West relations.

Some Western observers (for example, the British Foreign Office) have urged caution, arguing that Soviet military cuts will occur whatever the West does because of major problems in the Soviet economy. This may be the case, but it is in the West's interest to help the Soviet Union to achieve reconstruction by peaceful means and without major internal conflicts which could provoke a resurgence of conservatism in the Politburo and possible attendant slowing of military reforms. The advice is also misguided because there would be a danger of not achieving as much as possible in the way of arms control in Europe, quite apart from this type of approach completely losing any support from the Western public. Fortunately, the US Bush administration seems set on attempting to match the stream of Soviet arms proposals.

The programme of *perestroika* initiated in the Soviet Union under Gorbachev, appears to have the necessary vision to take up the challenge of major cuts and restructuring of nuclear and conventional forces and strategies. NATO appears in contrast to be still wedded to an excessive dependence upon nuclear strategies. NATO sometimes appears inflexible, unimaginative and defensive in response to the challenges posed by the Gorbachev administration.

Taking the Gorbachev peace rhetoric at face value, Pact military reforms require support from the West and pressurising towards further changes. NATO requires pressurising to initiate a process of military review and reform. Both need guidance and feedback as to the correct way to proceed. This is a vital role for a renewed peace movement, for the political opposition parties in Western Europe, together with some of the occasionally dissenting NATO members such as Spain, Greece, Norway, Denmark and Belgium. There is truly a unique opportunity for concerted political pressure to influence NATO and the Warsaw Pact in a way which would simply not have been possible a few years ago.

For such political pressure to be brought to bear, there needs to be an informed public debate and the evolution of a clear positive agenda, rather than the more usual agenda of opposition to things as they are. It is part of the purpose of this book to inform such a process and to begin writing the new agenda.

If this process can be started, NATO and the Warsaw Pact have a great opportunity to regenerate their economies and, with sufficient vision, to make a great and lasting contribution towards world peace for the 21st century.

Part I
The Present Danger

Introduction

THE 'FOG' OF WAR

General von Clausewitz coined a much quoted phrase 'the fog of war', sometimes called the epitaph of failed command, to describe the uncertainty, confusion, disorganisation, misunderstanding, unreceived communication, lost formations, chance, accident and plain stupidity which typify real combat.

The 'fog' and its attributes, however, are not confined to the undertaking of war itself. Many of the same factors can also be used to describe international relations, particularly in rapidly developing and, especially, rapidly intensifying crises.

The initiation of crises is often caused by combinations of quite chance events acting in combination with existing military structures. The escalation to war once the crisis has been initiated is also not totally under rational, political, or deliberate control but is more a function of the nature and dynamic interaction of the existing potential conflict systems (in our case NATO and the Warsaw Pact). How such systems may react in practice, and how the system may best be influenced back to relative stability is usually not known or understood. As a result, the best-intentioned actions of decision-makers may produce a result quite at variance with their intended result.

All this being the case, some knowledge of the types of events which might trigger or escalate conflict is important so that their likelihood or effect may be minimised.

SCENARIO: WAR BY MISTAKE

Naval Conflict

There is a major NATO naval exercise in the seas off the major Soviet port of Murmansk in the Kola peninsula, east of northern Norway and in Arctic waters. Six US carrier groups are manoeuvring, shadowed closely by surface and sub-surface Soviet naval vessels. Both fleets continually update each other's position and input the coordinates into the command systems of their on-board tactical nuclear weapons. Soviet naval shore batteries do likewise. The

NATO forces are rehearsing NATO maritime strategy, the destruction of the Soviet surface fleet and the bottling-up of Soviet nuclear-launch submarines in their 'sanctuary' in the Barents Sea. The Soviets are taking the opportunity to practise repelling them. Supersonic Backfire bombers carrying tactical nuclear stand-off missiles capable of destroying the largest surface vessel, are flying low-level supersonic sorties to within 100 miles of the US carriers before pulling away.

Unbeknown to the potential combatants, in a top-secret undersea operation close by, a specially silenced US submarine in the 'Holystone' programme is slowly and stealthily moving into Soviet territorial waters to set undersea listening devices and to collect taped sound signatures of Soviet vessels for later analysis.

But the US submarine has been detected and once in territorial waters does not come under the protection of the laws governing international waters. A Soviet vessel discharges a small depth-charge to force the submarine to the surface and a Soviet submarine closes in from the sea. The US submarine commander has orders to evade capture at all costs and launches two torpedoes in self-defence. The torpedoes miss their intended targets but carry on, hitting a US frigate on the fringes of the carrier battle group. The US vessel believes that it is under attack from Soviet surface vessels nearby and retaliates by firing upon a Soviet frigate. A Soviet Backfire deliberately overshoots its approach run, and is shot down by the US battle group.

In the rapidly escalating chaos and confusion, a tactical nuclear weapon is used with the complete loss of a large surface vessel with all hands. The conflict escalates to naval installations in Norway and the northern Soviet Union.

One more accident or unlucky chance and the conflict will escalate to strategic nuclear devastation.

Insurrection in Uzbekistan

In the wake of *glasnost* in the Soviet Union, Armenians are demonstrating for their own independent state. In Afghanistan, the Soviet Army has departed and fundamentalist Islam is spreading to Uzbekistan and Turkmenistan bordering Iran and Turkey. The Soviet Army suppresses riots near the Soviet border. The forces of fundamentalist Islam in Iran arise to aid their brothers across the border. An opportunity is seen by previously oppressed minorities in Eastern

Turkey who revolt against the Turkish state. Fighting breaks out and spills across the borders of Iran and the Soviet Union. Soviet and Iranian Army units exchange fire with the Turkish Army.

Outrageous Fortune

A plane carrying 200 passengers, including thirty US and NATO citizens is mistakenly shot down in Soviet airspace after ignoring warnings from Soviet jets and mistaken for an electronic intelligence mission.

A US spy satellite, one of the few high-resolution units left after the space shuttle disasters suddenly breaks off its communication. Has it been blown up by a Soviet 'killer' satellite? Is an attack coming?

A 42-cent 'chip' in the NORAD early warning system malfunctions. As a result attack practice tapes are released by the computer and interpreted as a major nuclear attack upon the USA. ICBMs, warplanes and submarines are readied for nuclear retaliation.

The President (or the General Secretary) is seriously ill. A deputy eager not to leave his country undefended is in control of the nuclear fire command codes.

A US 'Blackbird' spy plane is shot down and its pilot captured (or did the pilot defect?).

If some of these possibilities sound familiar that is because some of them have already occurred. Others have not. Neither has an unfortunate combination of two or three such events . . .

1 Problems with Nuclear Strategies

The nuclear arsenals of NATO and the Soviet Union have been designed to be able to devastate almost all inhabited areas of the globe. In NATO terms this is the basis of the Alliance's nuclear deterrent capability and a chief reason for the absence of NATO–Soviet conflict in Europe since 1945.

NATO nuclear strategy, as described by the Supreme Commander Allied Forces Europe (SACEUR), General John R Galvin, has two chief components:

> *Deliberate escalation*, to include the possible first-use of theatre-based nuclear weapons (weapons based on land in Europe);
> *General nuclear response*, the ultimate guarantor of Alliance deterrence.[1]

Both these nuclear options would come if the initial NATO option, 'direct defence' (conventional battle with armed forces) failed.

Soviet nuclear-strategy statements specifically reject the concept of first-use of nuclear weapons.

But in the creation of nuclear arsenals, constantly ready to unleash nuclear devastation at a few minutes notice, both NATO and the Soviet Union have created a new type of danger, one created by the nature of the nuclear systems themselves. These dangers can be classed into two main categories:

1. those arising from the necessarily complex nuclear command and control structures;
2. those caused by aggressive, destabilising strategies and contingency plans for the use of nuclear weapons.

Europe faces additional particular problems created by the local deployment of large numbers of shorter-range nuclear weapons which are closely integrated with large conventional (non-nuclear) forces. The widespread nuclear deployments on the land mass of Europe and the seas surrounding it, pose grave problems both for our present security and the possibilities of a workable defence strategy

16

based upon principles of defensive deterrence.

The danger is not one which arises primarily out of the possibility of deliberate aggression but out of misadventure or inadvertence. This possibility has been largely overlooked by analysts of nuclear-deterrence strategy but is now attracting increasing attention by strategic analysts.[2]

THE NUCLEAR ARSENALS

In Europe in peacetime, there are over 5000 nuclear warheads stored and deployed by NATO and a similar or larger number by the Soviet Union. These warheads are deployed on land upon short-range missiles and in artillery shells; on aircraft as nuclear drop bombs, 'stand-off missiles' and cruise missiles; at sea, in nuclear cruise missiles and nuclear depth-charges carried upon large naval task groups; finally, under the sea, upon long-range submarine-launched missiles allocated for use in Europe by the UK, the French and the USA (see Table 1.1).

Table 1.1　European nuclear warheads after INF, for use in the NATO/Warsaw Pact area

	NATO and USA	Soviet Union	France	UK
Land forces				
Short-range				
missiles	700	311+	58	—
(launchers)	(48)	(311)+		
Artillery shells	1670	2000+?	—	—
Neutron shells	600　(in US)	??	—	—
Air forces				
Drop bombs	1740	2000 ?	140	100
Naval forces				
Tactical	3500*	700+	??	30
Submarine launched	400	200 ?	180	120
Grand Total:	14 449+			

* not all deployed in Europe (this figure to be reduced by about 1000)
Sources: See Note 3.

Extraordinary though it may seem, none of these weapons are covered by the provisions of the Intermediate Nuclear Forces (INF) Treaty signed on 8 December 1987, neither are they covered by the draft provisions of the Strategic Arms Reduction Treaty (START). First, INF covers only weapons which are actually launched from the ground; thus all the sea-based weapons are exempt. Nuclear weapons carried on aircraft which are based on land are exempt because the nuclear warhead would be launched (or, in the case of a bomb, dropped) from the air. The INF Treaty only includes land-based missiles with ranges between 500 and 5000 kilometres (intermediate range). This leaves several land-based nuclear weapons with ranges shorter than this. The British and French have also deployed long-range (strategic-range), submarine-launched missiles which despite being of strategic range are not covered by START because the UK and France have refused to include these nuclear weapons in arms reduction talks at this stage.

In addition to these nuclear weapons allocated for use in Europe, the USA and USSR have another 12 000 and 10 000 strategic nuclear weapons respectively, based on air, land and sea, adding a further 22 000 warheads. The draft provisions of START would reduce this number to around 12 000 over a timetable covering several years.

NATO is also considering the deployment of a new generation of nuclear weapons in Europe (nuclear 'modernisation'). The new weapons under consideration are an extended-range version of the existing Lance missile, nuclear 'stand-off' cruise missile type weapons for strike planes and additional deployments of sea-launched cruise missiles. Additional deployments of US strike planes are another possibility along with updated artillery shells including the controversial 'neutron' bomb.

These proposals are the subject of much tension and disagreement within NATO because of the strong public and political opposition to the deployment of new Western nuclear weapons at a time when East–West relations appear to have improved dramatically. In March 1989, NATO agreed to defer any decision upon deployment of any new missiles until 1992. In any case the overall number of nuclear warheads deployed by NATO in Europe seems likely to continue to decrease as further numbers of the large stocks of nuclear shells are removed.

In peacetime, and the normal alert conditions, some 220 Western warheads are held on 'Quick Reaction Alert'. Within minutes, thirty-four bombers carrying 150 nuclear warheads could take off

Box 1.1   The nuclear arsenals

Over 55 000 nuclear warheads are deployed around the world by the nuclear powers, the USA, the Soviet Union, France, the UK and China. The Soviet Union and the USA possess the vast bulk, France, the UK and China possess a few hundred warheads each. India has demonstrated the ability to detonate a nuclear weapon, Israel and South Africa probably have warheads ready for assembly in an emergency, many other nations such as Pakistan and Iraq are seeking nuclear materials and weapons.

The nuclear warheads in existence range in destructive power from the equivalent in explosive power of 100 tons of TNT up to warheads with powers of over 10 million tons of TNT, 10 megatons. The bombs which destroyed the Japanese cities of Hiroshima and Nagasaki had an explosive power of 12–20 kilotons of TNT (12 000 to 20 000 tons). Nuclear warheads are carried on 'delivery systems', usually missiles or aircraft. Nuclear-tipped weapons are currently deployed in a bewildering plethora of types. Nuclear weapons are deployed on land deep in reinforced silos, on mobile missiles as nuclear shells for howitzers, as knapsack detonation charges, at sea on ships, under the sea in submarines and in the air in aircraft as drop-bombs and 'stand-off' air-launched missiles. The ranges of the delivery systems range from zero (the knapsack) or a few kilometres (the howitzer) up to several thousand kilometres (intercontinental ballistic missiles, ICBMs). Weapons with ranges of over 5000km are classed as 'strategic'. Weapons of range 500–5000km are called intermediate-range nuclear forces (land-based systems being the INF category) and sometimes 'theatre' forces. Those of ranges below 500km are called shorter-range intermediate nuclear forces (SRINF) otherwise known as 'battlefield' or 'tactical' nuclear weapons.

Collectively, these weapons comprise a massive and quite unprecedented capability for destruction. Some idea of the destructive power can be gained by the fact that either the USA or the Soviet Union could destroy world civilisation several times over should they choose to do so. Even the detonation of the smaller number of warheads possessed by China, the UK or France, if detonated over cities, could be catastrophic for the whole world. A few hundred warheads (only half of 1 per cent of the current arsenals) would be sufficient to destroy the world's 200 largest cities causing initial casualties of some 200–400 million at the minimum. Many millions of other people not directly targeted would die because of the destruction and disruption of world economy and trade. The other effects that could follow are not clearly known or understood but what we do know strongly suggests that all the possible outcomes would be catastrophic for the world as a whole. Possibly the worst outcome would be the so-called 'nuclear winter'. This phenomenon would be caused by

continued on p. 20

Box 1.1 *continued*

> immense fires raging unchecked through built-up areas which would
> inject massive amounts of smoke and soot into the upper atmosphere
> where the particles could remain for many months. These particles
> would blot out the sun's rays and the land masses beneath would suffer
> a long period of cooling. As a result, crops would fail, monsoon rains
> would be disturbed, tropical forests would die, people would starve.
> This is only one possibility. The effects of massive amounts of radiation
> in the world's food chains would have severe long-term effects. Overall
> the possibility exists that the human race itself could create its own
> self-extinction.[4]

from seventeen Allied air bases across Europe allocated to some
seventy key Warsaw Pact targets. 'Normal' peacetime is defined as
US DEFCON 5, corresponding to NATO LERTCON 5. As the state
of alert is raised through DEFCON 4 (general alert), DEFCON 3 or
NATO LERTCON 3, (initial force movements to wartime operating
positions); to DEFCON 2 or LERTCON 2 (general dispersal and
reinforcement of forces); and to DEFCON 1 (LERTCON 1) (outbreak of war or war imminent), the number of nuclear weapons
ready for immediate use rises to a total which would be increased by
crisis redeployments of US nuclear weapons from storage sites in the
USA to forward deployments in Europe and in a parallel and largely
unknown process by Soviet nuclear forces.

MISPERCEPTION AND MISADVENTURE

The command and control systems which have the awesome task of
controlling the immense nuclear firepower, have the conflicting demands of not firing accidentally yet of being capable of very rapid
retaliation or possibly of preemptive attack in the event of hostilities.
From launch, Soviet and US weapons can hit their targets in opposing countries in mere tens of minutes. Such short time-periods for
decision-making and reaction, coupled with the very high cost of a
serious mistake pose quite unprecedented human and technical
problems.

   High-powered computers are used to process vast quantities of
potential early-warning data in time. Immense worldwide communications networks have the task of sending electronically coded control messages reliably to numerous locations in the nuclear network

before, during or after nuclear attack. The human commander (the US President in the West, the Soviet Secretary General in the East, or their survivors in the command chain) at the apex of the command pyramid would, in a crisis, be faced with the task of deciding whether or not to fire, and if so, which nuclear response (if any) to choose, in as little as five minutes (it takes only a few minutes for a missile launched from off the coast to reach the USA or USSR). In the worst case, a decision would have to be taken by a commander immediately after he had been woken from sleep by a crisis message from the military command.

A mistake is even more likely when a commander is not familiar with the strategic options, and when the likely results of these options is based upon underestimates of the longer-term effects of nuclear exchanges. Both these factors have been true for every US President to date with the exceptions of Jimmy Carter and George Bush. The degree of briefing in the Soviet Union is not known.

Box 1.2   The President and the nuclear button

President Carter was the first US President actually to take a ride in the 'Nightwatch' plane, the Presidential airborne command post. He also initiated a thorough review of US nuclear strategy and a series of Presidential Directives culminating in PD-59 in the summer of 1980. PD-59 was the first executive order requiring US forces to be able to fight and endure a prolonged nuclear war. Carter's administration was also the first to test the emergency Presidential evacuation procedure from Washington – with farcical results. When the helicopter of the President's flight arrived to whisk him away, it narrowly avoided being shot down by his own security guards.[5]

All these factors create the very real possibility of nuclear war starting by misperception, misjudgement, misinformation, or even computer error in a crisis which blows up suddenly. Misperception, fatal misjudgements, chaos and confusion have been common experiences in the 'fog' of past wars. The advent of nuclear weapons with short flight times to target has added to the potential for confusion and error a totally new factor – computer error undiscovered or uncorrected in the minutes available. In a severe crisis the very real threat of imminent nuclear destruction and the awesome power of the weapons under command would create an immense pressure upon a commander to take the 'right' decision in a few minutes, in the absence of complete information or time for discussion and reflection. By creating the potential need to take decisions – and decisions with awesome consequences in very short time periods – nuclear weapons have created a new mechanism for the escalation of crises.

Even the purely precautionary defensive action of raising the state of alert may have destabilising repercussions. This destabilising effect occurs because all raising of alert states bring additional nuclear and conventional weapons to a state of immediate readiness. Whilst this may be a purely precautionary act, a potential adversary will interpret it as an increased capability for a surprise preemptive attack or in the worst case actual preparation for such an attack. If the adversary then raises his alert state this then appears to the initial raiser of the alert as evidence that the danger is very real. In this way a vicious cycle of raised alert states can occur until both sides are on the brink of war and at states of alert quite inappropriate to the initial cause of higher alert.

The whole subject of the details of raised nuclear alerts is shrouded in secrecy, thus most evidence of the actions actually taken during raised alerts is based upon data available from the USA.[6] Up to the present time the highest states of alert reached have been LERTCON 3 in Europe and DEFCON 2 by US Strategic Air Command during the Cuba Missile Crisis in 1963. There is no firm evidence that the Soviet Union has ever raised its state of nuclear alert. This may be extremely fortunate. It is widely acknowledged that the Cuba crisis represented the nearest to nuclear war the world has yet come.

Even an alert to the lowest level above peacetime may have unwanted repercussions. US forces declared such a DEFCON 4 alert in 1968, when Soviet forces moved into Czechoslovakia. European high command (EUCOM), however, expressly forbade the commander of the US Seventh Army to prepare armoured cavalry to move towards the border.[7] This action was taken in an attempt to avoid unwanted escalation. This illustrates the danger implicit in an alert even to the lowest level above normal. At DEFCON/LERTCON 4, nuclear forces in regional theatres such as Europe have standing orders to take steps to ready more warheads for immediate firing and to disperse command and control networks. Such action is taken at a very low level of alert because of the vulnerability of the entire nuclear command and control mechanism in peacetime to 'decapitation' surprise attack upon key command centres. According to a 1989 US joint CIA and military intelligence report, in the 1968 crisis Soviet Strategic Rocket Forces assembled nuclear warheads and mated them to missiles on their launch pads. They were apparently 'ten minutes from launch'.[8]

Alerts to DEFCON 3 occurred in 1960, and in 1973 during the Arab–Israeli conflict. In 1960 the alert followed a vague order from the US Defense Secretary who later testified before the US Congress that he had only wanted to test out the system following the interception of a US U–2 spyplane some two weeks earlier. As a result, a Paris summit between Khrushchev and Eisenhower collapsed. In 1973, a DEFCON 3 alert followed an hour-long session of the National Security Council called by Henry Kissinger. Extraordinarily, the President was not consulted but Defense Secretary Schlesinger and Joint Chief of Staff Moorer ordered all US military commands to raise their alert to DEFCON 3. The Soviet Union had hinted that they were considering military intervention to enforce a ceasefire and to save the Egyptian Third Army from annihilation by Israeli units. The US alert was intended to deter this and was meant to be perceived as a veiled threat of US military action against the Soviet Union if they were to take action on behalf of the Egyptians.[9] Again, as in the DEFCON 4 alert in 1968, the alerting action was immediately followed by orders rescinding items on the alert checklist to avoid unwanted escalation in Europe. The USA, however, desired an escalation of tension in the Mediterranean and three US carrier groups closed ranks and manoeuvred south-east of Crete. These forces were trailed by advance Soviet naval units backed up by ships in the rear carrying cruise missiles. For eight days the opposing task forces maintained continuous high readiness to engage the other in battle. Even after the DEFCON 3 condition had been cancelled, the tense and mutually reinforcing battle formations were maintained for several days before de-escalation was achieved. Should any event have occurred during this period to trigger conflict, deliberately or inadvertently, both fleets were poised for their mutual nuclear destruction and the targeting of land targets in Israel and Egypt with longer-range weapons such as cruise missiles.

Other alerts raised in limited geographical areas occurred in the Berlin crisis of 1961, the Pueblo incident in 1968, the 1970 civil war in Jordan, the Korean incident in 1976 and the leadership crisis in the aftermath of the assassination attempt upon President Reagan in 1981.

In any one of the DEFCON 3 alerts, an accident or chance unfortunate event could have taken US forces to the equivalent of DEFCON 2, and the very brink of war.

The dangers of raised alert states are an inescapable result of the integration of aggressive nuclear strategy and extremely destructive nuclear weapons with conventional military forces. The particular problems created by this nuclear–conventional force integration in Europe is dealt with next.

AGGRESSIVE AND DESTABILISING STRATEGIES

'First Use' and Nuclear War-Fighting

NATO and US training manuals do not reserve the use of nuclear weapons solely for retaliation to nuclear attack as one might expect from a simple appreciation of the idea of deterrence. NATO has a professed policy of using nuclear weapons *first*, *before* the Alliance has been attacked by nuclear weapons. NATO thus either threatens to initiate one-sided nuclear war deliberately with the aim of deterring further attacks or to use 'small' 'tactical' nuclear warheads (some are as large as the bomb which destroyed Hiroshima), as some kind of more efficient explosive to destroy enemy tank formations. The former is called NATO's 'first-use' strategy; the latter, nuclear war-fighting. A similar strategy is practised by NATO naval task groups, and is called NATO Maritime Strategy.

Contingency plans exist for the use of nuclear weapons in close conjunction with chemical and non-nuclear weapons. Talk of nuclear war-fighting strategies has never reached a high profile within NATO because of the public fear they provoke, but the concept of nuclear war-fighting is closely connected with the deployment of several thousand short-range nuclear warheads in Europe. Most of these warheads cannot possibly hit the Soviet Union from bases in West Germany but would be used to strike invading forces in West Germany or targets in East Germany. This planned use is one reason why nuclear war-fighting is unpopular, because the strategy would destroy tracts of West Germany and kill many of its citizens in an effort to save them from the Russians.

NATO sources have indicated privately that in the event of severe non-nuclear East–West hostilities, NATO commanders would seek the political sanction of the use of a few relatively low-yield nuclear weapons to devastate a military target such as a major air-base in East Germany or a tank-marshalling area.[10]

However, in 1986, NATO's Nuclear Planning Group adopted new

'general political guidelines' for the use of nuclear weapons.[11] The guidelines were tested for the first time in NATO's two-yearly Wintex–Cimex exercises in February/March 1989. In the exercise scenario, NATO struck first with seventeen nuclear warheads of 100 kiloton, followed up by a second nuclear strike of twenty-five more warheads, two exploding in West Germany and two in Turkey.[12]

That such a nuclear option should be chosen by NATO high-level planners, illustrates a dangerously narrow way of thinking by NATO military planners, together with a very NATO-centred perception of the likely results of such an act. As senior NATO policy-makers present the scenario, the Soviet Union would be the aggressor, clearly in the wrong and attempting some kind of aggressive adventurism in Germany. As such, NATO's nuclear use would be intended as a clear signal to the Soviets that NATO would not let them get away with such opportunism and that the aggression must cease. Nuclear use would indicate NATO's serious intent to use further nuclear weapons should hostilities continue. The ball, as NATO sees it, would be firmly back in the Soviet Union's court.

This is quite absurd. First, war may not have started in such a clear way. Wars rarely do. Even if it did, the aggressors would surely not feel guilty of aggression and thus somehow more ready to pull back should their bluff be called. In a real East–West conflict both sides would rightly or wrongly see the other as being in the wrong. There would be considerable chaos, confusion, fear and paranoia. From the Soviet perspective, NATO using nuclear weapons first would most likely be interpreted as a clear signal of NATO aggressive intent. Should the Soviet Union detect NATO's preparation for imminent nuclear use, the Soviets would have to consider seriously their own nuclear response or preemptive attack if they were not doing so already. Any moves the Soviets took which NATO detected would further spur NATO on, thus forming a vicious spiral of escalation rapidly leading to nuclear conflict. First-use, far from deterring or halting conflict would almost certainly escalate it. The mechanism for escalation can perhaps be best envisaged by considering the most likely NATO response to first-use by the Soviet Union. How would NATO respond if the Soviets devastated a major USAF base in West Germany? By giving up? Surely not. Yet NATO officials questioned at regular private briefings in NATO HQ about their consideration of the Soviet perception of NATO contingency plans to use nuclear weapons in this way consistently profess not to have considered it.[13] This is quite staggering because the whole purpose of deterrence is to seek to influence the mind of potential aggressors. Therefore it is most important that the likely effect one's actions will have upon potential aggressors must be carefully considered. Yet NATO has neither a central intelligence section nor a department specifically studying the Soviet Union. NATO relies largely upon US perceptions of the USSR with inputs from other NATO countries. These inputs are often far from objective or accurate. 'Soviet Military Power', published annually by the Pentagon to justify US military spending by reference to the Soviet threat is a good example. The errors in this document are so numerous and extensive as to enable a leading US defence expert to publish an 'Annotated and Corrected Version of the Pentagon's Guide' listing errors page by page.[14]

Further cause for concern arises from a reading of some US field manuals which describe how the USA envisage that war, nuclear war, would be fought in Europe. These manuals indicate an unrealistic attitude to the use, likely effects and results of using nuclear weapons but are the basis of US military training and instruction. The training manuals in question describe the strategy of Air-Land Battle and associated doctrines.[15] Air-Land Battle envisages the very early use of pre-planned 'packages' of tens or hundreds of nuclear weapons over a limited geographical area to achieve a tactical goal.

NATO's professed strategy is Follow-On Forces Attack (FOFA) which refers to NATO's plan to attack reinforcing Warsaw Pact forces 'following on' behind front-line invading forces. NATO adopted FOFA after a public controversy which Air-Land Battle aroused because of Air-Land Battle's manifestly aggressive nature involving the very early use of nuclear weapons. In fact FOFA is little more than a re-packaging of Air-Land Battle in more acceptable terms and with the overt references to the more unacceptable elements of Air- Land Battle removed. The concept of FOFA is actually described in Air-Land Battle as a 'sub-concept' of the overall US Air-Land Battle approach to warfighting. In Air-Land Battle, the FOFA phase occurs 12 to 24 hours before Soviet reinforcements reach the front line, 30 to 150 kilometres behind it. At this stage NATO would launch a combined air-and-ground attack in coordination with the use of nuclear weapons if release permission had been obtained.

A significant factor is that almost all the nuclear warheads that could be considered for use either in Air-Land Battle or, as NATO says it intends to use them, as a forthright demonstration of nuclear intent, are owned by the USA. US forces train in Air-Land Battle.

Whatever NATO says its strategy is, US forces which form a substantial contribution to NATO will fight in the way in which they are trained. US forces do not have to ask for permission from NATO before firing nuclear weapons. The USA can decide on its own to fire nuclear weapons. 'Consultation' with the Allies would occur only if there were time. US forces, as part of Air-Land Battle, could use nuclear weapons in, say, the Fulda region in West Germany, thus precipitating nuclear use amongst the Allies. Unilateral US use would avoid the very likely refusal of nuclear use permission from the West Germans who would vigorously oppose the devastation of Germany. Presumably taking account of such factors, in the 1989 NATO Wintex–Cimex exercise, the nuclear scenario assumed that all the weapons were fired by *non*-West-Germans. US and British forces were tasked with firing the weapons.

The use of such a nuclear strike could have two aims: in NATO's 'general political guidelines' to achieve some kind of intra-war deterrence and to persuade the Soviets to give up and go home, and in Air-Land Battle to annihilate enough Soviet forces to make further Warsaw Pact conventional attack impossible. In both cases the result seems very likely to be the same, Soviet nuclear preemption or retaliation and escalation to the destruction of Europe. There is hard evidence of this, in that usually when NATO plans to go nuclear in an exercise, it precipitates a Soviet nuclear strike exercise. In the NATO 1976 REFORGER exercise, the Soviet Union took the unprecedented step of publicly announcing that NATO 'was going nuclear' two hours *before* NATO planned to do so. This was apparently achieved through routine Soviet monitoring of coded NATO nuclear communications.[16]

US Field Manual FM–100–5 describes the concept of Air-Land Battle in its introductory pages as being 'consistent with NATO doctrine and strategy'.[17] The manual goes on to describe the 'Basic operational concept . . . Air-Land Battle doctrine', about which it says: 'This doctrine is based upon securing or retaining the initiative and retaining it aggressively to defeat the enemy.' The manual stresses initiative, depth agility ('depth' being deep inside the Warsaw Pact) and synchronisation in a fluid battle in which decisive battles may last hours instead of weeks (as in previous wars) and in which decentralised decision-making is used to ensure speed. Coordinated conventional and nuclear 'fires' are seen as one means of obtaining this initiative. In Air-Land Battle ground and air forces are very closely coordinated and aim to break through enemy weak spots in outflanking manoeuvres, to isolate attacking enemy formations and to defeat them piecemeal. NATO forces, having limited depth in which to manoeuvre before losing West Germany and unwilling to defend in depth, in Air-Land Battle would take the battle into East Germany or Czechoslovakia, thus giving themselves more space for manoeuvre.

Air-Land Battle strategy clearly plans that US forces should use nuclear weapons first. This is not particularly surprising: it is after all NATO strategy. What is very surprising is just *how* early it is thought that nuclear weapons would be used.

US Training Manual TRADOC 525–5, upon which much of Air-Land Battle is based, gives a clear sequence of how a conflict is seen as developing. Three distinct stages are envisaged; the Deep Battle, the Corps Battle, and the Air-Land Battle. In Deep Attack and Deep Battle, commanders are expected to collect intelligence of, and to engage, enemy forces which could join or support battle as early as *three days before* they reach the front line, known by yet another Army acronym as the FLOT (Front Line of Own Troops). Commanders are told that such an attack will create an 'opportunity window' three days ahead by destroying support vehicles and command and control of the attacking force. Three days after the attack by US forces, the defence would have a respite or 'window' to exploit by counter-attack. What is so surprising is that it is at this very early stage, when Soviet forces could be over 180km (100 miles) behind the FLOT, that US commanders are taught to think of asking for permission to use nuclear weapons.

The TRADOC manual defines the Corps Battle as the period 24 to 60 hours before enemy forces reach the front. At this time the manual envisages nuclear strikes with weapons such as Lance or air-launched nuclear bombs. It is 24 hours before Warsaw Pact forces reach the FLOT that we move into Air-Land Battle. The manual states: 'if tactical nuclear weapons are to be used, they must be used now'.[18] At this stage the battle would be commanded by divisional commanders who would use nuclear-tipped artillery shells if they had permission. Later, 12 hours before the FLOT we are down to brigade commanders and the possible use of chemical weapons 'to isolate parts of the battlefield', but only if chemical weapons have been used first by Warsaw Pact forces.

One reason why the manuals argue that nuclear weapons must be used a whole day at the minimum before Soviet forces actually reach the front line, is because otherwise these weapons would devastate West Germany and kill West German citizens. The FM–100–5 manual notes the extensive urban sprawl in West Germany, noting that 'the fluid [Air-Land] battle would be fought only outside urban areas'. It is rather difficult to see how this could be achieved except by taking the battle into East Germany because much of West Germany near the border is extensively urbanised (see Chapter 5, Figure 5.2).

Air-Land Battle strategy, apart from having a very aggressive conventional component, makes no fundamental distinction between conventional and nuclear weapons. Smaller 'tactical' nuclear weapons are seen as quite usable, albeit much more destructive weapons to be used in conjunction with, and in similar ways to, conventional weapons. The strategy does not encompass nor envisage escalation to all out nuclear conflict. Yet the strategy is so aggressive that the Soviet Union would surely be forced into a nuclear response. Air-Land Battle strategy assumes that war and nuclear war fought with shorter-range nuclear weapons could be fought, limited and won in Europe. The term for this is a nuclear 'war-fighting' strategy. This concept is described very clearly in descriptions of specific contingency plans for exactly how and in what number nuclear weapons would be used in Air-Land Battle. Field Manual 100–5 states that:

> Using nuclear weapons requires advance planning, training, and logistics support. One technique is to develop preplanned packages. A package is a group of nuclear weapons of specific yields for use in a specific area and within a specific time to support a specific tactical goal. Each package must contain nuclear weapons sufficient to alter the tactical situation decisively and to accomplish the mission.[19]

A US Army reference book entitled 'Conventional–Nuclear Operations',[20] an early coordination draft for the 'How to Fight' manual FM 100–5–2, describes a US 3rd Corps Package code-named ZEBRA. Package ZEBRA consisted of 141 nuclear warheads:

CORPS NUCLEAR WEAPONS PACKAGE
[ZEBRA]

NUMBER: 141 nuclear weapons not to exceed the following limits:

Number	Yield
48	0.1 KT
40	0.5 KT
6	1.0 KT
20	2.0 KT
14	5.0 KT
13	10.0 KT

> Except that a lower yield weapon may be
> substituted for a higher yield weapon on a
> one-for-one basis.

TIME: Timeframe – To be requested when needed.
                     Timespan – Not to exceed 120 minutes.

AREA: From NB9668 to NBO838 to NA3757 to
                     NA9886 to NB9668

CONSTRAINTS: Preclude personnel casualties in urban areas
                     and damage to single-story masonry buildings
                     in communities over 1000.

US 3rd Corps are deployed in the vicinity of the town of Fulda, West Germany and the coordinates define an area in that vicinity. This area is identified by NATO as an important attack avenue for invading Soviet forces in the event of hostilities. The ZEBRA package was evaluated in a mock Soviet attack. About one third of the weapons were detonated north of Fulda and between it and the Hersfeld–Alsfeld autobahn, the E40. Half of the weapons were detonated along the E45 autobahn running north–south through Fulda. The remaining one sixth, of larger yield, were detonated in East Germany, particularly on road, rail and river crossings such as Dorndorf and Kaltersundheim. The reference book, commenting on the exercise states:

> The employment of package ZEBRA immediately caused approximately 37 per cent of the threat battalions in contact to become ineffective. The threat supporting attack against the 2d [*sic*] division had ceased even before the pulse was completed. After the pulse, only isolated company-sized threat units continued to attack in the northern sector and these were easily repulsed by the 1st division.
>
> Shortly after midnight on the 24th, 3d [*sic*] Corps initiated an attack to re-establish the pre-conflict international boundary. Some enemy equipment was recovered, decontaminated, repaired and used in the offence. Three US mechanised infantry battalions in the 1st Division and two in the 2d [*sic*] division became tank battalions (equipped with threat tanks) by the end of the war.
>
> The threat division located near Hunfeld when package ZEBRA was employed received only light casualties and subsequently established a firm defence just west of Hunfeld. To maintain the momentum achieved by the corps attack on the night of 24–25

May, the NCA [National Command Authority] authorized the use of another nuclear weapons package by 3d [*sic*] corps. This second package, much smaller than ZEBRA, was used primarily against the threat division defending at Hunfeld. Although the physical damage to the city was heavy, Hunfeld suffered less damage than it had during the German retreat in 1945.

Initial reports of civilian casualties . . . were inflated. Post-conflict analysis revealed that, of the 150 000 civilians . . . 16 000 were casualties. As a result of increased West German civil defense training . . . half . . . suffered only minor radiation sickness, first-degree burns and minor wounds . . .[21]

The scenario is extraordinarily unrealistic. The most likely result of such a nuclear 'pulse' would surely be a Soviet nuclear response and escalation to larger-scale nuclear conflict and the destruction of Europe at the very least. It is not realistic to assume that a Soviet force determined enough to fight its way through to Fulda, or some other objective – a nuclear-armed force at that – is going to allow NATO to inflict 35–50 per cent casualties upon it with nuclear weapons without a fight. The use of nuclear weapons might indeed occur inadvertently *before* this deliberate use in which case the US forces might themselves be annihilated or at the very least their nuclear weapons and their ability to command and control them reliably severely reduced.

The scenario is also extremely optimistic about casualties. Even assuming that there was no escalation to nuclear war and no Soviet nuclear strike, the number of casualties would be far worse than this. A study by the World Health Organisation (WHO) suggests that civilian casualties would number some 50 000 rather than the 16 000 the scenario suggests.[22] Further escalation would kill many millions. One cannot not feel reassured as to one's security knowing that people such as the authors of this manual, who were then and presumably are still, representative of a major strand in US military thinking consider the possible use of nuclear weapons in such an unrealistic light.

More recent NATO nuclear scenarios are if anything even less reassuring. In NATO's Spring 1989 Winter–Cimex exercise scenario, NATO fired nuclear weapons first, detonating seventeen 100kt nuclear weapons mainly on targets in East Germany and neighbouring Warsaw Pact countries to try to halt invading Soviet forces. Only one weapon was detonated on the Soviet Union, this being delivered somewhere on the Kola peninsula by a British Tornado bomber based in West Germany.[23] This nuclear scenario is *six* times the destructive power of the ZEBRA package and could easily cause a million civilian casualties, largely in Germany. In the scenario, the Soviet Union rather conveniently does not respond with nuclear weapons but presses doggedly on through the German towns and villages now devastated by blast and radiation. The Wintex scenario then called for a further NATO unilateral nuclear strike of 25 additional warheads, this time including two strikes upon West German and two upon Turkish targets. This resulted in an early withdrawal by the German participants in the exercise because of its unreality and the killing of Germans by NATO forces.

In Air-Land Battle, a similar package to ZEBRA would be targeted much more predominantly on East Germany or Czechoslovakia, or completely within these countries. The intention in Air-Land Battle would be to use nuclear arms early to avoid too much damage to US forces. As the Air-Land Battle training document TRADOC Pam 525–5 says:

> In a review of innumerable planning exercises in which assumed enemy penetrations were drawn with great care to reflect that point 'beyond which the integrity of the defence is jeopardized,' it was found that if the penetration was allowed to develop as it was drawn in the defended territory, it was always too late to react successfully.[24]

In other words, if Soviet forces battle their way successfully as far into West Germany as Fulda, US forces would be too damaged to counter-attack.

Unrealistic and dangerous as the scenario surrounding the use of package ZEBRA is Air-Land Battle and the Wintex 1989 scenario is even more dangerous, if possibly a little more realistic. Air-Land Battle by hitting targets in the Eastern Bloc would be even more likely to bring about nuclear retaliation. Because the strategy threatens such early nuclear use, Air-Land Battle makes Soviet preemptive nuclear strike much more likely. The Soviets would naturally try to limit the ability of NATO to fire nuclear weapons and gain any sort of advantage. This is borne out by American and NATO simulations:

> without exception, American exercises have shown that whenever NATO is about to use nuclear weapons it prompts a Soviet nuclear pre-emptive strike.[25]

and from US General Don Starry:

> Several thousand simulations suggest . . . if you wait until they
> [Warsaw Pact forces] get into your territory, to ask for the use of
> nuclear weapons it is always too late.[26]

As I mentioned before, during the NATO 1976 REFORGER exercise the Soviet Union took the unprecendented step of publicly announcing that NATO 'was going nuclear' two hours *before* NATO planned to do so. It is extremely odd that NATO's 1989 exercise chose to ignore these factors.

Thus the nuclear 'logic' comes full circle. Using nuclear weapons when Warsaw Pact forces have already invaded is too late, results in the devastation of Germany and will probably result in Soviet nuclear retaliation. Planning to use nuclear weapons earlier and deeper into the Warsaw Pact countries will probably bring about a Soviet nuclear strike too.

Maritime Strategy

NATO's aggressive land-based strategy of Air-Land Battle has its counterpart in naval strategy. Since the early 1980s, NATO naval military strategy has been quite openly aggressive. In two key battle zones, the North Atlantic and the North Pacific, the aim of NATO and US naval task groups is not purely defensively to contain Soviet naval forces but is to take the war to the Soviets, to destroy Soviet ports, surface ships and submarines. US naval battle groups between them carry some 3500 nuclear weapons (this number is to be reduced by about 1000), some of which (cruise missiles) have a range of 1000 miles and can threaten strategic targets well inside the Soviet Union.[27] All these weapons are capable of being fired on the authority of officers on the ships carrying them. A command or code from higher authority is not physically necessary.

The Soviets have a considerable geographical disadvantage at sea since their ports are iced up in Winter and they are limited to operating from two main basing areas: Murmansk in the Kola peninsula in the north-west Soviet Union, and out of the Sea of Okhotsk from Petropavlovsk on the Kamchatka peninsula to Sakhalin, north of Japan. The latter contains many sensitive military installations and was the area over which flight KAL 007 strayed and was shot down by the Soviets in 1983. Western naval strategy seeks to take advantage of this Soviet disadvantage. Another justification for the US aggressive strategies is that the aircraft carriers themselves are very high-value targets and would be a very high prize in a Soviet attack. As long as the USA forward-deploys such units they will be vulnerable to tactical nuclear attack, thus the USA feels obliged to have a highly aggressive strategy to protect them.

Since 1982, US and NATO naval aircraft-carrier battle groups have conducted large-scale exercises off the northern tip of Norway and off the Kamchatka peninsula and Sakhalin Island in the North Pacific. These forces practise operating well forward, sinking Soviet submarines and attacking operating bases of Soviet Backfire bombers on land in the very early stages of any conflict. NATO's assessment is that the Soviets would deploy only a small fraction of their forces forward, thus massive forward deployments of Western forces cannot be justified upon the basis of holding the line and of defending NATO and US lines of communication. The objective is to defeat Soviet maritime forces decisively early on.

> We must fight on the terms which are most advantageous to us. This would require taking the war to the enemy's naval forces with the objective of achieving the earliest possible destruction of his capability to interfere with our use of the sea areas essential for support of our overseas forces and allies. In this sense sea control is an offensive rather than a defensive function. The prompt destruction of opposing naval forces is the most economical and effective means to assure control of the sea areas necessary for the successful prosecution of the war . . . Our current offensive naval capabilities centered [*sic*] on the carrier battle forces and their supporting units, are well suited for this strategy.[28]

In accordance with this offensive strategy, 1982 saw the first multiple-carrier battle-group exercise held in the Northern Pacific since the Second World War. The exercise was held within 500 miles of the Soviet naval base at Petropavlovsk. The Soviets dispatched Backfires on mock attacks against the carriers, some 100 sorties to within 100 miles, a response which is encouraged by the US so that they can achieve more realistic exercises. In 1983 a similar exercise was held, the objective to test 'our ability with the Air Force to coordinate strikes at Petropavlovsk and Alekseyevka'.[29] In 1984 a similar exercise was held off the northern tip of Norway and the fleets practised attacks upon the Kola peninsula. Backfires again made mock attacks upon the fleets approaching to within a few minutes flight.[30] In a real conflict the Backfires would have launched air-to-surface 'stand-off' missiles aimed at the US carriers.

The NATO Naval Maritime strategy increases the risk of nuclear escalation in several ways:

1. If NATO achieved its objective of destroying the bulk of Soviet surface ships, the Soviet Union would be unable to protect its strategic submarines in the Barents Sea sanctuary, north-east of Norway, from a concerted attack from Western anti-submarine forces. The Soviets would be under immense pressure to launch their intercontinental-range missiles from these submarines before they were lost.

2. Soviet strategic submarines would be sunk directly, further adding to this pressure. All naval vessels, East and West, carrying nuclear weapons, have the *ability* to fire them without permission (although they do not have the authority except in extreme circumstances). Such conditions as the imminent defeat of the entire Soviet navy and the extreme vulnerability of all Soviet submarine-launched nuclear weapons would surely seem extreme enough to prompt some Soviet commanders at least to unleash nuclear weapons under extreme contingency standing orders of which we are not aware, such as exist for Western commanders, even if central command did not or was unable to directly order such a response.

3. Air strikes would hit vital targets on Soviet territory making a fierce response with other forces on land seem highly likely. Despite these mechanisms for inadvertent escalation to nuclear war, the production and deployment of tactical nuclear weapons deployed on US ships 'has never been accompanied by any clear or coherent doctrine for their use'.[31]

A survey of journals over the five years up to 1985 failed to reveal a single article devoted to these problems.[32]

In 1989, the US Navy decided to eliminate some 1100 tactical nuclear weapons from its ships in what some sources described as a 'radical shift from . . . nuclear war-fighting at sea', or even 'maritime unilateralism'.[35]

However, this change seems to stem from an appreciation that elimination of tactical nuclear weapons at sea would favour the US Navy. The Discussion Group On Strategic Policy comment in 'Deterring through the Turn of the Century':

Box 1.3   War games under the sea

Both the USA and USSR engage in highly dangerous undersea surveillance and tracking activities undertaken by nuclear submarines,
often within foreign coastal waters and even within each other's ports.
Very little is officially known of Soviet activities, but Western reports
have given details of close undersea encounters with Soviet submarines
and discoveries of submarine bottom-scraping tracks in coastal waters.
The Swedes in particular have had something of a running battle with
unidentified submarines around their coasts and reports of midget
submersibles and frogmen landing to 'have breakfast' on remote
coasts.

The USA has a highly risky undersea surveillance programme called
Holystone. In this programme, US submarines gather intelligence just
outside or just inside Soviet territorial waters. In the mid-1960s a
Holystone submarine collided with an E-class Soviet submarine inside
Vladivostok harbour whilst photographing the underside of the vessel.
In November 1969, the USS *Gato* collided with a Soviet submarine
15–24 miles off the entrance to the White Sea off the north of the
USSR, one of at least six collisions between 1961 and 1975.[33] Such
incidents contain the potential to initiate a nuclear exchange. In the
Gato incident, the submarine commander readied a SUBROC anti-
submarine rocket carrying a 1–5kt warhead and three other nuclear
torpedoes. According to one report, only one authentication would
have been needed to prepare the torpedoes for launching.[34]

In naval warfare, nuclear SLCMs would allow the Soviets to
compensate for poorer accuracy. The US advantage in accuracy
should enable us to succeed – indeed, to prevail – in a conventionally armed SLCM contest.[36]

The US TLAM-C, a conventionally armed cruise missile with a range
of 1130km, is claimed to have an accuracy of 10 metres, enabling it to
make pinpoint attacks upon coastal installations. The Soviets do not
possess a weapon of such accuracy.

CONVENTIONAL FORCES AND STRATEGIES:
THE NUCLEAR FACTOR

NATO's nuclear strategies and the existence of nuclear weapon in
and around Europe undermine conventional forces in many ways:
expectations, morale, stability and fighting ability, linked conventional and nuclear alerts and conventional attacks.

Expectations

In time of war, NATO could draw upon a large combat force: around one million combat personnel, up to 20 000 tanks together with artillery and all the other equipment for war. Naively, one might expect these forces to have the task of repelling Warsaw Pack attack. Yet, despite the impressive combat power of these forces, to a large extent they form a 'trigger' or 'trip-wire' – costly in financial and human terms – to the nuclear arsenals. NATO says that it does *not* expect them to be able to repel any conceivable conventional Warsaw Pact attack.

As we have seen, NATO expects the use of nuclear weapons early in any conflict in Europe. On top of this, NATO military sources have publicly predicted on numerous occasions that NATO's conventional forces could fight for 7–10 days before being driven back or substantially penetrated by incursions arising from a determined and reinforced Warsaw Pact attack.[37] The most basic reason NATO gives for this is the superiority of Warsaw Pact conventional forces (an assertion which I seriously question later in this book) but there is another important and somewhat surprising reason. NATO states that European NATO forces simply do not have enough ammunition or fuel stocks to fight for longer than one or two weeks of intense conventional conflict (NATO makes the assumption that Warsaw Pact forces would still have enough ammunition and fuel after this time period). Lord Carrington in his post as NATO Secretary General, referred to NATO's apparent lack of ammunition and supplies as 'ludicrous'.[38] US forces however, apparently have enough supplies to go on fighting for a month or two. One has to ask why the European NATO forces are not provided with more ammunition, when clearly this is a prerequisite for the usefulness of almost all their combat equipment. It seems to indicate either that European NATO does not take the Soviet threat very seriously, or at the least is incapable of organising itself sensibly to respond to it. Part of the reason undoubtedly lies with NATO's famed bureaucratic nature, which I describe in some detail in the next chapter, but another significant factor may be connected with NATO's nuclear strategies. If NATO expects to resort to nuclear arms in a week or less, then it clearly makes no sense to have ammunition to fight for a period much longer than this. This is quite consistent with the reasoning in the nuclear war-fighting manuals and the contingency plans for very early use of nuclear weapons. If, as a result of deliberate policy, conventional forces can hold out for no more than, say, ten days, then political permission in principle for nuclear use must be called for well before this – say at five days into a conventional conflict. Again this has been NATO SACEUR's (Supreme Allied Commander Europe, always a US General) known professed intention for some years.[39] Thus the underprovisioning of conventional forces enables the military to justify early calls for use of nuclear weapons consistent with their plans for nuclear war-fighting. Whatever the real reason for this state of affairs, the only war which NATO professes to be really ready to fight in Europe is a nuclear war. NATO advice to nuclear civil defence planners is that nuclear war may be expected as little as 48 hours after the outbreak of hostilities.[40]

In any case, NATO strategies plan for the early use of nuclear weapons in Germany, which would lead to further uncontrollable nuclear escalation. In this eventuality, any concept of any conventional force imbalance in Europe would become increasingly meaningless as conventional forces themselves were rapidly obliterated.

Morale

Once nuclear weapons are used and the Soviet Union retaliates conventional forces become largely irrelevant to the outcome of the conflict. This is not a reassuring prospect for conventional forces. They are aware of NATO's overall strategy, which effectively predicts and plans for the possibility of their annihilation two to ten days after conflict breaks out. The conventional forces, if NATO's information is taken at face value, cannot expect to throw back Warsaw Pact aggressors; the best for which they can hope is a negotiated settlement in circumstances when previous attempts at a political settlement have clearly failed. In this important way the NATO's nuclear strategy undermines the morale of their conventional forces. Soldiers on the ground cannot expect to win a victory. They are expected to lose. They also know that they may be the target of a Soviet preemptive nuclear strike. If NATO fires first they will still be the target of nuclear retaliation. Either way their destiny is out of their hands and their likelihood of survival is seriously threatened by forces which they cannot counter.

In no sense do the nuclear weapons 'bolster' the conventional forces. Once war has actually started, nuclear strategies can only hasten or guarantee the destruction of the conventional forces.

Before conflict has broken out, it is difficult to see how the making of nuclear threats which imply one's own destruction (which is the essence of nuclear deterrence) can possibly stabilise the situation in the long term, however terrified everyone is in the short term.

The Stability and Fighting Ability of the Alliance

Some full NATO-member-countries – Norway, Denmark, Greece and Spain – dissent from NATO's nuclear strategy. Probably most seriously, NATO's nuclear strategies have contributed to the fact that French forces have not been completely integrated into NATO. This has been the case since 1966 and is also in part due to disagreements over the US domination of NATO. This supposedly reduces the potential conventional strength of NATO. However, it seems that secret US–French agreements would allow the use of relatively safe military supply routes from Italy via France, or from southern French ports or French airfields.[41] These agreements were revealed in the summer of 1989. Until then NATO had kept up the pretence that vulnerable routes from northern ports via the Low Countries and Germany would be the only available re-supply routes for heavy military equipment.

Linked Conventional and Nuclear Alerts

At present, the alerting system alerts both conventional and nuclear forces alike. NATO needs to go to LERTCON 3 to bring in conventional reinforcements, to ready artillery and tanks to operational positions up to firing positions and to deploy additional strike aircraft. The very act of reinforcing the conventional forces to enable them to hold out for longer may create an increased likelihood of Soviet nuclear strike because of the perception by the Soviet Union that a NATO nuclear strike is being prepared.

Conventional Attacks upon Command and Control and Nuclear Forces Themselves

Conventional attacks would be aimed at command and control centres (which also control nuclear forces) and nuclear-capable launch vehicles such as aircraft and artillery battalions. In this sense conventional attack inevitably has a nuclear component and, in as much as it was successful, would increase pressure for nuclear use as nuclear 'assets' were knocked out. This factor is particularly true for nuclear-armed surface naval task-groups operating off European coasts.

Nuclear installations such as nuclear power stations, of which there are many dozens in Eastern and Western Europe, are also likely to be hit deliberately or inadvertently. This, along with the vaporisation of radioactive elements in nuclear warheads hit by conventional strikes means that a conventional attack may release significant amounts of radiation – in the case of a nuclear power station equivalent to the amount that would be released by a small nuclear weapon.

Quite apart from the additional hazards caused by extensive release of radioactive materials even in 'conventional' war in Europe, there is the severe danger that the radiation release may be mistaken for actual nuclear attack and bring about a nuclear response.

CONCLUSIONS

Despite all their efforts, the nuclear strategists have not been able to think up a convincing scenario for the use of nuclear weapons in the NATO area on land or at sea, which does not carry a significant and unacceptable risk of escalation to the destruction of Europe.

The stark logic is that actually *detonating* nuclear weapons in Europe makes no military or practical sense. As long as either side could credibly respond with nuclear retaliation, no longer-term military or political advantage can be gained by the use of nuclear weapons. Also, because nuclear weapons are so destructive, and because radiation, depending upon the wind direction, could spread over the aggressor as much as the defender, there is significant doubt whether the use of nuclear weapons could result in any military or political advantage for their user even if they were possessed by one side alone.

These arguments hold whatever the rationalising behind the proposed use. Once some nuclear warheads are detonated it really makes no difference whether they were detonated as 'first-use', in 'flexible response' or in FOFA or in Air-Land Battle. The result would be the same, destruction.

This being the case, the presently interlocking nuclear systems of East and West amount to some kind of a nuclear 'doomsday machine' designed to go off should war break out. Any ideas of trying to gain any advantage in such a situation, as in Air-Land Battle, or Maritime Strategy or Soviet equivalents, are illusory.

A serious, specific danger is that US forces may use nuclear weapons in certain circumstances earlier than would be counselled by their European Allies, in a mistaken US attempt to keep nuclear war 'limited' to non-Soviet Europe and to avoid intercontinental nuclear war and the targeting of the USA. This may drag European NATO into early and unwanted nuclear escalation. NATO's General Political Guidelines for the use of nuclear weapons also build in the option of first-use of nuclear weapons on a widespread scale.

The ludicrous nature of NATO's nuclear strategy is most clearly brought out in West Germany. Should war break out and NATO be losing the conventional battle, NATO plans to use nuclear weapons to halt the Soviet attack. First US commanders would order the bombing of East Germany and neighbouring Warsaw Pact countries to persuade the invading Soviets to give up and go home. The Germans assume that this would result in nuclear retaliation and the general nuclear destruction of Europe. It is difficult to see how such nuclear destruction by the West would not bring about a nuclear response. NATO also has plans for a second nuclear strike should the first fail, this time upon its own territory. In other words NATO (or at least the US nuclear commanders) would devastate parts of West Germany and Turkey to save them from being taken by Soviet attacking forces. This is not an attractive prospect to the inhabitants of West Germany and Turkey. There are bound to be other secret contingency plans, such as package ZEBRA, where NATO would hit West Germany in its *first* nuclear strike should invading forces have penetrated too far before nuclear release permission is obtained.

NATO's nuclear strategy would amount in part to a grisly re-enactment of the Second World War – only this time the killing of Germans with nuclear weapons by their *allies*. The scenario of one's own allies killing you to save you is worthy of Ionesco in the 'theatre of the absurd' or a scene from Kafka, it is not fit to be called a military 'strategy'. Yet just such a scenario was played out in the Wintex–Cimex exercise of Spring 1989. The German participants withdrew three days early in protest. They protested at the size of the first nuclear strike and managed to get it reduced from nineteen to seventeen warheads. This strike alone would have killed many East Germans. But the second NATO strike of twenty-five nuclear warheads was partly targeted on West Germany and Turkey. This caused a storm of German protest. As one German politician pointed out at the time: 'all anyone who wants to drive the Germans out of NATO needs to do is conduct such games'.[42] One would have to presume that if similar levels of political expression were permitted in Turkey that the Turkish Government would have felt pressured to make a similar protest.

With the mounting public opposition in West Germany to short-range nuclear weapons, nuclear 'modernisation', and noisy and dangerous low flying by NATO bombers, the Wintex scenario could hardly have been better chosen to inflame German worries epitomised in the neat aphorism 'the shorter the range [of nuclear weapons] the deader the Germans'. With the key political and geographical position of West Germany in NATO and the breaking down of the Berlin Wall between East and West Germany, strong German pressure could ultimately force a revision of NATO nuclear strategy.

The basic requirement of a defence policy is that it should make sense and provide a rationale for action capable of bringing about desired political goals. The use of nuclear weapons in Europe cannot do this. Furthermore, modern nuclear strategies create a *new* type of cause for war which has not previously existed to any great degree: inadvertent war or war by mistake.

My conclusion is that it is simply not possible to use nuclear weapons to replace or back up conventional forces in Europe. In fact, nuclear weapons and strategies *reduce* the capability of European conventional forces. NATO's nuclear strategy undermines its conventional forces by engendering an 'expecting to lose' mentality, by encouraging low stocking levels of fuel and ammunition and by creating disunity amongst NATO and potential NATO members.

The only solution is to construct conventional forces that are in themselves strong enough to hold off conventional attack and to design nuclear and conventional strategies with built-in stability. I explore various options available to NATO in this respect in detail in the final section of this book and deal with possible responses to nuclear 'blackmail' in such a defence.

Part II
New Weapons, New Strategies

Introduction

SCENARIO: SOMEWHERE IN EAST GERMANY

In the grey light just before dawn a sentry patrols the perimeter fence of Grossenhain AB, a Warsaw Pact main operating base 20km north of Dresden, East Germany, normal base of a regiment of nuclear-capable SU-17 'Fitter D' aircraft. The base is in a high state of alert. SU-17 ground-attack aircraft are fuelled-up and waiting under curved-roofed, camouflaged, concrete shelters. Five MiG-23, 'Flogger G' air-combat fighters are loaded with four R-60 'Aphid' and two R-23 air-to-air missiles and preparing for take-off near the end of the main runway.

All is quiet. The only sound that can be heard is the rushing sound of the wind in the trees. The noise grows and seems too constant to be the wind. Suddenly, looking towards the south, the sentry spots what looks for all the world like a miniature space shuttle. It is gliding low over the trees, jinking from side to side in flight and seems to be the source of the noise. The sentry radios in to his command to raise the alarm and watches transfixed. Warning sirens sound. The glider, which despite being too small to have a pilot on board, manoeuvres almost as if to land on the main runway. Dark objects start to be ejected sideways on small jets of flame. In a set of muffled explosions the objects appear to break up into smaller sections. These then drop quickly on small parachutes. The planes on the runway are screaming their engines up to temperature ready for take-off.

The grey glider flies neatly down over the main runway, which suddenly erupts into violent activity. The cylinders dropping by parachute suddenly emit tongues of flame and plunge at incredibly high speed towards the reinforced tarmac. As they hit it, intense blue-white bolts of light illumine the scene with an unearthly glow making a roaring tearing noise. Fractions of a second later there are several explosions and several of the 8-foot-thick concrete slabs beneath the runway heave up creating huge obstacles. Some of the explosives do not seem to work and leave only a fairly neat hole. More cylinders lie scattered about on the grass and on undamaged stretches of the runway surface. The soldier sees the squat cylinders sprout curved vanes which had formerly been wrapped about them. The vanes cause the cylinders to stand upright on end. They then extend short aerials from their tops. The cylinders have rather ominous-looking apertures in their sides.

Despite the severe damage to the runway, the Warsaw Pact pilots think that they have a good chance of take-off by careful choice of taxiing path. They start to taxi forward. But as the first plane passes the first of the waiting cylinders, the horrified pilot sees it *rotate* as if to face him, followed shortly by an intense blast of red hot shrapnel which sets the plane on fire. As the pilot escapes from his plane the second pilot taxis forward and reaches a relatively clear area of runway. Just as he reaches it, another huge section of concrete rears up from another underground explosion, blocking his path completely.

Ground crews move out quickly in armoured bulldozers ready to clear away any mines and to fill holes with ready-mixed quick-setting concrete. The heaved-up slabs of the airfield runway offer no easy purchase to the bulldozer blades. At random intervals, further underground mines explode, raising more huge slabs. The other mines sitting on the grass also explode at random intervals intended for any ground crews foolish enough to venture out unprotected. The ground crews have to set them off slowly, one by one, by shooting at them from a distance.

Only two planes manage to escape and take off, several remain as burned-out shells on the runway, while yet others are trapped in their shelters, useless, pinned down with all their unusable fuel and weapons. Other planes away on sorties have to be diverted to other less-well-protected and supplied bases further afield. The anti-aircraft guns sit useless, waiting for attacking aircraft which do not come.

Even as the ghastliness of the situation becomes apparent to the hapless Warsaw Pact base, more silent, gliding, low-flying objects fly in dealing out more death and destruction. Ground forces near the base discover more lethal mines waiting in the woods to destroy lightly armed tanks or personnel carriers and to kill or maim unwary soldiers.

This may sound like the science-fiction fantasy of some Dr Strangelove or deranged General, but it is not. If US and NATO arms initiatives in Europe are pursued and stay funded to the tune of billions of dollars, such a scenario would be only one of many possible should war ever break out.

In fact such weapons as described above are now the state-of-the-art of the military technology of airfield destruction weapons which have already undergone extensive testing and feasibility studies in three or more variants. The low-flying powered glider was a 'dispenser system', precision-guided to its target after launch from an aircraft some distance away and 'dispensing' a range of specialised bomblets, mines and other so-called sub-munitions. Such weapons are now being discussed and developed in line with plans for new NATO weaponry for the mid-1990s and beyond.

SCENARIO: THE SPECTRE HAUNTING MOSCOW

Images of a fierce Soviet attack upon the West have been commonplace in the NATO lexicon and gained a certain credibility from sheer repetition. One can argue that this is as unlikely as NATO attacking the Warsaw Pact and heading for Moscow, but if East–West relations were to become strained to breaking point in some unknown crisis, the Soviet military have to consider the worst case. Soviet worst case scenarios centre around the spectre of a powerful German state in Central Europe and some kind of repeat of the Second World War – a blitzkrieg attack through the Pact states into the Soviet Union. This scenario mirrors the NATO worst case – the Soviet Union attacking NATO.

If we assume that NATO deploys all its new highly technological weaponry and that the Soviets who lag behind in this technology by up to ten years have no equivalent response, how would these developments fuel or reduce Soviet fears of attack and hence our mutual security in a crisis?

The scenario which I describe assumes that when war breaks out there are some Soviet forces in Eastern Europe. With the removal of most or all of these forces, the scenario, as much as it may appear more unlikely to western political perceptions, would be more *militarily* feasible because Soviet forces would no longer be forward-based in large numbers in Eastern Europe.

The scenario in the Soviet mind's eye could go something like this:

In response to a crisis in Eastern Europe which western observers interpret as a Soviet threat to the security of a newly democratic Eastern European state, the US Marine Corps and Tactical Airlift squadrons are moved into Europe and European ground forces are on high alert and reinforced.

At 0200 hours on 8 November, NATO launches operation 'Liberate'. 500 non-nuclear cruise missiles are launched under cover of extensive, thick, low cloud from the US 2nd fleet in the North Atlantic and air-launched from adapted military transport planes and bombers on 'routine' patrols over Western Germany. They fly circuitous routes to their known, fixed targets in East Germany, Poland and Czechoslovakia. The following targets are hit; in order of priority:

    10   underground command and communication bunkers;
    72   main airfields;
    119 fuel dumps;
    113 railway marshalling yards, bridges road and rail intersections;

NATO blitzkrieg formations of main battle tanks supported by heavy multiple launch rocket systems (MLRS) fire and air cover, decimate surprised Soviet front-line garrisons in East Germany and carry on through heading for Warsaw. In western Czechoslovakia, MLRS, tanks and Patriot air-defence formations are dropped behind enemy lines by US Air Cavalry and tactical transport. As they attack in the rear, Western forces pour down the Ohre and Berounka river valleys across the German–Czech border, then branch North towards Warsaw in a flanking manoeuvre, and East towards Prague.

Fierce urban fighting erupts in Berlin, Magdeburg and Leipzig as the beleagured Soviet forces re-group for counter-attack against Western forces. Streams of refugees cross the East–West frontier as high-level discussions proceed on the 'Hot Line'.

What military plan are the NATO forces following? Will they halt before the disputed border? Or is their objective Byelorussia and the Baltic States?

The West has fired no nuclear shell upon Soviet territory, but threatens massive nuclear response to any Soviet nuclear response. Western anti-submarine forces and 'hunter-killer' submarines trail Soviet submarines out of Murmansk into the North Atlantic and out of Vladivostok into the Sea of Japan, threatening their destruction should they prepare for firing. NATO is in a commanding position.

2 The Armed Bureaucracy

Every year through the late 1980s, NATO countries spent $320 000 000 000 ($320 billion) on military forces in Europe (1988 figures).[1] Out of this, most – about $280 billion a year – was spent on non-nuclear forces: armies, navies and air forces. These massive levels of military expenditure are already declining. Further cuts can be expected through the 1990s.

The forces in Europe form the basic starting resource from which any alternative non-nuclear defence strategy would have to be fashioned. The size of the conventional forces budget illustrates the importance of any possible savings in this area. This chapter describes some of the underlying forces and tensions controlling and influencing decision-making within NATO. Understanding the influences upon decision-making within NATO is highly relevant to assessing the practical difficulties and institutional resistance that will be faced by proposals for military and political reform.

NATO is bureaucratic alliance of sixteen nations with differing histories, backgrounds, world outlooks and interests. The major national influences within NATO, in order of political importance and influence, which is closely linked to the economic and military contributions made to NATO's common defence, are: the USA (by a long way), West Germany, the UK, France (although not formally a full member of NATO) and Italy.

Other influences and forces are connected with the aims of military–industrial initiatives and fierce commercial competition for lucrative arms markets which exists between the USA and Europe, and between individual European countries. These commercial factors and forces pressure weapons choices, and even military strategy, in ways which I argue are not always consistent with the requirements for peace and stability in Europe nor with what might be realistic preparations and precautions for the possibility of actually having to fight a war with the Soviets, with or without nuclear weapons.

ALLIES AND ENEMIES

NATO has actually deployed over ten types of tank, over two dozen different anti-tank weapons, about one hundred different tactical missiles and more than fifty kinds of ammunition. There are over twenty families of combat aircraft with different payload capabilities and operating ranges. When the aircraft land some require differing refuelling nozzles, differing spares and electronic 'conversion' kits to enable the same missile to be fitted. Some cannot even be re-armed in certain countries' airfields because of differing bomb-loading facilities. The British Tornado for example, cannot be re-armed at German and Italian airfields because of non-standard bomb pallets.[2] On top of this, NATO's armies have four different major communications systems which are incompatible.

It is impossible to find any explanation for this incredible plethora and range of weaponry purely in a military response to a perceived Soviet military threat. Although national military requirements do differ, having such a wide range of largely non-standard weapons, requiring totally different ammunition and spares makes little overall military sense for NATO as a whole.

A substantial answer to this conundrum lies in the fact that while NATO member-countries are military allies, they are economic competitors. This competition is most keenly felt between the USA and European NATO.

Arms are very big business, involve huge sums of government money and provoke great competition between Western arms manufacturers who vie fiercely with each other for NATO or national contracts.

As arms have become more and more expensive to produce and the number of arms companies has dwindled, individual European NATO governments have ended up supporting a few of their own large, surviving arms manufacturers. Having made such a large financial and political investment, each government often feels obliged to push the products of their own arms industry and to buy them for their national forces. This political factor, which works strongly against cooperation in arms manufacture, accounts largely for the very wide range of weaponry in NATO.

This is in sharp contrast with the forces of the Warsaw Pact who have a high level of standardisation of equipment, which is used by all national forces. Individual national political interests are not allowed to influence the military sphere which is dominated by one major political interest, that of the Soviet Union. This leads to a high degree of military coherence; thus the Warsaw Pact fields only two types of new tank and around three families of combat aircraft.

In NATO all the many types of weapon are produced by many

companies all essentially doing the same thing, working upon the same types of project, each struggling to solve the same problems but working in isolation and secrecy. Analysts of manufacturing inside NATO estimate that:

- eleven firms in seven countries work upon anti-tank weapons;
- eighteen firms in seven countries design and make ground-to-air weapons;
- eight firms in six countries make air-to-air weapons;
- sixteen companies in seven nations make air-to-ground weapons;
- ten firms spread among seven countries make ship-to-ship missiles.[3]

All this activity is clear evidence that the 'threat from the East' is not perceived to be so great, or that NATO has no political leaders who dare to forsake national interests for group European interests. Nevertheless, Warsaw Pact forces and Warsaw Pact arms spending are used as major justifications for NATO spending. A continual source of friction within NATO is the overall military budget and the relative contributions made by respective NATO members. Surprisingly, the NATO member-countries have no formalised arrangements for member-countries to contribute some proportion of the GNP to a military pool in the way, for example, that the EC works. The USA tends to see Europe as shirking its responsibilities and continually expecting the USA to pay out more. The Europeans are suspicious of US dominance of NATO and the large market penetration of European arms markets by US weaponry.

NATO Spending versus Warsaw Pact Spending

As long ago as 1977, the US Carter Administration, pointing to an apparent continuing increase in Warsaw Pact arms spending to the tune of 6–8 per cent per annum, persuaded NATO member-countries to agree to a real increase, above inflation, of 3 per cent per annum for five years in order to offset these imbalances and to deploy new high-technology weapons. Ever since, NATO has continued to re-assert a desire to increase spending on military forces by 3 per cent a year.[4]

Few NATO countries have kept to these spending requirements. During the US Reagan Administration, US pressure on NATO manifested itself in threats by Congress to remove several thousand US troops based in Western Germany unless NATO countries kept to their 3 per cent spending agreement. Republican Senator Sam Nunn proposed an amendment to the $291 000 million (£210 000 million) Defense Authorisation Bill, 1985, that would have meant a phased withdrawal of up to one-third of US troops in West Germany unless the European NATO allies spent more, as they had agreed on infrastructure, for example, ammunition sufficient for up to thirty days and additional hardened aircraft shelters for US air reinforcements.[5] The amendment was defeated by 55 votes to 41 after fierce lobbying against it by the Reagan administration who felt that it would 'embarrass the Margaret Thatchers and Helmut Kohls of the world'.[6] In the end a compromise measure was reached in which US troop levels would be held constant at about 326 000 unless the Allies showed that they had taken steps to meet their defence commitments.

This was the first time that such a proposal had caused serious concern in the White House. Of course, even with the amendment having been defeated, the USA could exert significant pressure upon NATO to do what they wanted.

There is, however, strong evidence that these US administration figures for Warsaw Pact spending were inflated estimates in the first place. Estimates of Soviet arms spending depend largely on how they are done and what assumptions are made.

Up until May 1989, the Soviet Union maintained that their military spending was a mere 20 billion roubles a year, whilst Western sources estimated figures in the range of 150 billion roubles. In fact, until 1989, it seems extremely likely that the Soviets themselves did not know what they were spending because of the lack of Western-style accounting methods and the inextricable links between the Soviet military and civilian industries.[7]

In the USA in the middle-1980s, there was a sharp running dispute between two establishment intelligence agencies. In June 1984, the Defense Intelligence Agency (DIA) took the unprecedented step of giving an unattributable briefing to the effect that Soviet spending had increased by 5–10 per cent on 170 weapons systems. Previously, the CIA had released figures showing a 2–4 per cent increase in the Soviet arms budget. The US media interpreted the Defense Department release as 'buttressing the Defense Department's case for continued strong defense spending',[8] as the briefing was given on the same day as the Senate was voting and before the Congressional vote. The New York Times, in protest, refused even to send a reporter. The calculation methods employed by both agencies have been repeatedly criticised as grossly inaccurate. The Center for Defense Information in Washington has pointed out that when Reagan agreed to increase forces' pay this had the bizarre effect of immediately increasing apparent Soviet spending. This is because the CIA assume that US and Soviet forces receive equal pay, whereas in fact Soviet conscripts actually received 3.8 roubles per month (roughly $6), while US volunteers were paid about $550 a month (1984 figures).

Probably the best independent figures for comparison are those of the Stockholm International Peace Research Institute (SIPRI). SIPRI devote a large effort to understanding the economics of Warsaw Pact arms production. They came up with a 2.5 per cent Soviet spending increase for the years 1982 and 1983 in constant price figures, which compared closely with the CIA figure,[9] and was well below the DIA estimate.

One point which needs to be made relating to all these arms spending comparisons is that is extremely difficult, if not impossible, to compare Western and Soviet/Warsaw Pact military spending directly. The Soviet 1989 figure of 77 billion roubles corresponds to about $123 billion using official Soviet conversion rates (far less than US spending of $300 billion). This rate, however, is artificial, as the rouble is not an exchange currency, and overestimates the 'market' value of the rouble in comparison with the dollar. 77 billion roubles, however, does correspond to about 9 per cent of Soviet GNP which compares with 6 per cent in the USA and 4 per cent in the UK. Some Western intelligence sources, however, estimate Soviet spending as being as much as 16–20 per cent of Soviet GNP.[10]

Burden-sharing

In 1988 the European defence spending issue resurfaced in a new guise – 'burden-sharing'. In August 1988, the US Defense Burden-sharing Panel warned the Europeans in very strong terms that budgetary pressure upon the US budget (primarily arising from the huge US budget deficit) would lead them to cut US forces in Europe:

> The Panel is aware of internal political influences in Japan and Europe, but believes that our allies are not sufficiently aware of the strong political pressure in this country to reduce our defense commitments to our allies unless they are willing to share more of the burden . . . the Panel states in the strongest possible terms that

the Europeans had better be prepared to defend their own territory without a large-scale US ground force commitment, because
that commitment cannot be guaranteed forever.[11]

This is a US line of argument more divorced from US estimates of the
Soviet threat than before, but the background US threat to Europe is
the same. The US is highlighting – in its eyes – the European's
lackadaisical approach to their own security and the low priority the
Europeans give to military spending. The difference in attitudes on
the opposite sides of the Atlantic between the USA and Europe
illustrates a different perception of the Soviet threat. Historically,
and especially in the wake of the reforms in the Soviet Union,
Europe sees the Soviet Union as far less of a threat then than does
the USA.

It seems, however, that President George Bush has turned this
US–European problem into an opportunity by linking US troop cuts
to the present conventional arms talks in Vienna. In this way the US
hope to cut their forces in line with Congress pressures, whilst also
getting reductions in Soviet forces in Europe.

The burden-sharing issue represents a resurgence of another perennial argument. Arms lobbyists have long argued that NATO,
despite having a technological lead, has had an inability to convert
this into large numbers of usable, and – most importantly – affordable
weapons. As weapons are becoming more and more sophisticated,
they are also becoming more and more expensive. Some NATO
analysts have even gone so far as to suggest that if current trends in
increases in costs of military equipment continue, NATO will be
forced to disarm 'unilaterally' in a process of 'structural disarmament'.[12] Not something that NATO strategists are keen on. They
argue that while the Warsaw Pact may not be spending as much as
was thought, they are actually getting far better value for their
money, more 'bangs for the buck'. They are also getting equipment
which is standardised and interoperable between all Warsaw Pact
forces, a feature dramatically absent from NATO national forces
who often compete to produce several different and incompatible
sorts of the same weapon, which are then all bought by their host-
countries'/forces.

In response to these pressures, there have long been calls within
NATO for more standardisation and co-production of weapons. The
USA has argued that the way for NATO to utilise its technological
lead is to use the latest technological developments in a new range of

'smart' weapons to be produced by a range of US and US–European consortiums.

These US proposals for new weaponry have elicited a mixed European response because of European suspicions that the new technological initiative is just another way for the USA to sell Europe another whole breed of costly, advanced weaponry. NATO's European members, and particularly the industrialists, tend to be more worried about unfair economic practices by the US than by possible Soviet weapons developments. Besides NATO's apparent competition with the Warsaw Pact in terms of military power, Europe itself is in fierce competition with the USA for a share of the market. Europeans see the USA as having a large, captive home arms market well protected by Congress and specific legislation such as the 'Buy America' Act of 1933 and the 'Specialty Metals' rider to the Department of Defense Appropriations Act – a rider introduced every year since 1973. This rider seeks to ban the import of metals such as titanium and specific composite materials. As most aircraft and missiles have some of these components in them these are all prohibited imports. Each year the Department of Defense has obtained special waivers for imports from NATO countries, but the rider can be reinstated at any time.

The Europeans assert that the USA sells 7–9 times as much arms to Europe as NATO sells to them. To use the NATO parlance, not so much a two-way (trade) street, more a one-way system. Some US sources maintain that the real imbalance is not this bad, more like three to one in their favour.

Such bald figures however, do not tell the full story of some blatant cases of American protectionism and the bitterness caused in the companies affected in Europe. A clear example was the case of the British Martin-Baker ejection seats, traditionally preferred by the US Navy for fitting to its F/A-18 combat aircraft, after they had come out best in open, competitive testing. But the US Navy decision was overturned by a Congressman on the grounds that buying from abroad would cause erosion of the US industrial base. This objection arose not 'from any consideration of pilot safety or productive efficiency, but from murky machinations of American politics'.[13] The machinations were not so murky, the Congressman was merely ensuring votes from workers employed in a competing arms company in his state.

An even more blatant case of US protectionism is the case of the British 81mm L16 mortar, which is in service with eighteen armies around the world. Nevertheless, the US Army's test agency 'tested' the L16 for seven years. At one point, the round was frozen in a refrigerator to $-10°C$ then fired in the August heat of the testing ground. Needless to say, once the round was removed, a thick layer of ice was formed from water vapour condensing out of the warm air. The round came out of the mortar tube 'like a snowball' and fell far short of its target. The Army test report said that the round 'doesn't work in cold weather'.[14] – a statement which is nonsense, because in cold weather when everything was cold, a layer of ice would not form. This mortar was in fact used in action in the tundra conditions of the South Atlantic in the Falklands–Malvinas conflict.

NATO and European Cooperation and Decision-making

It is ironic that although fear of the armed forces of the Warsaw Pact has not been sufficient to induce European–NATO cooperation, worries about competition with the USA sometimes is. Many of the somewhat dormant mechanisms designed to bring about European cooperation are seeing something of a revival. The Independent European Production Group (IEPG) had its first ministerial level meeting in its eight-year history in November 1984. This group is particularly important because it includes the French who are members of NATO but are not fully integrated into its military structure.

The Western European Union (WEU), until recently a fairly inactive alliance of France, West Germany, Belgium, Luxembourg, Italy, the Netherlands and the UK, dating from the breakdown of talks on a European Defence Community in 1952 and predating NATO itself by a year, is also seeing a revival. Talk is of the need to 'strengthen the European pillar of NATO'. Again this grouping includes France and excludes the USA. Politically, the three key countries in the WEU are France, Germany and the UK. The WEU has already led to increased French–German links and facilitated German arms production. The original terms of the WEU agreed in 1952 prohibited the Germans from producing atomic, chemical or biological weapons, warships over a certain size, and aircraft and missiles over a certain range. These terms were modified in 1984, and from January 1986 the West Germans have been allowed to build conventional weapons without any restrictions, a point attacked at the time by the Soviet Union. The French and Germans are also collaborating closely in joint military exercises and talking about possible roles for French nuclear weapons in Germany's defence.

For many years, various of the many NATO committees and subcommittees, which briefly report their activities in *Atlantic News*, a twice-weekly Brussels publication, have been talking about arms cooperation without anything changing very much. In one scathing report in November 1983 by the Norwegian State Secretary Holst, it was stated that 'the IEPG could not even identify one single draft that had been established within its framework'.[15]

Now, several very large collaborative projects are being considered which will show whether NATO can really cooperate. At present the Conference of NATO Armaments Directors (CNAD) has discussed a NATO frigate, a Defence Research Group (DRG) study on long term planning, various new technology projects, seven working papers on improving conventional defences (CDI) and an Identification Friend or Foe (IFF) system (a way for NATO planes to identify themselves to other planes or ground-based missiles to avoid being shot down – at present all planes are assumed hostile and NATO planes returning from sorties have to avoid the hazards of being shot down by their own air defences). The Common Frigate project is one of the largest joint ventures NATO has ever attempted. The Defence Research Group drew up plans in 1984 entitled Land and Maritime Operations (LO 2000) and (MO 2005) respectively, envisaging military requirements into the next millenium, the NATO counterpart of the US Air-Land Battle and Air-Land Battle 2000.[16] Other elements of the bureaucracy which would be involved are the NATO Industrial Advisory Group (NIAG) – controlling over 200 sub-groups and involving industry the Periodic Armaments Planning System (PAPS) and the National Armaments Planning Review (NAPR).

Some of these NATO committees formalise a relationship which has grown in any case – a close linkage and relationship between senior political and military figures, and arms manufacturers. NIAG is one such committee. Other *ad hoc* groups regularly organise seminars where the military talk about the weapons and strategies that they would like, while the manufacturers tell them what is possible now and in the future for what level of funding. One such invitation-only seminar, held in Cologne, West Germany on 4 and 5 October 1982, was organised in the name of General Franz-Josef Strauss, former Commander-in-Chief of Allied forces in Central Europe. Funding came from the German Association for Military Technology (DWT). The seminar concerned itself almost exclusively with the sensors and weapons which could make a 'deep strike' strategy work and was attended by senior members of Germany's Bundestag; US Defense, State Department and Congressional officials; Luftwaffe officers; and executives from leading West German and US Aerospace firms involved in the proposed manufacture of the new weaponry. Informed sources speculated that the meeting was 'clearly a Worner initiative'.[17] Manfred Worner was at that time a prospective West German Defence Minister and since May 1988 has been NATO General Secretary, replacing Lord Carrington. Similar seminars are regularly held by such 'non-profit making' organisations as the International Defense Electronics Association (IDEA), 'State of the Art Limited' (SAL), the Technical Marketing Society of America (TMSA) and Advanced Technology International (ATI). Attendance at a two-day seminar in, say, Munich, Oslo, Stockholm or London costs some £400 to £500 (sterling). Recent seminars have covered subjects such as 'legal aspects of penetrating the NATO market' (TMSA, March 1987); 'anti-submarine warfare' (SAL, February, 1987); 'anti-tactical ballistic missile systems' and 'contracting to the [UK] Ministry of Defence' (ATI, January, 1987); and 'Smart to Brilliant Munitions' (IDEA, January 1985). Attendance is limited to 'United States citizens or citizens of an allied nation with whom the United States has a memorandum of understanding or a memorandum of agreements relative to reciprocal defense procurement'. Such memoranda are classified agreements which form the written basis of arms-dealing between the USA and European NATO.

Such seminars are the way in which the arms industry mobilises support and funding for its activities and seeks to influence key decision-makers in NATO. The arms industries need to keep producing more products and to diversify production to survive in a competitive market. Because of the jobs created by the arms manufacturers there are domestic political pressures to keep arms manufacturer's order books full in individual NATO countries, in the absence, as NATO sees it, of alternatives. The workforce involved is considerable. Over 40 per cent of Western scientists and engineers work upon various aspects of military research and development. Their job is to apply the latest developments in science and technology to the battlefield. Thus new potential weapons are continously being made possible if the money can be found to develop them beyond the drawing board. This is a technological pressure to stay ahead, the 'if we don't develop them they will' argument. Another driving force is provided by sectors of the US Republican Party who fundamentally mistrust the Soviet Union and argued against the INF treaty to the extent of accusing President Reagan of being an 'apologist' for the Soviet Union (criticism voiced by Senator Dole) and of being a 'weak man dominated by a woman'.[18] Quite an extraordinary experience for Reagan who originally coined the 'evil empire' description of the Soviet Union. Original members of the US Defense Department such as Caspar Weinberger and Richard Perle share similar views of the Soviets and have voiced similar arguments both in and out of office.

Such industrial influences combined with right-wing US figures combine to lobby European NATO powerfully. As the NATO bureaucracy for decision-making is ponderous and obscure (Lord Carrington has described it as 'labyrinthine') this leads to a situation where the various 'market' forces often decide issues and effectively lead decision-making in advance of European politicians, who are then cast in the role of justifying policy after the practically available range of policy options has been significantly narrowed or virtually set. This is not the entire story and a determined politician who has some independent ideas can have a major influence, but a politician's real power to change things depends upon his or her ability to understand the system and how to manipulate it, rather than letting the system manipulate them.

As such, the latest generation of weapons, new non-nuclear, highly accurate and destructive devices capable of finding their own targets after being fired, which go under the general title of precision-guided munitions, are the latest product of a military-technological process rather than a more rational process of objectively establishing the political requirements of NATO's defence policy and then looking for a suitable strategy to fulfil it. It can be argued that the latest technological developments fit in neatly with NATO's plans for conventional force modernisation. Or perhaps put more cynically, NATO's new plans fit in neatly with the new weaponry. I would suggest in fact, that both arguments are correct as far as they go but that they bear much of the same relation to each other as the arguments about which came first – the chicken or the egg? The 'chicken or egg' debate does however rather miss the point. Both were produced in this case by military-industrial pressure upon a ponderous bureaucracy.

SUMMARY AND CONCLUSIONS

NATO's decision-making structure is complex and obscure, and linked to powerful political and economic forces connected with major arms manufacturers. The current set-up has considerable institutional momentum and is highly resistant to change. Never the less there are strong internal pressures for change in NATO. The USA, which contributes over half of NATO's military budget, has committed itself to reducing its large budget deficit. The military budget is a prime contender for cuts. For their part, the European allies have their own budgetary pressures generated by domestic-spending requirements created by high unemployment and the need to revitalise the European economy. These are strong pressures to reduce European military spending. All these factors pointed to an almost inevitable decline in military spending and force levels in Western Europe even before the sweeping changes in Eastern Europe. Following these changes and assuming that no longer-term threats are perceived, NATO countries along with the Warsaw Pact countries will find it well nigh impossible to justify any arguments for the maintenance of high levels of military spending.

Implications for an Alternative

NATO's response to any alternative is to resist it, raising the spectre of alliance disunity should the idea of NATO's dependence upon nuclear weapons be challenged, and the spectre of an 'overwhelming' Soviet threat in the face of possible conventional arms reforms. However, viewed objectively, military reforms towards defensive defence need not challenge the profit motive of the arms industry. Defensive defence does, however, imply a change of emphasis to different types of military production. Reforms toward defensive defence, if only NATO could seriously consider them, could also provide a desirable goal towards which to work in response to pressures to reduce arms spending. Military reforms towards defensive defence could then provide a positive agenda as the goal of arms negotiations. Instead of continual opposition against the tides of change, NATO should take up the challenge and institute positive reforms towards greater international security.

3 Pandora's Arsenal

At the present time, NATO is engaged in a conventional force rearmament programme. NATO plans to bring a wide range of new technology weapons into service during the 1990s. Some of the new weapons are already in service in small numbers. The programme also has some important implications for NATO's nuclear forces, as many of the new weapons have a designed or potential 'dual use' or 'dual capability' (that is, they could be used with conventional or nuclear warheads, and in some cases with chemical warheads).

One justification which NATO spokespersons put forward for the need for NATO to increase its conventional capability, is to raise the so-called nuclear 'threshold' (that is, the likely delay before nuclear weapons would be used would be longer).

On the face of it, this is a laudable objective. But will this objective be achieved by the new developments? And, importantly will the new weapons combined with NATO's strategy of 'Follow-On Forces Attack' (FOFA) achieve greater conventional crisis stability?

NEW WEAPONS AND STRATEGIES

It is possible to identify the time when the military–technological process first specifically addressed the issue of new technology weapons. As early as 1981, the US Defense Science Board identified particular technologies which could be applicable to new weaponry. These included very high-speed integrated circuits (VHSIC), advanced computer programming languages, machine intelligence, supercomputers, advanced composite materials and very high-density sensor arrays (focal plane arrays) for computer imaging. Some of these areas of technology were also being highlighted by the Strategic Defense Initiative Office (SDIO) in the USA. Advanced new semiconductor materials for missile sensors such as gallium-arsenide and mercury-cadmium-telluride were also highlighted.

In December 1982, Weinberger presented a paper (classified, but substantial information was 'leaked' or can be gleaned from unclassified sources) to NATO on possible applications of new military technology.[1] This paper was subsequently discussed in various NATO committees including the Executive Working Group, the

Military Committee and the Conference of National Armaments Directors (CNAD). The CNAD drew up a list of four areas to be emphasised:

1. stopping the 'first wave' of attacking Warsaw Pact forces with the aid of weapons such as the multiple launch rocket system (MLRS), artillery with 'smart' munitions, and using remotely piloted vehicles for reconnaissance and targeting;
2. attacking following-on forces with new longer-range weapons;
3. specialised airfield-attack weapons for both offensive and defensive counter-air operations;
4. improving battlefield information by means of interconnected networks of command, control, communications and intelligence (C3I);

By April 1984, CNAD had suggested no fewer than eleven large defence projects as the initial 'emerging technology' (ET) applications programme. It was indicative of disagreements between the USA and Europe, that none of the weapons finally selected were of very long range. US proponents of 'deep strike' concepts, hitting far behind Soviet lines (as far as 600 miles 'deep') were not successful. NATO's Defence Planning Committee (DPC), however, did shortly afterwards formally adopt a new strategy of FOFA, referring to Soviet forces following the front-line forces, ready to 'pour through' any holes breached in NATO defences. In May 1985, the DPC launched the Conventional Defence Improvements Initiative (CDII), followed in February 1986 by the selection of six CDII projects to be pursued cooperatively.

The strategies of FOFA, Air-Land Battle and deep strike were under debate for two years before NATO formally adopted FOFA whilst also re-endorsing the long-held strategy of forward defence, in which NATO says it will defend as far forward as possible so as not to be seen by the West Germans as being willing to give up any depth of Germany even for a short period.

FOFA, which as we have already seen, is a 'sub-concept' of Air-Land Battle, can be seen as a political compromise between the US proponents of deep strike and NATO's long-standing strategy of 'forward defence', whilst avoiding the public fears likely to be associated with the term Air-Land Battle connected with fears over the use of nuclear weapons.

FOFA, incorporating forward defence, according to one observer means attacking 'with conventional weapons those enemy forces which stretch from just behind the troops in contact to as far into the enemy's rear as our target acquisition and conventional weapons systems will permit'.[2] As such, this definition does not rule out attacking at any depth, but the weaponry planned and in existence has ranges up to several hundred kilometres, sufficient to span right across East Germany and to hit targets in the west of Poland.

I will describe the weapons and strategies in order of type and range, starting with weapons designed to fight the first wave of Warsaw Pact forces up to 50km behind the front line; then the more strictly FOFA type weaponry: ground-based missile systems and air-launched missiles. I then look at battlefield command and control, and at new developments in Soviet advanced technology weapons.

STOPPING THE BLITZKRIEG

According to NATO planners, stopping the first wave means engaging possibly as many as 800 battalions (thirty-eight divisions) of Warsaw Pact forces comprising many tank, motorised-rifle and artillery battalions together with supply vehicles, deployed within 30km or so of the intra-German border.

At present NATO would engage these forces with helicopter-delivered anti-tank mines, artillery barrages, tanks and large numbers of new anti-tank missiles such as Swingfire, Milan, TOW, HOT and Hellfire carried by infantry in dug-in positions and by attack-helicopters and air-strikes.

HOT and Swingfire are due to be replaced in about 1995 by the Third Generation anti-tank (TriGat) missile, which is being developed by a combined French, British, German and Italian consortium including British Aerospace, Aerospatiale and MBB. British Aerospace are the prime British contractor with a UK cost contribution of £2400m. This weapon is being designed in two variants: one-man-portable of 2000 metre range and using a gallium arsenide (GaAs is one of the new semi-conductor materials) detector to follow a carbon dioxide (CO_2) laser beam; and a 4500 metre 'fire and forget' variant with initial radar guidance and an advanced infra-red (heat) sensor for final targeting (see Box 3.1). The warhead may be a new 'tandem' type, designed to cope with new tank armour (see Box 3.2). These

---

Box 3.1   Fire and forget

'Fire and forget' weapons are designed to cut out the need for human guidance. After being fired the weapons guide themselves to their targets by a wide variety of mechanical 'senses' including radio, radar, heat, laser beams, ordinary light, noise and vibration. Some carry maps of their target areas, to which they can navigate to within a few tens of metres and then compare the scene they 'see' with their on-board map to finally home-in on the target.

Box 3.2   HOT 2

The HOT 2 anti-tank missile, produced by the Euromissile consortium, has a range of 4000 metres and can penetrate 1250mm (*four feet*) of rolled-steel homogeneous armour plating.

The HOT 2T has been designed with a tandem warhead. A small front charge detonates any reactive armour (this is an overlayer attached to some Soviet tanks intended to deflect anti-tank warheads) whilst a second main charge punches a hole through the tank armour. The warhead is now designed to kill the tank crew by the addition of an incendiary device together with anti-personnel steel balls.[3]

Box 3.3   New warheads

The new warheads may be deployed in the future upon a hydraulically raised weapons platform up to 13 metres (44 feet) above a cross-country truck. This mode of delivery enables the missile-launcher to hide whilst the weapons platform peeps over seeing oncoming threats. The MAN system is fitted with day-and-night sights, has an air-conditioning system to protect against chemical attack, and is envisaged as deploying anti-tank, anti-helicopter or anti-aircraft missiles. The system was first displayed in 1988.[4]

---

developments, if successful will make NATO's anti-tank weapons much more lethal.

For improved infantry air defence 70 000 'Stinger', (a shoulder-fired anti-aircraft missile used by the Mujaheddin in Afghanistan) are to be deployed to replace 'Redeye'.

Other weapons being developed are various 'smart' munitions for the 203mm and 155mm calibre howitzers already possessed by NATO.

Box 3.4   HELIK and BRAVE 200

Boeing have recently developed a robotic air vehicle (BRAVE 200) designed to fly slowly over the battlefield looking for enemy helicopters with an advanced radar system. The drones could be deployed singly or in pairs. After identifying their target the 'Brave 200' drone performs a terminal dive on to its target, destroying it with a warhead. The system is designed to operate day or night in any weather. The intention is to 'deny an enemy the use of airspace, disrupting synchronised operations-level attacks by eliminating second-echelon weapons in their own territory before they cross the forward edge of the battle area'.[5]

To translate, the weapon would attempt to shoot down anything resembling a helicopter behind enemy lines. One has to presume that Boeing have developed a means for the drones to recognise each other, otherwise they could well shoot each other down.

Multiple Launch Rocket System

With the expected advent in the near future of so-called 'third generation' precision-guided munitions, a major part of NATO's planned new conventional weaponry will be the multiple launch rocket system (MLRS).[6] MLRS is intended to replace much of NATO's present role for ordinary artillery or air-strikes upon attacking forces. Instead of waiting for Soviet forces to come up and be shot at by NATO's forward defences, NATO intends to take the battle more to the Soviets and to longer range.

Seven NATO countries – the USA, Germany, France Britain, Italy, the Netherlands and Turkey are deploying or will deploy MLRS.

The MLRS, as its name implies, consists of a mobile, tracked launch-vehicle carrying twelve missiles in two 'six-pack' canisters. The MLRS, carries a massive destructive power. According to LTV, its US manufacturers, a single MLRS vehicle with its three-man crew represents firepower equivalent to twenty-two M109 155mm howitzers manned by nearly 200 personnel. In one minute, one launcher can 'ripple'-fire twelve rockets to a range of 30km where, with the Phase I warhead, it distributes no fewer than 7728 M77 submunitions (644 per rocket) over an area the size of four football pitches, (an area 400–600 metres in diameter) resulting in a density of coverage of about six metres between each bomblet. This submunition carries a shaped charge that can penetrate up to 100mm of armour, thus the

66

Figure 3.1 Multiple-launch rocket system (MLRS)
Source: Photograph courtesy MLRS International Corporation.

Box 3.5   Precision-guided munitions

Precision-guided munitions (PGMs) are a revolutionary military technological development. Due to immense technological developments in micro-electronics, sensors and automatic guidance systems can be made small, light and above all, cheap enough to be fitted into the nose-cones of missiles, bombs or bomblets, the last-named often referred to as 'submunitions'.

The reason why PGMs are such a major development is that, unlike most other weapons, they have a better than 50:50 chance of hitting their intended target and in addition are almost certain to destroy it when they do. This is achieved by the conjunction of accurate targeting with the development of new, very specialised and controllable explosives known as 'shaped' or 'hollow' explosive charges. In a shaped charge, the explosive is shaped and detonated in such a way that the resulting blast wave is highly directional and concentrated, generally along the direction of the warhead's flight and is capable of burning and punching a hole through thick metal or concrete.

PGMs are often referred to as 'smart' or 'brilliant' by the arms manufacturers selling them.[7]

---

whole area is devastated by withering fire. Some of the advertising copy for this extremely lethal weapon system refers to this capability with the slogan: 'MLRS turns a ripple into a tidal wave.'

The MLRS is designed to be operated night or day and under chemical or biological attack; the crew can move from site to site and fire all the rockets without leaving the sealed cab. The loader-container holding the rockets is designed to have a ten-year storage life without special protection or maintenance. The launcher has an inertial guidance navigation system that is accurate to within 0.4 per cent of the distance travelled and which is normally updated every two hours or so. Less than two minutes elapse from the vehicle stopping, to the launcher being aimed at the first target, and the interval between successive firings can be as little as four seconds: two seconds to re-aim and two seconds to allow turbulence from the previous round to subside. The computerised fire-control system can communicate in English, French or German. At the heart of this is an automatic positioning determining system which, when requested, automatically finds true North and gives azimuth and elevation directions for firing the rockets. For multiple targets the system re-aims automatically.

The Phase II warhead and rocket can carry twenty-eight RTG AT2 anti-tank mines (336 per MLRS vehicle) to a longer range of some

40km where they form a minefield 1000 × 400m. The Phase III version of MLRS carries terminally guided submunitions to attack moving targets. 'Terminal guidance', means that the munitions home in to their targets using their own heat and radar sensors. Entry into full production is planned for 1992–1994.

The US army fielded the first operational MLRS battery of nine launchers in early 1983 and plans to spend a total of some $4000m on more than 300 launch vehicles and approximately 400 000 rockets. France, Britain, Italy and Germany have set up a European production group (EPG) to manufacture MLRS Phases I and II. Once this is complete the UK will order sixty-seven launchers with Phase I rockets; Germany 200 launchers, and Phase I and Phase II rockets; France eighty launchers, with Phase I rockets; while Italy wants twenty launchers with Phase I and II rockets. The Netherlands are ordering twenty-one systems direct from the USA and the other countries another thirteen.[8]

Thus the total European orders, excluding the USA, make a total of about 400 MLRS launchers with some 200 000 rockets. The US will deploy another 300 MLRS making a total of about 700. By the most conservative of estimates, these weapons, once deployed, would alone represent the equivalent of some 1300 additional artillery battalions in Europe and a roughly fivefold increase in the destructive power of NATO's artillery.

The MDTT Consortium (consisting of Martin Marietta, Diehl, Thomson-CSF and Thorn-EMI) is developing the Phase III warhead, intended to be operational in 1992. The submunitions in the Phase III Sense and Destroy Armor (SADARM) warhead would be ejected over the target area and descend spinning as they fall like sycamore seeds. As the high-explosive 'seeds' fall, the submunition's heat-sensitive seeker spins with it and thus scans over a large area searching for a warm target. Once a target is found, the munition homes in on it and – at a predetermined height above a tank measured by radar altimeter – detonates, firing a 'self-forging' fragment through the top armour. In the explosion, the blast energy is precisely channelled, causing molten metal to flow and forge into a warhead shape which is propelled at supersonic speed to its target. In tests the most recent Soviet engine-compartment armour including advanced reactive armour has been penetrated even though covered with several sandbags.[9]

One salvo of the MLRS would deliver seventy-two SADARM munitions into a target area of about 800 metres across. As each heat-seeker scans an area of about 75 metres radius, the entire target area is thoroughly scanned, and assuming that the system worked as expected, would hit any metal vehicles, tanks, support vehicles and so on in the area. Any munitions which cannot find targets as they drop, retain a deadly effect when they hit the ground where they become deadly anti-tank mines. Current US spending on SADARM (see Figure 3.2) is running at $450m per year.[10] It is expected that some 560 000 submunitions will eventually be bought. The Phase III Terminally Guided Warhead (TGW) version is under development by a US-European consortium and will contain three anti-tank sub-missiles per MLRS rocket (thirty-six per twelve rocket salvo).

The destructive potential of the MLRS is such that some of its proponents compare the possible killing power of the Phase III warhead with 'tactical' neutron nuclear warheads.

Calculations show that the tank killing power of one MLRS salvo, with the coverage described above, would have the same effective killing radius for tank crews of a 0.1kt nuclear shell.[11]

Finally, lest it be forgotten, the MLRS rocket, in common with much existing NATO artillery, is capable of firing a binary chemical warhead.

New Shorter-range Conventional Weapons and Conventional Stability

The deployment of several hundred MLRS Phase II and III systems in Europe will have important implications for NATO strategy. Once these weapons are deployed and, most importantly, providing that NATO could obtain good intelligence of Warsaw Pact forces positioning and strength in a conflict, then NATO would have substantially increased available firepower to bring to bear than at present. With well-organised coordination of fire and prepared defensive positions for MLRS systems to hide in and to move between, concentrations of invading forces could be killed not by concentrations of opposing NATO tanks but by dispersed MLRS which would be relatively invulnerable to counterfire providing they were well hidden. Such a development would be stabilising providing that NATO resists the temptation to deploy a nuclear warhead on the MLRS.

There is little doubt that relatively short-range PGM-dispensing systems such as MLRS, are highly 'effective' in a purely military

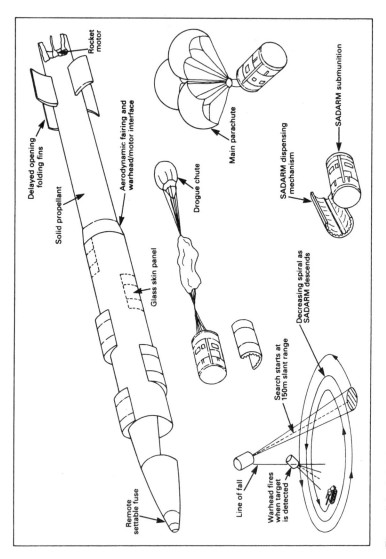

Figure 3.2 MLRS phase-III rocket with 6 SADARM (Sense and Destroy ARMor) munitions

sense. Warheads carrying small amounts of explosive are now capable of guiding themselves to and destroying valuable military targets such as tanks, aircraft and bunkers. Because the methods of destruction are much cheaper than their highly valuable targets, simple economics dictates that as long as the PGMs are capable of finding and destroying their targets, small and simple PGMs can be deployed in large numbers ready to overwhelm tank attacks and to limit severely the power of the offensive. To hope to compete, offensive weaponry must become smaller, cheaper and less complex.

PGMs favour the defence, because the offence – particularly armoured forces – have to move out of cover and across ground where they are vulnerable to fire from forces in better-protected positions. Western forces are now already armed with some of the latest PGMs which allow the firer to be completely out of sight of the target tank. Defensive forces armed with large numbers of such PGMs could make a blitzkrieg look like a suicide mission. These developments are stabilising, because in a crisis they favour the defence over offence and in a crisis the priority is not upon firing first, but upon survival, hiding and waiting quietly for attack to come.

All these new developments are part of exactly the same military dynamic that has operated in the past. In the continual battle of measure and counter-measure the balance between defence and offence continually swings from the one to the other. The Soviets will use as many counter-measures as they can and they are developing their own PGM weapons, which is again a stabilising development as long as they do not decide to develop and deploy long-range weaponry of this type. Most military analysts now agree that the new short-range weapons favour the defence and will do for some time in the foreseeable future. This analysis is based upon the fact that many of the shorter-range weapons have been shown to work, in contrast to some of the longer-range weaponry which relies upon new and relatively unproven exotic technology.

One major problem which the new weaponry creates and which NATO faces, arises from its highly effective and destructive nature. Any conventional conflict is likely to be much more swift and far more intense than in the past. Decisive battles may take hours not days and the strain upon troops and equipment will be considerably higher. There would be no time for resupplying ammunition once the battle has started, thus stocks need to be much higher than before. This type of intense conventional warfare was seen clearly in the so-called 'six day' war between Israel and Egypt. The consequences of this are that NATO would need to be able to respond more quickly and to keep higher stocks of ammunition. Both these measures create additional costs and pressures upon the organisation of military forces.

Another problem for NATO, with its current nuclear strategy is that intense and swift as the conventional conflict is, any delay achieved before escalation to nuclear use could be markedly reduced because it would be clear relatively early on who had 'won' or 'lost' the conventional battle. At this stage, with nuclear weapons deployed in close proximity with the conventional forces, the urge to fire nuclear weapons would be very strong. Another problem is that intense conventional warfare will result in very high civilian casualties.

NATO's problems of planning for intense, swift and costly warfare are very relevant to my proposals for a more stable system of conventional defence for Europe. It is necessary to create a deployment scheme using precision-guided munition weapons so as to avoid too rapid or intense conflict and the 'forcing' of escalation to nuclear use. Part of the answer is to remove nuclear weapons which are in such close proximity to conventional forces. The alternative strategy which I propose in the final section of this book seeks to avoid too high civilian casualties by aiming to slow down and bottle-up opposing forces rather than to achieve a quick and decisive 'victory' at great cost of life. I also address methods of avoiding the weakness of 'forward defence' which do not rely heavily upon aggressive strikes into the Eastern bloc.

ATTACKING FOLLOW-ON FORCES (FOFA)

This aspect of the new NATO initiative means attacking invading forces roughly 30–300km behind the front line or forward edge of the battle area (FEBA) as military strategists refer to it. NATO strategists estimate that out of roughly 425 fixed targets (airfields, bridges, etc.) and over 2000 mobile Warsaw Pact targets (tank battalions, missile-launchers, etc.) of which about 50 per cent would be deployed within 300km of the FEBA (see Table 3.1). According to NATO, the objective of the FOFA strategy is to prevent these 'following-on' forces from reaching the 'close' battle and to keep the ratio of NATO to Warsaw Pact forces at a 'manageable' level.[12] The main problems in actually achieving this are:

Table 3.1   FOFA targets

Type of target	Range beyond border (km)				
	0–30	30–100	FOFA 100–300	Deep strike 300–800	Total
Fixed targets					
Airfields (main operating bases)	–	13	31	28	72
Choke points (bridges, railyards, highway obstructions)	12	10	91	78	191
Underground (nuclear storage, communications, fuel)	5	27	87	43	162
Total fixed targets	17	50	209	149	425
Mobile targets					
Tank and artillery battalions (76 division force)	832	132	426	294	1684[†]
Nuclear missiles and support units	256	129	104	87	576[*]
Total mobile targets	1088	261	530	381	2260
Total targets	**1105**	**311**	**739**	**530**	**2685**

[†] Subject to reductions negotiated in the Conventional Forces in Europe (CFE) Talks.
[*] These targets are being reduced in number by the INF Treaty and would be removed completely by a nuclear 'third zero' short-range nuclear forces agreement.
Source: As note 13, this chapter.

1. having a weapon with sufficient range, accuracy and penetration capability to destroy fixed targets which would be heavily protected from attack from the air by air-defences;
2. knowing where the mobile targets are and being able to reach and destroy them before they move again.

Previously, these missions were to be handled almost entirely by air-strikes; now, the argument goes, aircraft are much too vulnerable (and too costly) to risk them again and again on conventional bombing runs against improved Warsaw Pact air defences.

As yet, although FOFA has been official NATO policy since November 1984, the only existing weapons to enact it (at least at ranges beyond 30km which can be covered by the MLRS) are improved ways of 'bombing' targets from the air using various munitions 'dispenser' systems (see Box 3.6). New technology FOFA weapons are in the process of development and initial testing.

FOFA Now

Beyond the range of the MLRS, NATO has an extensive air-strike capability. Most of this air force is allocated not to air defence or ground support, but to 'airfield denial'. This is the jargon term for striking Warsaw Pact airfields early in any conflict to deny their further use, making further Pact air operations much more limited. A large part of the Warsaw Pact air forces are designed to stop NATO achieving this objective and to support Pact ground forces. As such, NATO has a preponderance of ground-strike aircraft which would fly low, deep into the Warsaw Pact countries which have a preponderance of fighters and interceptors.

Both sides know exactly where each other's main operating bases (MOBs) are, and are well aware that these airfields would be prime 'sitting' targets in the event of any conflict. Most MOBs are thus located well behind the intra-German border out of easy striking range. MOBs have reinforced ('hardened') concrete shelters and fuel dumps, plus heavy anti-aircraft defences. The Warsaw Pact possess seventy-two such bases of which forty-four are within 300km of the German border. If these main operating bases are knocked out of action, then aircraft have to be dispersed to 'dispersed operating bases' (DOBS) where air defences, fuel supplies and hardened aircraft shelters would all be in short supply. Here the Warsaw Pact is at a severe disadvantage because it has virtually no short take-off and landing aircraft (STOL and VSTOL – the latter for vertical take-off). The Warsaw Pact has no equivalent to the NATO Harrier 'jump' jet.

NATO has been developing very specialised weapons to attack these prime targets. Weapons already deployed by NATO are various dispenser systems, particularly the French Durandal, the US low altitude dispenser system (LADS) and the German MW-1. These weapons demand that the pilot fly over the airfield runways under what would be very heavy fire, albeit at extremely low altitude. To increase the pilot's chances of survival, weapons known as anti-radiation missiles would be released. Missiles such as the homing

---

Box 3.6 'Dispenser' systems

A 'dispenser' is essentially a large canister full of tubes containing submunitions which is loaded underneath an aircraft enabling it to deliver large quantities of bomblets in a very short space of time and often from very low altitude.

Practically every country in NATO has developed its own version of such weapons; the British JP233 (see Figure 3.3), the French Durandal, the West Germans MW-1 and the US Low Altitude Dispenser System (LADS). Generally, two such weapons can be carried by a Panavia Tornado or a US F-15, F-16 or F-18 strike aircraft. The submunitions designed for FOFA are specifically meant to kill or destroy concentrations of armour, supply columns and personnel. Some create directional showers of shrapnel designed to penetrate light armour, others shaped charges to destroy tanks, together with small anti-tank mines to delay further advances.

The Raketen–Technik–Gesellschaft MW-1 is widely deployed in Europe and consists of a four-part container with a total of 112 launch tubes allowing a load of more than 3000kg or 4.6 tonnes. The device can carry 7800 MIFF, 4500 KB-44 or 668 MUSA/MUSPA submunitions 200 STABO bombs or various combinations of all five. These submunitions can be dispensed from an aircraft flying at an extremely low altitude, as low as 100 feet. After ejection from the tubes, air-bags explosively inflate and separate and spread out the individual weapons. MIne Flach Flach (MIFF) is a flat anti-tank mine which is activated by ground-vibration sensors. One MW-1 can deploy its full complement of these along a strip 3.2 metres wide and 2500 metres long to halt or 'fence in' tank formations. The KB-44 itself consists of seven bomblets each of which fragments to kill troops or armoured vehicles. All 4500 KB-44s can be dropped into an area 300 x 400 metres providing a 1:3 chance of killing anything in that area. MUlti Splitter Activ (MUSA) sends a shotgun-like blast of fragments designed to destroy truck convoys. The very similar MUSPA is designed to destroy taxiing, taking-off or landing aircraft. The Startbahn Bombe (STABO) is a runway cratering bomb (*startbahn* is German for runway).

According to the literature: 'Dispensed in various permutations and combinations . . . the submunitions make it difficult, discouraging and dangerous for Warsaw Pact ordnance teams to "sanitise" an airfield or tank assembly area once it has been attacked'.[14]

---

anti-radiation missile (HARM) are designed to fly in advance of a ground attack-aircraft and to home-in on any radio or radar signals with the aim of knocking out air-defence radars and rocket-battery sensors, thus clearing a relatively safe path for the aircraft through air defences. A new version of this weapon, the short range anti-radiation missile (SRARM) is being designed by a US, Canadian,

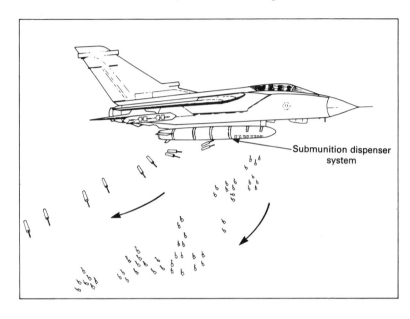

Figure 3.3 JP233 'dispenser' system operating from Tornado
Source: Courtesy of Hunting Engineering Ltd

Italian, Dutch and British team. If successfully delivered, the airfield attack weapons sprinkle specialised submunitions designed to heave up runways, hinder repair operations, destroy any aircraft still on the ground and to kill ground personnel.

The US bought the first 350 Durandals at $9.2m, for deployment on the US F-111 aircraft and bought a further 16 190 weapons during 1987 at a cost of some $499m.

The French Durandal with the BAP100 bomb, carries kinetic energy penetrators which are deployed at low altitude, slowed by drag-chutes, then fired at 850ft per second into the runway surface, breaking reinforced runway surfaces up to 8 feet thick.

The German MW-1 and the US LADS can carry more specialised munitions. The MW-1 can carry 200 STABO or 668 MUSPA submunitions or combinations of both. STABO makes a hole in the runway then explodes a charge beneath it heaving up huge slabs of concrete which offer no purchase to bulldozers coming to repair the damage. MUSPA sits on the ground and listens for the sound of taxiing aircraft; when it computes that any are within range, the head swivels towards them and fires a swathe of fragments over a lethal

---

Box 3.7   The French have a word for it

One cannot fail to be struck by the way the French consistently choose beautiful names for their highly destructive weapons: Matra's *Mimosa* fragmentation weapon for use against troops or light vehicles, the *Arcadie* (Arcadia) 'semi-smart' anti-tank weapon or mine, *Samanta* (Samantha) runway-cratering munitions. The *Mimosa* weapon is probably named as such after the multiple-forked pattern left in the air after the explosion of such a fragmentation device, which resembles a mimosa in blossom. There of course the resemblance ends.

---

radius of tens of metres. The anti-shelter weapon (ASW) penetrates shelters then fires an explosive through the resulting hole, destroying aircraft (or people) sheltering within.

The British airfield attack weapon JP233 has proved something of an expensive embarassment. The USAF pulled out of the project in 1980, after spending $103m, because Congress vetoed it because of escalating costs, delays, and evidence from trials that the weapon would not work properly. The weapon was eventually produced more than two years behind schedule at a development cost of £890m, £190m over budget. No NATO countries have bought it. A former USAF officer was quoted as saying that the JP233 would work only 'if you are up against a Third World power'[15] – this is apparently because the runway cratering bombs are not powerful enough. A former RAF officer also had severe reservations because of the need for the pilot to fly low *along* the enemy runway. JP233 was also intended to be used after enemy radars had been knocked out by specialist radar-seeking missiles, but the UK air launched anti-radiation missile (ALARM) missile is five years behind schedule (each of these missiles costs £813,000).

As a result of these delays and problems the UK MoD have issued a new Staff Requirement (Air) 1232 for a new laser-guided bomb and an anti-radar drone (pilotless aircraft) as a short term stop-gap.[16]

NEW FOFA WEAPONS

Two main new types of new weapon are envisaged: (i) missiles of various types deployed from aircraft out of range of air defences ('stand-off' missiles), and (ii) missiles to be launched from the ground. A vital necessity for all systems is accurate information about where their intended targets actually are.

Ground-based Missiles

Many possible weapons have been tested under what was originally known as the 'assault breaker' programme. Original contenders were the Vought Lance T-22 and Patriot T-16 missiles, essentially longer-range versions of the MLRS. The weapon now chosen is known as the Army Tactical Missile System (ATACMS) (see Figure 3.4). In the period 1986–9, $500m has been spent upon development and procurement.[17] Two ATACMS can be launched from a standard MLRS launcher to targets 100km away. The rockets would deploy 1000 M-74 bomblets over a target area some 400 metres across, with a design accuracy of 150 metres. LTV Corporation is to deliver sixty-six ATACMS by late 1990.

There is some controversy and speculation surrounding the development of the ATACMS because of its possible nuclear or chemical warhead. If ATACMS were fitted with a nuclear warhead it could possess a range of about 400km (this is because the nuclear warhead is lighter and leaves more room for rocket propellant).

It is widely expected that the ATACMS would provide the 'follow-on' to the present nuclear Lance missile if at some stage NATO goes ahead with its nuclear 'modernisation' programme.

The US Department of Defense is pressing the US Congress to allow development of a nuclear capability for ATACMS. With some modifications, ATACMS could use Pershing II missile warheads spare after the INF agreement. Because of its 400km range, ATACMS would be classed as short-range nuclear weapons (SNF) and would escape the INF Treaty conditions. If Pershing II warheads were used in this way, it would certainly cause strenuous complaints from the Soviet Union and the German peace movement because of what would be seen as rather cynical avoidance of the Treaty conditions.

'Stand-off' Missiles

A variety of new weapons is being developed, described by various relatively unpronounceable acronyms: Modular Stand-Off Weapon (MSOW); Short-Range Attack Missile (SRAM); Advanced Cruise Missile (ACM); Tactical Air-to-Surface Missile (TASM); and Joint

Figure 3.4   ATACMS missile firing from a MLRS launcher
Source: Photograph courtesy of MLRS International Corporation

TACtical Missile System (JTACMS). There is also the French *Apache*, the Hughes *Maverick* and the MBB vertical ballistic dispenser. They are all essentially new air-launched cruise missiles (basically a small pilotless glider or plane). They have design ranges between 20 and 1000km. Some are undoubtedly being designed with nuclear or chemical variants amidst high levels of secrecy. The design of new nuclear missiles for NATO is of the utmost political sensitivity.

MSOW/APACHE

Until September 1989, when the US and UK pulled out of the project, the modular stand-off weapon was being developed by a large US–European consortium (General Dynamics, Brunswick, Hunting Engineering, Sener, Dornier, Agusta). The Matra/Aerospatiale Apache programme, however, has an almost identical specification. Each weapon will cost around $1m and is being designed at least two variants. One version (UK Air Staff Target 1236) with a range of about 20km, will have the task of airfield 'denial', by means of airfield-cratering munitions – a stand-off version of NATO's existing dispenser weapons which have to be delivered from over or very near to their target.

The weapon would be programmed to fly low over the main runways of enemy airfields dispensing bombs sideways to cover the entire area. The glider would locate its target using inertial guidance (see Figure 3.5).

Another version would be designed to attack mobile armoured columns, although at present it is not known how the missile would find its target. The UK are particularly interested in a longer-range weapon which could be fitted with an anti-hardened-aircraft-shelter warhead. The UK Ministry of Defence's Royal Aircraft Establishment is working on this at present. Similar work is going on in West Germany and the USA. The warhead would home-in to its target using radar- and heat-sensing to distinguish the shelter from other buildings around the runways. The bomblet would be designed to penetrate 1.5 metres of reinforced concrete ($4\frac{1}{2}$ feet). Once a hole had been made, the second part of the warhead would detonate inside the shelter killing any occupants and destroying aircraft sheltering inside.[18]

The extremely complex conventional warhead design represents the warhead designer's way of achieving with a conventional explosive what could formerly be achieved only with a nuclear warhead. This having been said, many of the stand-off weapons are being

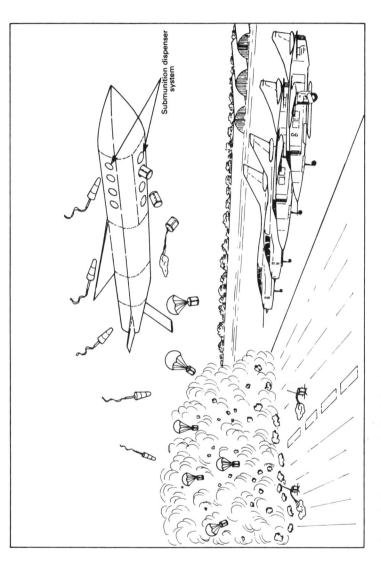

Figure 3.5   A 'stand-off' airfield attack weapon

considered for deployment with a nuclear warhead. With the lighter and smaller nuclear warhead the MSOW or APACHE or Maverick would have a range of around 400km. If deployed in a nuclear mode these weapons would greatly complicate arms control because the nuclear and non-nuclear versions would be indistinguishable without a very close examination. The intention is equip all NATO's nuclear-capable bombers such as the Tornado and the F-16 with a weapon of this type.[19]

SRAM and TASM

Both weapons are cruise missiles with ranges of several hundred kilometres. Both carry nuclear warheads. US planned spending on the TASM in 1990–1 is $134 m. The SRAM will be available for service in 1992 or 1993 for F-111 bombers, possibly those based in the UK. 1600 will be procured. SRAM development costs have been $231m a year.[20]

ACM and JTACMS

Both these weapons are long-range cruise missiles designed to carry sophisticated conventional or nuclear warheads. JTACMS is now a classified 'black' project. It is likely to have a range of around 550km and could be fired from Tornado or the F-16. Targets would be found by the complementary Joint Surveillance Target Attack Radar System (JSTARS) radar system. This radar system will be carried on the USAF C-18 (Boeing 707) aircraft carrying a large amount of on-board processing equipment and eight to ten radar operators. Information would be exchanged with ground stations and missiles in flight via digital data links. Spending on this project is running at $300m a year.[21]

The ACM is designed to have a range of 3000 miles and is a 'stealth' version of the existing air-launched Cruise missiles. 'Stealth' means that the missile would be designed to be very difficult to see on conventional radar systems. This weapon would equip the heavier bombers in the US Air Force such as the F-111 and the F-15 Strike Eagle. The USAF has a 'requirement' for more than 1000 ACMs.[22] Both missiles are being designed with extremely accurate mid-course and final (terminal) guidance so that small targets such as hardened aircraft shelters could be destroyed with 'dumb' munitions.

The UK and France are also secretly spending money on similar projects. British Aerospace Dynamics has been working for some years on a cruise missile version of the Sea Eagle, known as the P4T.

There is a possibility of collaboration with the French to spread research and development costs.[23] The UK Government is believed to be prepared to spend £3 000 000 000 (£3000 bn) on this project.[24]

Counter-Air 90
This was the name of a US proposal to attack enemy air-bases with ballistic missiles within the first few hours of a European war.

Martin Marietta proposed the use of a conventionally armed extended-range Pershing-II missile called Conventional Counter-Air Missile (CAM-40). Lockheed suggest using a system based on the Trident C4 missile called Ballistic Offensive Suppressive System (BOSS). BOSS would reach a maximum altitude of 160 000 ft (outer space) travelling at Mach 6 (Mach 1 is the speed of sound, about 700mph, Mach 6 is therefore about 4500mph). The warhead would arrive at Mach 2.4, dive and pull up to deliver submunitions, possibly the Boosted Kinetic Energy Penetrator (BKEP). This submunition would have been designed to penetrate the hardest targets, such as runways built on permafrost in summer, which then become an integral part of the permanently frozen ground in winter. Such a weapon would be deployed against air-bases in the Kamchatka and Kola peninsulas in the northern USSR. Such weapons as these have not been approved by US Congress nor are they likely to be so in the current climate, they do however illustrate the quite incredible 'no holds barred' approach of the arms designers. The furore that would have resulted from the siting of what appeared to be new ballistic missiles in Europe and the extreme threat which these weapons would pose to Soviet air bases, only a few minutes from destruction can only be imagined.

BATTLEFIELD COMMAND AND CONTROL

Although the next generation of precision-guided munitions (PGMs) will be designed to a greater or lesser extent to find their own targets, and are thus very deadly, all this cleverness is of no avail unless the PGM is released in roughly the right area, where there are actually targets to hit.

Unless a defender has enough PGMs to mount a continuous 'wall of fire', or can sow enough mines to defend a sizeable portion of the front line, intelligence about enemy-force concentrations is absolutely vital.

Here again technological developments are revolutionising the type and quality of information that a commander in the field can expect to get. These developments are largely a result of the widespread military use of microprocessors (devices at the heart of all home-computers), originally produced in bulk for the home-computer market. The US Army, for example, at one stage used Apple II computers on the field for targeting and intelligence because they are cheaper and more reliable than specialised military developments. The microprocessing is necessary to process and correlate the sheer volume of information coming in from various sources. Sensors now carried in Airborne Warning And Command System (AWACS) planes, reconnaissance planes, remotely piloted vehicles, phased-array radar systems and ground-sensors now provide information across the whole electro-magnetic spectrum, from radio, radar and microwaves through heat, to ordinary visible light and beyond into the so-called ultra-violet. Thermal (heat) and light sensors are now available tuned to particular wavelengths at which the atmosphere is most transparent. By a suitable choice of wavelengths – usually two heat and two visible – it is possible to see through cloud, smoke and rain, day or night.

In a 'remotely piloted vehicle' (a small plane or helicopter under 'radio-control' from the ground) information can be gathered by such sensors in high-resolution electronic cameras. This information is then encoded into a series of digital messages and relayed back to a ground- or air-based command and control centre. Such a ground centre would be very vulnerable to attack so the latest systems are designed to be operated from a dispersed 'nervous system' of units all mutually communicating with each other and sharing information. The British system, built by Plessey, is called Ptarmigan after the bird which is so good at concealment. The system consists of dozens of trucks positioned randomly behind the lines which share the total workload. If one or more trucks are destroyed, the system is still supposed to work, except that the processing of information is slowed down because of the loss of part of the system. The West Germans have their own system called AUTOKO, so an important problem for NATO lies in ensuring that each system can communicate with the others and that all the NATO forces can actually be commanded centrally at high level.

One of the problems which any such high-technology system creates, even if it is working properly, is the sheer volume of information produced. In a picture released in 1982, but actually taken in

1979, a strip photograph of Los Angeles was taken from a range of 12 miles, showing an area of 3 miles by 22. The resolution was high enough to count the players in a football stadium, to distinguish between the makes of cars moving along the freeway and to count the wires emanating from a power station. The photograph was not even taken conventionally upon film but was printed out 100 miles away from the sensors within thousandths of a second of the readings being taken.[25] Processing of the image on the ground can be computer-enhanced to sharpen the edges, filter-out smoke or haze or to zoom in for more detailed images. The images obtained can be transmitted by conventional telephone lines to more sophisticated processing centres or printed out as required. The US Army is running experiments in Europe to see how best to use such technology. But if such information was available for the whole of the European Front it would represent a massive processing problem in literally 'seeing the wood for the trees'.

As an example of this technology, Itek use a Charge-Coupled Device (CCD) imager which can generate a good-quality image in conditions ranging from clear skies down to half full-moon lighting, or in very poor and cloudy conditions, or in dusk lighting. The entire mini-camera, installation in a light plane and ground processing-station costs under $1m.

The complementary approach to reconnaissance is the purely electronic form of surveillance. NATO is conducting tests on various new forms of radar systems to find fixed and moving targets. Again the concept is to have the system spread over many units, both on the ground and in the air. 'Phased-array' radar scanners have no moving parts but consist of an array of sensors which can be tuned to get information from various directions. Such systems are being designed to detect missiles travelling at speeds of 2000 m.p.h. to within an accuracy of 40 metres range and 500 metres altitude. Linked to a computer, the information can be transmitted directly to guide a fighter or bomber aircraft accurately to the correct location or even to fire weapons directly in response. Miniature planes and helicopters are being considered as 'spies in the sky', whilst other sensors would be dropped behind the lines to transmit their information back in coded form.

The US JSTARS project is a highly accurate radar system designed to detect and track force concentrations such as armoured regiments or artillery battalions many miles behind the front line.

The US Defense Advanced Research Projects Agency (DARPA) has even investigated the possibility of a walking land vehicle to creep around the battlefield on legs. Designed by Martin Marietta the self-contained vehicle would move around at up to 20km an hour making observations by means of video cameras, imagers, laser range measurements and acoustic sensors. It would have a computer 'memory' of the lay-out of the land provided by prior satellite radar measurements made of key areas of the globe as part of the US cruise and Pershing-II world targeting programme, so that it could find its way around.

For all this amazing futuristic information-gathering technology to be of any use at all it must work reliably and accurately. Also, the information must be up to date and someone somewhere must be able to make use of it. That 'someone' is the battlefield commander in a bunker somewhere, who, particularly if he wants to take full advantage of all the technology and direct attacks at long ranges beyond conventional sensor range, is now more reliant than ever before upon good communications. Different sectors of the armed forces, particularly the army and air force – and within the army, artillery, infantry and armour – must also communicate and coordinate operations very well if they are not to start attacking each other in error.

Communications are thus the Achilles' heel of all the new technological developments and one reason why some weapons are specifically designed to attack control bunkers in a 'decapitation strike'. Air-launched cruise weapons with nuclear warheads could achieve this task, formerly assigned to the Pershing-II missile. Nonnuclear bunker attack weapons are being designed which are accurate enough to navigate themselves to a bunker, blast through tens of feet of reinforced concrete and then fire another explosive charge through the hole, killing the occupants and wrecking the equipment. This may be a very destabilising development, because, knowing their potential vulnerability to some of these new conventional weapons, military commanders and politicians may feel forced to make contingency plans should communications irrevocably break down in a conventional conflict. With the existence of nuclear weapons, which are controlled by the same commanders from the same bunkers, some of these contingency plans mean the firing of nuclear weapons by the majors or colonels commanding missile batteries, effectively out of political control and in circumstances which may inevitably lead to escalation to an all-out nuclear holocaust.

Another worrying possiblity is the detonation of even a small nuclear weapon high up in the atmosphere, generating a huge nuclear electro-magnetic pulse, a sharp pulse of intense radio-waves generating as much as thousands of volts in sensitive electronics over thousands of square miles, damaging them beyond repair. In the chaos and loss of centralised control which might follow such an event, commanders controlling nuclear weapons might fire nuclear weapons in – as they saw it – self-defence.

NEW SOVIET TECHNOLOGY

There is, as yet, no Soviet equivalent to the Western initiative for new technology weapons. However, the new generation of Soviet military men are now demanding their own new weapons in response to developments which are taking place in the West.

Up to now the Soviet approach to weapon-system design has often been markedly different from that of the West. When a Soviet defector landed a Soviet 'Foxbat' advanced fighter plane in Japan, the Western engineers who took it apart to see how it worked, were surprised to find just how heavily constructed it was compared with a Western plane. When they started to look at the electronic systems they were stunned to find that the plane did not have any electronic integrated circuits ('chips') at all. A comparable Western plane such as the Phantom is literally packed with such devices. Instead all the aircraft's avionics were handled by miniature valves (about the size of torch bulbs). The fairly obvious conclusion to draw is that the Soviets are well behind in electronic avionics technology. This is certainly true for such devices as micro-miniaturised electronic circuits which can contain thousands of active components inside the same space as a miniaturised valve. Advanced electronic components are banned for export to the Soviet Union by the USA and NATO, in an attempt to prevent high-technology transfer. The fear is that advanced components would be incorporated into weapon systems. A consignment of very powerful, high-speed Vax computers was seized in Sweden *en route* to the Soviet Union, marked as 'engineering equipment', proof, if needed, that Western computers are much in demand. These computers would have had the capacity to run the entire Soviet early warning system for example.

The best that can be said of the Foxbat electronics is that while electronic valves may be large and crude (and unreliable), they are very resistant to large overloads. When nuclear weapons are exploded, intense radio energies are given off in the electromagnetic pulse (EMP), capable of destroying circuits miles away. Thus, if a nuclear weapon was exploded, the Foxbat might well stay flying, while the Phantom (or Tornado) might lose many flying aids and possibly crash. The resistance to nuclear EMP may of course be simply fortuitous and follow merely from out-of-date technology, but the Soviets do seem quite concerned about the possible effects of EMP upon their communications.

In a Soviet journal describing their tank units, a picture is shown of a helicopter hovering over the leading tank in a column.[26] A soldier is leaning out of the helicopter and handing a clipboard with orders to another soldier standing upon the tank turret for the Soviet tank commander. The original Soviet caption reads that an 'urgent message' is delivered this way during an exercise. The significance of this is that no NATO document would show such a photo. They would show a highly sophisticated communications system operated by a computer in a bunker or flying command centre. Having to communicate by helicopter is the modern-day army's equivalent of sending a runner instead of using the phone. This point is highlighted by a Western analyst who suggests 'The weakness of the Soviet command and control network at battalion/regiment level is a point to be exploited by Western defences'.[27] The only thing that can be said for such a method of communication is that, again, it is EMP-proof, a point stressed by an ex-Soviet tank commander, although one wonders if the command centre sending the message or the helicopter would have survived a nuclear strike.

Such examples as these, do not deter some US authors from suggesting that the Soviet Union has technical 'superiority' in some fields. One such analyst, Philip A. Karber, is a vice president of the BDM corporation, and until summer 1983 headed Defense Secretary Caspar Weinberger's Strategic Concepts Development Center. Through BDM, Karber has been a consultant to the Pentagon for over a decade. Karber gave an unclassified briefing to the German Strategy Forum in Bonn in March 1984, which was attended by several senior political and military officials from West Germany and the USA. He asserted that America's technological leadership had fallen behind, that the Soviet Union was working very hard on tactical lasers, the forward-deployed SS-22 missile (now removed by the INF Treaty) had an advanced warhead for attacking NATO airfields, that a general rocket support system, the BM-27, had been deployed five years ahead of the US MLRS with an advanced warhead, and that new nuclear artillery systems were being deployed.

In all these areas he gave remarkably little detail, even saying that his fears were 'inferential' concerns over what could happen, not predictions based on observable evidence of what would happen. He said that he 'would rather be called wrong – even called an alarmist – than remain silent and see NATO unprepared'.[28]

An artist's impression was shown of a two-vehicle laser system, with one vehicle to transport the power supply and another to hold the laser. In the 1986 edition of *Soviet Military Power*, Caspar Weinberger suggests that Soviet theatre force lasers may be ready sooner than the late 1980s and that they 'are likely to be capable of structurally damaging aircraft at close range and producing electro-optical and eye damage at greater distances'. A US Army spokesman, Major Robert Pilnacek, stated that the US Army recently cancelled its work on a similar battlefield laser, the so-called Close Combat Laser Assault Weapon – in part because of humanitarian concerns that it could blind enemy soldiers.[29] Roughly $14m was spent on the programme before it was cancelled.

It is at this point that one's belief, if not already wavering, becomes very strained when one considers that 'humanitarian' concerns have not prevented the development of chemical poisons, nerve gases and minelets which fragment into plastic shards designed not to show up on X-rays, thus making treatment difficult. A more basic reason for the particular laser project cancellation was that it cost a fortune and did not work very well. Lasers tend to be very inefficient and require a large energy supply. In tests the laser beam has to be held on the same part of the target for some time before it melts. In a much-publicised US test, the target drone aircraft had to fly very straight and slowly for the laser system to do this. Even if one can achieve this difficult task it is far simpler to fire a shell through the same point.

Regarding the other weapon systems, other authoritative sources such as *Jane's*, *Brassey's* and *World Armies*,[30] simply contradict Karber on the issues of advanced warhead designs. This leaves the advanced nuclear artillery, by which Karber means neutron shells. Here the USA has long had the technology but made the political decision not to deploy such weapons in peacetime in Europe. We have to conclude that Karber was expressing the fears of US hawks rather than what is really going on.

Following authoritative sources, it is clear that the Soviet Union lags behind the USA in electronics technology by five to ten years. In areas such as tank design, modern Soviet tanks are engineered to similar standards to NATO tanks. The Soviets however until recently have had a policy of keeping all their old tanks 'just in case' and have problems with engine and clutch reliability. Their artillery and rocket systems are inferior in quality but make up for this in large numbers.

The US Department of Defense in fact publishes a very detailed assessment of Soviet military technology in comparison with US technology. The Federal Year 1983 figures put the USA 'very superior' to the Soviet Union in no fewer than eleven categories, including micro-electronics, computers, propulsion, signal processing and optics. The Soviet were only superior in conventional warheads and mobile power sources. In deployed systems a similar picture emerged. The USA was ahead in bombers, cruise, fighters, PGMs etc, while the Soviet Union was ahead in surface-to-air missiles, infantry combat vehicles and mine warfare. The USA had a clear edge in offensive weaponry.[31] A director of the CIA implied that as many as *30 per cent* of US weapons were beyond the capacity of the USSR to produce. The US Department of Defense said the same thing in 1989, referring to the seven-year lead possessed by the USA over the Soviet Union in advanced integrated circuit technology.[32]

Following this analysis, in no sense can the new Western weapon developments be called 'a response' to known Soviet technical developments. In the vast majority of cases, Soviet weaponry lags far behind that of the USA and NATO. The Soviet way of thinking is also somewhat suspicious of high technology in the 'friction' and chaos of war. The Soviets tend to rely upon using older weapons as back-ups for more modern weapons and for spares. This type of thinking is a strong reason why the balance-of-force analyses often seem biased towards the Warsaw Pact. NATO on the contrary, believe in using high technology in the form of high mobility, firepower and accuracy, to compensate for any inferiority in numbers.

The lag of Soviet military technology behind the West is relevant to the possibility of the Soviet Union adopting a strategy of defensive defence and replacing more offensive tanks with more defensive precision-guided munitions. Until the Soviet Union develops advanced PGMs capable of knocking out Western tanks' advanced armour, the Soviet Union will have to rely upon its best anti-tank weapons, its own tank guns and heavy artillery. Rather underlining this point, in 1989 the US Pentagon claimed that the new steel-uranium armour for the M-1 Abrams tank led the Soviet Union by 'a decade' and that it was impenetrable to Soviet PGMs and *all those known to be under development.*[33]

FOFA, NEW WEAPONS AND CONVENTIONAL STABILITY

The strategy of FOFA contains some flaws and dangers. One flaw is that weapons to attack follow-on forces can only work if Soviet forces are there conveniently drawn up behind the front line waiting to go into battle. The strategy relies upon there actually being such targets moving up to the front to be hit, or choke-points to be hit in the advance path of reinforcements. This would not be the case in either a 'standing start' surprise attack which utilised forces solely from East Germany, or an attack after a long period of reinforcement. In both these cases, enemy forces would be deployed much nearer to the front and FOFA would not be possible at anything like the ranges planned. Thus, to work really well FOFA needs some elements of Soviet cooperation, which is of course not going to happen.

A second flaw is that all the longer-range, potential FOFA weapons systems would have to rely upon accurate intelligence and guidance to hit moving concentrations of forces. This is a major problem. The UK Nimrod air radar system has now been cancelled because of problems, and the US equivalent, the flying AWACS radar system, is not capable of distinguishing numerous multiple targets in a full battle environment because its computers become overloaded with information.

FOFA also contains the seeds for escalation of conventional conflict and, with NATO's present nuclear strategies, inadvertent escalation to nuclear war. The longer-range conventional FOFA weapons may be mistaken for tactical nuclear attack and thus provoke a nuclear response. The longer-range nuclear FOFA weapons such as air-launched cruise and ground-based Lance would be used as part of NATO's first-use strategy. As long as nuclear weapons are deployed in Europe, FOFA is thus potentially destabilising.

Another major problem is the burgeoning numbers of new air-launched nuclear missiles. This is a major problem for arms control. Just as one treaty (INF) has removed one class of ground-launched weapons, another set is being considered for deployment. In some cases there have been direct references to 'replacing' the gap left by INF.[34] In other words the effect of the INF treaty is being subverted by new military developments (as many other treaties have been in the past). Even if the Conventional Armed Forces in Europe (CFE) talks limit the numbers of warplanes deployed by East and West, the smaller number of planes negotiated may be well able to carry far more destructive power than their predecessors and at much longer range. Even if operating bases are pulled back beyond operating ranges, the increasing range of the stand-off weapons will cause immense problems. Just how far back will planes have to be deployed? 500km? 1000km?

Even considered as purely conventional systems, longer-range systems such as ATACMS carry greater military benefits only if they are used early, before force concentrations have crossed a vulnerable crossing-point and before these forces are near to engaging NATO forces.

NATO plans in FOFA to attack targets several hundred kilometres behind the lines. Targets such as bridges over the Oder and Neisse Rivers which carry seven vital rail lines (for carrying heavy equipment such as tanks) from the Soviet Union to East Germany. These would have to be hit at present by precision bombing with 2000lb bombs, or a new air-launched cruise warhead could also be given this task (but the target could, of course, be far more efficiently destroyed by a 'small' nuclear weapon). Whilst NATO could quite justifiably argue that hitting these targets was a purely defensive measure, from the perception of the Soviet Union this would surely appear very aggressive particularly as, to be most effective, such attack would have to be made very early in any conflict before reinforcements had passed over the bridges.

Another severe problem is that any attack upon a nuclear power station, with sufficient power to breach the containment and vaporise some of the core (even if the reactor was not operating at the time) would have direct radiological consequences far worse than the Chernobyl accident. Nuclear power stations are conceivable targets in their own right but could also be hit inadvertently. There are dozens of such plants in East and West Germany. So even conventional war could have devastating radiation effects, poisoning Europe and Europeans for many decades.[35]

Airfield-attack weapons deserve special mention as weapons likely to cause sudden escalation of conventional conflict. An MSOW attack upon a Warsaw Pact airfield could wreak as much damage as a small nuclear weapon, but without the associated radiation, and deaths of nearby civilians. Sudden destruction of an airfield in this way would be interpreted as a highly aggressive act likely to lead to further escalation.

These are all mechanisms for the rapid escalation of conflict to higher levels including nuclear war. This escalatory nature of modern weaponry arises from its highly destructive nature and the extensive range and depth of possible operations planned in FOFA.

For all these reasons, conventional conflict is likely to escalate quickly in intensity and in geographical area to rapidly encompass all of East and West Germany. The time for negotiation is likely to be short before escalation to nuclear war. The strategy is based upon a war of high fire-power and mobility based upon principles developed in the Second World War. In the precursor to a Third World War, tactics such as those in the First World War where mobility was low and gains and losses were costly and slow would be more appropriate and could gain valuable time for negotiations to reach a political solution before nuclear weapons were used. In this sense, NATO conventional strategy, as much as it can be divorced from NATO's nuclear strategy, is inappropriate for the nuclear age, where the prime need should be to gain time for negotiation. To delay, to avoid a rapid conclusion of the conventional phase, when nuclear use would seem highly likely.

To a large extent, many of my criticisms of NATO conventional strategy have been just as relevant to Soviet strategies. Some Eastern Bloc military officers found the public anguish which NATO went through over Air-Land Battle strategy quite amusing when, in their judgement, it had actually been NATO and Soviet strategy all along but not until then in the public eye.[36] Nevertheless, Mikhail Gorbachev has at least adopted the language of defensive defence and is unilaterally removing some of the most offensive elements of Soviet forces deployed in Eastern Europe.

Another important factor is that the Soviet Union at present simply does not have either the capability or the resources to design, produce or finance the profligate range of weapons designed by NATO, many of which never get past the design stage. The advanced guidance systems and microprocessing technology necessary for the smart missiles for example. Even if the Soviet Union wanted to do so, they could not match NATO's new range of FOFA weaponry.

NEW WEAPONS IN AN ALTERNATIVE MILITARY STRATEGY

When considering the applicability of longer-range FOFA-type weapons systems for use in an alternative defensive approach, it is clear that some of these weapons have possibilities, but only if a clearly non-nuclear environment can be created for their use. FOFA weaponry could be used to achieve delay of conflict without severe risks of escalation if a deliberate policy was made of limiting the depth of offensive strikes into the Eastern bloc. If this was done, weapons systems such as airborne dispenser systems could be used to block and bottle-up invading forces rather than enacting the present role of destroying air forces on the ground. Air-to-ground operations in front of enemy forces would also pose far smaller hazards for pilots and mean a greater chance of mission success than at present.

The new shorter-range precision-guided munitions could be used to stabilise the East-West military stand-off because they favour the defence, not the attack. The offensive superiority of massed tank formations is seriously in doubt for the coming years. New weapons such as the MLRS, *providing that the nuclear (and longer-range) options are not deployed*, could enhance defensive options by enabling mobility of fire to replace mobility of offensive forces over ranges of up to 40km.

The new NATO initiatives for obtaining additional intelligence of enemy movements and more robust command and control systems are on the whole stabilising. More assured advance warning should diminish fears of surprise attack and diminish pressures upon NATO to plan to fire nuclear weapons first or to preempt aggression.

Part III
Towards a New
Direction in Defence

Introduction

Up to this point in this book I have identified various problems in current defence strategy. I have argued that NATO places too much emphasis on nuclear weapons and strategies, looked briefly at the NATO military–industrial–political arms production complex and some of the implications of the new conventional (and, in some cases, nuclear) weapons planned for the 1990s.

In a sense, up to now I have defined in my own terms what to *avoid* in a defence strategy. Many may question whether it is possible to construct a viable defence policy for the modern world, in which nuclear weapons play such a significant role, without nuclear flexible response, nuclear first-use, nuclear war-fighting strategies or potentially destabilising conventional strategies. I am sure that it is possible. Over the next four chapters I gradually build the case for defensive deterrence.

The rejection of what I consider highly dangerous nuclear strategies or options has some very important military and political implications. Some reject such ideas as defensive deterrence for the political problems facing substantial changes to nuclear deployments and strategies alone. I deal with these more political questions in Part IV, Chapter 8.

Apart from the more political questions, the rejection of nuclear war-fighting has two very important military implications:

1. NATO's conventional forces must be strong enough to withstand and repel conventional hostile attack;
2. NATO must have a viable reply to nuclear threats or actual nuclear attack itself.

The second point is so important that I feel obliged to deal with it, at least in part, before turning to the need for a strong conventional defence. After all, if there is no answer to nuclear threats or nuclear use then the whole idea of defensive deterrence is a political dead duck.

It is important to note that the strategy of defensive deterrence which I am developing and proposing here is not a purist non-nuclear defence policy. It requires very substantial reductions and the rejection of highly dangerous nuclear strategies and options but it acknowledges that some nuclear deployment modes can have a deterrent effect. Thus defensive deterrence is not a pure nuclear unilateralist policy but something of a hybrid. The terms unilateral and multilateral have in any case become relatively useless because of the political polarisation of the UK defence debate which has stifled positive debate concerning nuclear disarmament for some time now. This has benefited the nuclear *status quo*.

How precisely, or to what degree, a nuclear minimum deterrent should exist and who might possess and control it I leave to the final chapter where I deal with more political questions. But the important point is that in defensive deterrence the answer to a nuclear threat would be very similar to what it is now, the threat of unacceptable and unavoidable nuclear retaliation.

This takes me on to the second type of potential nuclear problem – actual nuclear attack. Here the answer is simple, if equally unsatisfactory to hawks or doves (unless either believes in the effectiveness of civil defence against nuclear attack).

The simple answer is that there *is* no military defence against nuclear weapons. This is true whether or not one has nuclear weapons. In the absence of a 100 per cent effective defensive system totally impervious to all nuclear weapons (there are severe doubts about the technical feasibility of a completely impervious 'space dome' defence in any case and the US Administration has now abandoned the goal of a complete Strategic Defense Initiative (SDI) shield)[1] there is no defence against nuclear weapons. Period.

Let me be very clear. If nuclear weapons *have been used* there is no defence (I class nuclear deterrence not as a physical defence but as a psychological defence – against deliberate use). If deterrence fails, there is no defence, only retaliation from the grave.

I will now return to the first of the two important implications: namely that NATO's conventional forces must be strong enough to withstand and repel conventional hostile attack. This issue is particularly important because most spending goes on conventional weapons and cuts in forces here can have a major economic impact. The next four chapters seek answers to this. First, Chapter 4 assesses the relative strengths of NATO and Warsaw Pact forces deployed and allocated for use in the European area, also taking account of Warsaw Pact withdrawals and possible conventional arms reduction treaties. Chapter 5 then assesses how these forces are deployed in Central Europe and the possible outcomes of various conflict scenarios with and without defensive reforms. Chapters 6 and 7 then describe the general principles of an alternative security system and how these principles could be applied to NATO in a practical system.

Before I go on to develop my arguments, however, what exactly is NATO defending against militarily? What is the military threat?

The two scenarios which follow are based upon some Western analysts' published and unpublished assessments (or fears) between 1984 and 1989.[2] The scenarios come as something of a bracing shock in the post-*perestroika* world but even after force cuts and withdrawals a Soviet threat is still the currency of NATO military exercises and contingency planning. NATO's plans are being reviewed as a result of *perestroika* and *glasnost*; but all military strategists plan for the unthinkable, the worst case. The worst case in Europe, however unlikely it may be thought to be, is an attack on NATO by Soviet forces.

SCENARIO: THE SPECTRES HAUNTING NATO

1 Blitzing NATO

It is Christmas Eve, and NATO forces are standing down. Although East–West tensions are high, the Soviet Union and its allies have not mobilised for war. But at 2300 hours, troops of the Soviet Third Shock Army move out of their garrison near Magdeburg, East Germany. Under cover of darkness, they head west through secret passages in their own minefields. The first detachments reach the West German border at midnight and plunge across without warning, raising the alarm at NATO headquarters. The main body follows only one hour later. To the north and south, other Warsaw Pact armies slash into NATO's defences at almost the same moment.

On each wing of the main attacking forces is a smaller group of forces, known as an 'operational manoeuvre group' (OMG). Each Soviet army would send out an OMG, a self-sufficient raiding party of divisional or larger size (up to 22 000 infantry, 450 tanks, 600 armoured vehicles, 300 artillery pieces, an anti-aircraft regiment and a company of engineers). This mobile force attacks of opportunity, but whenever it runs into stiff opposition, it disengages and drives deeper into West Germany to disrupt NATO defences. Meanwhile, Soviet war-planes, paratroopers and missiles tipped with non-nuclear warheads, are striking NATO targets even farther behind the lines, including airfields, missile-launchers, supply depots and communication centres. Behind the raiding parties, the Third Shock Army moves on. By 0200 hours on Christmas morning it reaches Brunswick and bypasses the city. By 0400 hours it enters the outskirts of Hanover, 50 miles inside West Germany. That city is bypassed too, as the Third Shock Army races towards the Rhine. The main bodies of each Soviet army likewise, thrust through the cracks in NATO's defences, with the aim of bringing about a collapse of the NATO political structure within a matter of days.

The British Army on the Rhine, the BAOR, charged with defending the Brunswick-Hanover sector, manages to get most of its troops out of the camps by 0400 hours. In neighbouring sectors, American, West German and other Allied forces also respond quickly. NATO, however, needs at least 48 hours to achieve full mobilisation. The Soviet surprise attack has left the defenders of West Germany with nothing like that time. Their surprised conventional forces in disarray, NATO's political leaders must soon consider the next fateful step – the use of tactical or intermediate-range nuclear weapons. But the advancing Soviet columns are already deep inside West Germany; nuclear strikes against them would endanger countless NATO troops and German civilians. And many of the airfields and missile-launchers from which a nuclear strike could be launched, have been damaged or occupied by Soviet attackers. In the end, NATO's leaders cannot agree on using nuclear weapon. The Soviets are left in a commanding position for the conventional war which follows. The West, outnumbered and outgunned on the ground, has lost without firing a single nuclear shot.

One can question what on earth the political gain of such an attack would be, but the military goal is to achieve a quick, relatively cheap conventional victory by neutralising NATO's tactical and intermediate-range nuclear forces before the leaders of the Western Alliance can take the awesome decision to use nuclear weapons. The scenario, despite NATO's nuclear first-use option, assumes that NATO could not use nuclear weapons early. In order to achieve surprise, the Soviets would mount no preliminary artillery barrage. The Soviets mount no preemptive nuclear strike because it is judged that this would almost certainly provoke a Western nuclear response before Soviet troops had penetrated very far into West Germany.

2 Attack after Reinforcement

East–West tensions have been high for four months, and NATO and Warsaw Pact forces are reinforced and in a high state of alert. Soviet Navy surface ships and submarines are deployed in large numbers out of Murmansk in northern Russia. A Soviet attack is expected, but despite continual military exercises and training near border areas, and continuing bad relations, an attack does not come.

Finally, the attack comes. NATO forces, although nearly fully reinforced, are gradually driven back by the sheer weight of over 100 Soviet divisions at full combat power against a NATO force of less than half this size. NATO forces hold in most places, but in others, concentrations of Soviet forces break through behind NATO's thin forward line of defence, disrupting supplies and communications. Reserve Soviet divisions pour through the gaps.

NATO is losing and commanders seek permission to use their nuclear weapons before they are overrun or destroyed by air-strikes. For some the permission comes too late, but when it does, Soviet forces fire first, destroying NATO's ground-based nuclear forces on the ground.

The Soviet forces reach the Rhine and halt. The American, British and French consider using their strategic nuclear weapons in silos and submarines, but do not do so, knowing that their nuclear strike upon the Soviet capital and other Soviet cities will undoubtedly bring about a savage nuclear retribution on Paris, London or Washington, and the destruction of their countries too. They have no choice but to negotiate. Germany is now no longer a potential threat to the Soviet Union. Germany's army, the *Bundeswehr*, has been destroyed fighting to the death. The remnants of the Allied forces regroup in Holland, Belgium and France, licking their wounds. The political map of Europe has once more been altered by war and Germany is devastated yet again.

It is even harder to see any political gain for the Soviet Union or Warsaw Pact in this attack.

The important question is: are these spectres mere chimera induced by fear and paranoia or do they have substance?

The first scenario, 'Blitzing NATO', only remains possible as long as several Soviet divisions are deployed in East Germany. But the general concept, surprise attack across an international frontier some-where in Europe will remain feasible as long as there are military forces in Europe capable of offensive action. Some senior military spokespersons argue that the risk of a smaller-scale conflict in Europe has increased as the inhibiting forces of the Cold War are progres-sively released in Eastern Europe.

The second scenario, 'Attack After Reinforcement', is quite

independent of Soviet force deployments in Eastern Europe because in a major crisis both NATO and the Warsaw Pact countries would deploy additional forces in excess of global and regional treaty limitations.

The scenarios have substance in the sense that a large part of NATO defence strategy is justified upon the basis of preventing or deterring an attack on Europe by the Warsaw Pact.

Another point is that if NATO's forces are not intended to stop some kind of attack like this, or if such an attack is simply not feasible, what precisely are all these expensive weapons systems *for*?

In the eyes of those who suggest such scenarios, the overall picture has not been drastically changed by the Gorbachev force removals. The talk is now of a 'leaner but meaner' Soviet Army. When questioned about the validity of such scenarios should the CFE talks result in conventional-force parity between East and West, one retort is that Hitler's armies fought to the gates of Moscow with a force of about 4000 tanks against available Soviet forces of a similar size, so less does not necessarily mean safer, and that presumably a Soviet offensive in the reverse direction would be far more successful. The International Institute for Strategic Studies (IISS) in its *Military Balance 1987–88* makes a similar point.[3]

To try to give some quantitative answers, the following two chapters look at the quantities, qualities and plans of NATO and Warsaw Pact forces deployed in, or allocated for, use in Europe.

4 The Numbers Game

Until recently, it has been generally taken for granted that Soviet and Warsaw Pact forces in Europe do have a numerical advantage which they could exploit in a conventional war in Europe.

The perennial NATO fear since the 1950s has been the view that while NATO forward forces could hold Soviet front-line forces in a conflict in Europe (i.e. Warsaw Pact forces deployed in East Germany and Czechoslovakia) NATO forces could not hold back a second or third 'wave' of 'follow-on' Warsaw Pact invaders for 'more than a few days'. The second wave or echelon would be Warsaw Pact forces deployed in Poland and the third echelon would be made up from Western Soviet military districts in the Soviet Union itself. General media sources continually refer to 3:1 to 5:1 force advantages in favour of Warsaw Pact forces or use phrases such as 'overwhelming advantage', or 'massive superiority'. Similar statements are repeated by politicians and a few specialist military sources.[1] This has been the perception received as accepted wisdom by the majority of the Western public for many years. In 1989, the impact of Mikhail Gorbachev's approach, rather cynically dubbed a 'peace offensive' by the media, created a substantial shift. Opinion polls across Europe showed that only a minority of the public (an average of some 20 per cent) still believed that the Soviet Union was a threat.[2] Whether this change of public perception remains a permanent feature of European politics remains to be seen and will no doubt depend in large part upon the perceived continuation or success of reforms in the Soviet Union and eastern Europe and success in the new arms talks.

THE IMPACT OF NEGOTIATED ARMS REDUCTIONS

The Conventional Armed Forces in Europe (CFE) talks have the goal of reducing the numbers of Soviet and NATO forces to common ceilings in various categories of military equipment including tanks and warplanes. The first-stage (CFE-I) level is 20 000 tanks each, together with cuts in military personnel in the central European region.

A second stage (CFE-II) goal could be further mutual cuts in NATO and Warsaw Pact forces of 30 to 50 per cent.

Whatever the talks achieve, the analysis of forces which I present in the next two chapters is important. The numbers of forces form the basic starting-point for discussion – the so called 'data exchange' in the negotiating process or the basis of any perceived threat.

In a very real sense, the 'numbers', or the forces deployed by East and West have been at the heart of the East–West confrontation. Over the years, various analyses of force imbalances, 'bomber gaps' and missile 'windows of vulnerability' have been used to justify military spending. In retrospect, all such gaps have been found to be illusory, but by then the money has been spent and the focus of attention is upon a new threat assessment.

The ways in which figures for the sizes of the military forces of East and West are presented for political ends, will doubtless continue as long as there are any forces confronting each other in Europe and any domestic and economic tensions between various partners in the two alliances of East and West.

THE BALANCE OF FORCES

In this chapter I try to establish whether the Warsaw Pact (or possibly NATO) could in any circumstances have a conventional military advantage which they could exploit in Europe, now, and after the negotiation of a CFE treaty bringing about East–West force 'parity'. First, in this chapter I compare the sizes of the forces facing each other in Europe. In the following chapter I try to determine what the possible outcome of a conventional conflict might be.

Before I do, it is very instructive simply to look at a map of Europe and the Soviet Union (See Figure 4.1). NATO Europe is a very small area in comparison with the vast expanses of the Warsaw Pact and the Soviet Union. All NATO's forces on mainland Europe, which would have the task of stopping any invasion from the East, have to be deployed in West Germany, the Netherlands and Belgium. These countries represent a depth for defence of 300–400km at most (up to 250 miles) a distance which can be driven in a day. The non-Soviet Warsaw Pact, East Germany, Poland and Czechoslovakia, are 800km across (500 miles) and twice the area of West Germany. Moscow is 1700km from the East–West border (1060 miles), as far to the east as Madrid, Spain is to the south-west. The Ural Mountains, which bisect the Soviet Union in a north–south direction and are often taken as a convenient dividing line between western and eastern USSR, are no

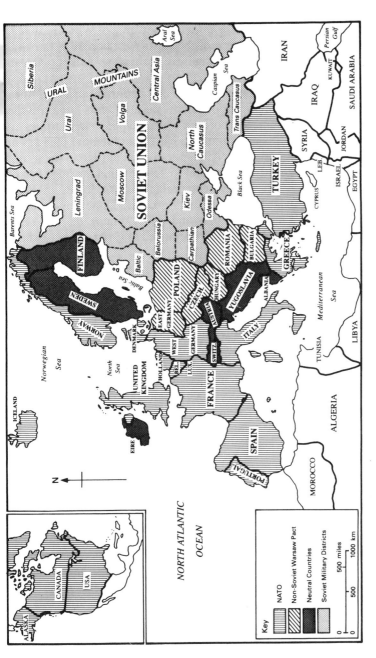

Figure 4.1 NATO and Warsaw Pact countries and Soviet military districts

less than 3900km (2400 miles) away. The area of the Soviet Union to the west of the Urals is *seventy times* the land area of West Germany. An equivalent point as far west of the East–West border as the Ural Mountains are east, is almost halfway across the Atlantic Ocean towards America.

These massive inequalities in size are important because they inevitably distort comparisons of forces. Because of its large size the Soviet Union has immense borders which require large armies to protect them. The Soviet Union also has three potential theatres of war: NATO to the west; Iran, Afghanistan and Pakistan to the south, and China to the east. It is important to bear in mind the huge size of the Soviet Union when, say, comparing NATO forces in West Germany with Soviet forces west of the Urals. These Soviet forces are spread over a huge land mass and would require massive reorganisation and mobilisation to be redeployed to East Germany where they could actually fight NATO.

The Mandate for the CFE Talks defines an area for negotiation which spans 'the Atlantic to the Urals' and covers all conventional (and dual capable) forces deployed on land (not at sea). This area acknowledges the fact that the Soviet Union has an Eastern border to defend facing China, which is not subject to Western negotiations. This area, as I have outlined above, is extremely large and the negotiations include sublimits for forces in smaller areas either side of the East–West border. The smallest area is the Benelux countries, the two Germanies, Poland and Czechoslovakia, the next an area including Western Soviet military districts and France, the UK and Italy. As the sub-areas gradually include more NATO (and Warsaw Pact) countries the negotiations become increasingly complex and difficult.

There is an old saying that there are 'lies, damned lies and statistics', or, as applied to the arms talks, 'the devil is in the details'. Certainly there are many possible ways of comparing Eastern and Western forces in Europe. Possible units of comparison, starting with the more conventional and moving to the more arcane, are: numbers of personnel; divisions; numbers of main battle tanks or artillery; armoured, standard or heavy divisional equivalents, and total firepower. The most commonly used units of comparison (used by almost all sources of information) are the numbers of troops and large pieces of equipment such as tanks or strike aircraft. Some other units of comparison, such as various 'divisional equivalents', try to take into account such factors as mobility and fire-power. There are

Table 4.1   Forces: Atlantic to Urals

	NATO's figures			Pact's figures		
	Pact	NATO	Force ratios	Pact	NATO	Force ratios
Personnel	3 090	2 213	1.5:1	3 573	3 660	1:1
	—	4 100*	1:1.3	—	—	—
Divisions	210	72	3:1	—	—	—
Tanks	51 500	16 424	3:1	59 470	30 690	2:1
	—	22 224*	2.5:1	—	—	—
Aircraft	8 250	3 477	2.5:1	7 876	7 130	1:1

NATO: CFE data released November 1988.
* Data released December 1988.
PACT: CFE data released January 1989.

still numerous other important factors, including terrain; morale; degree of readiness or reinforcement, training and reliability of equipment.

Before I go into a more detailed analysis, it helps to get a rough idea of the sizes of the conventional forces of East and West in Europe. Table 4.1 is a summary of the force data released by NATO and the Warsaw Pact in Winter 1988/9 before the CFE talks started.

Despite some obvious differences, there are some areas of general agreement between the two bloc figures. What the table shows is that both NATO and the Warsaw Pact have about 3–3.5 million military personnel each, and that the Pact outnumbers NATO in tanks by 50 000–60 000 tanks to 16 000–31 000 (by 3:1 or 2:1, depending upon whose figures you look at).

There is a sharp discrepancy between the two sets of figures regarding aircraft. The Pact's figures show that both sides have 7000–8000 aircraft, whilst NATO's figures show NATO outnumbered by 8 000 to 3500.

The discrepancy in NATO and the Warsaw Pact's tank figures is almost entirely due to the Pact counting much lighter armoured vehicles than NATO as a 'main battle tank'. The difference in aircraft is more serious. The Pact is counting several NATO aircraft, which whilst designated for Europe are based either at sea or in the USA. NATO excluded these aircraft precisely because they are not land-based, and thus escape the tight provisions of the CFE Mandate which only covers land-based forces.

Warsaw Pact Unilateral Force Cuts

In his speech to the United Nations Assembly, General Secretary Gorbachev announced that cuts and withdrawals of Soviet armed forces would be made by 1991. Since then, cuts in the forces of most of the Warsaw Pact countries have also been announced. The programme of cuts is as follows:

A reduction in the size of the Soviet Army by 500 000 soldiers and 10 000 tanks.

This figure includes cuts in the size of Soviet forces stationed in the Warsaw Pact countries of East Germany, Czechoslovakia and Hungary: 50 000 soldiers; 5000 tanks ; 8500 artillery systems and 800 combat aircraft; withdrawals of Soviet river-crossing equipment;

Cuts in Soviet European forces: 240 000 soldiers;

Cuts in Eastern Soviet forces: 200 000 soldiers;

5000 tanks converted to prime movers for construction and mining.[3]

It is important to note that withdrawals of Soviet forces from East Germany, Poland, Hungary and Czechoslovakia do not add to these cuts unless forces are verifiably disbanded.

Cuts announced in Polish, Hungarian, Czechoslovakian and East German armed forces in 1989–90 may eventually amount to over 2000 tanks and 100 000 soldiers.

In April 1989, Mikhail Gorbachev revealed for the first time an accurate figure for Soviet defence spending: 77 billion roubles. Cuts in Soviet arms expenditure are planned as 7 per cent in 1990 and 14.2 per cent in 1991.[4] Similar spending cuts have been announced by other Warsaw Pact countries.

Personnel

With the notable exception of the figures released by NATO, estimates of the numbers of military personnel of East and West released by all other Western more-or-less independent sources through the 1980s, and comparing personnel by various criteria, agree that Warsaw Pact and NATO forces are quite evenly matched (Table 4.2). The Warsaw Pact appear to have slightly larger numbers of troops – up to some 20 per cent more than NATO.

In 1984, NATO presented figures describing NATO and Warsaw Pact military personnel and equipment in two publications: 'NATO and the Warsaw Pact: Force Comparisons' (NATO, 1984a, in Table 4.2), and 'Western Defence: The European Role in NATO' (NATO, 1984b, in Table 4.2). Both detail NATO's forces, whilst only 'Force Comparisons' describes Warsaw Pact forces. Numbers of soldiers are presented in two categories: in 'Force Comparisons', 'rapidly deployable' and 'reinforced', in Western Defence 'Before Mobilisation' and 'After Mobilisation'.

Rather astonishingly, the two NATO publications, which were presented to the author at a NATO briefing in 1986 in Mons, Belgium, give totally inconsistent figures for the size of NATO's own armies (see Table 4.2). The differences are not small. In both categories, before and after mobilisation of forces, 'Western Defence' finds a NATO army *double* the size of 'Force Comparisons' and discrepancies of 1 700 000 to 6 200 000 soldiers. After mobilisation, taking the 'Western Defence' figures and comparing them with the largest estimate for the Warsaw Pact armies, NATO would outnumber the Pact by 10 700 000 to 6 000 000 soldiers. From these comparisons alone, the average reader should regard these figures with more than a little suspicion.

NATO's comparisons of the forces of East and West are also highly suspect. In NATO's 'Force Comparison', the figures for 'rapidly reinforceable' forces in Europe are 2.6 million NATO troops against 4 million Warsaw Pact troops. The NATO figure of 2.6 million is consistent with the IISS 'Atlantic to Urals' figure of 2.4 million troops, but NATO's figure for Warsaw Pact forces (4 million troops), is very much larger than the comparable IISS figure of 2.3 million for that year. NATO's figure can only be realised by adding in a further 2 million Warsaw Pact ground reserves, who are hardly 'rapidly' deployable, as they are spread all over the Soviet Union and would require some months to be called into action. NATO is neglecting to count in 2.3 million US and Canadian soldiers assigned to, or with a 'probable role' in Europe which are detailed in the other NATO publication.

Thus, in 1984, NATO was not comparing like with like. NATO was comparing figures for *un*reinforced NATO forces against reinforced Warsaw Pact forces, resulting in an artificially large disparity.

NATO's 1984 and 1988 figures for 'reinforced' forces were 4.1–4.5 million NATO troops facing 6 million Warsaw Pact troops. The size of the NATO forces is consistent with the equivalent IISS estimate of 4.4 million troops for NATO forces Atlantic to Urals', after reserves are added in. But, once again, the size of the Warsaw Pact forces is

Table 4.2   Forces in Europe: personnel (in 000s), 1984–9

Source		NATO	WTO	Remarks
GKL 1984[5]		360	300	'Combat ready'
		600	690	after nine days
		740	1080	after thirty days
Vienna MBFR[6]				
NATO figures		980	1132	ground plus air-force
				personnel
Pact figures		989	979	
UK Defence				
Estimates	84[7]	590	740	Fighting units
		800	980	'Total Soldiers'
IISS[8]	83/84	1075	1150	'Deployed in Europe'
	84/85	833	1303	(Northern Europe)
	85/86	1094	1648	"
	86/87	841	1668	"
	87/88/89	796	995	NATO Guidelines Area
	87/88	2385	2292	Atlantic to Urals
	"	4371	4276	(Atl-Urals plus reserves)
	"	5502	5348	Global
			6148–6848	(including 800–1500
			6148–6848	construction, rail, etc.)
NATO	1984a[9]	2600	4000	'Rapidly reinforceable'
	1984b[10]	4300–5500	—	'Before Mobilisation'
	1984a[9]	4500	6000	'Reinforced'
	1984b[10]	8700–10700	—	'After Mobilisation'
	Nov 1988[11]	2213	3090	'full-time personnel'
	Dec 1988[12]	4100	—	(with mobilisation)
Pact	1989[13]	3660	3573	

NB Soviet unilateral reductions in armed forces amount to 240 000 soldiers in Europe and 50 000 in the Central European region. These cuts are roughly 5 per cent of the relevant Soviet forces.

Table 4.2 *Notes*

Three reputable sources – Gottfried, Kendall and Lee (GKL), figures released from the Mutual and Balanced Force Reductions (MBFR) and talks in Vienna and the UK MoD – agree that the upper limits of ground-forces in Europe before reinforcement are some 1 000 000 NATO troops and 1 100 000 Warsaw Pact troops (these figures include some small numbers of air force personnel). GKL give some information about the forces which could be mobilised (brought up to operational strength and readiness) in various lengths of time, while the UK Statement on the Defence Estimates distinguishes between 'combat-ready' forces (fighting units) and those merely stationed in Europe or deployed in a support capacity. All three of these sources are counting forces *outside* the Soviet Union and the USA, i.e. NATO Europe, and East Germany, Czechoslovakia and Poland.

The figures are not too dissimilar from the IISS figures for forces 'deployed in Europe' (the figures shown are IISS figures adjusted to show only Northern Europe) for 1983–4. Subsequent IISS figures for the years up to 1986–7, show larger numbers of military personnel in East and West, particularly in the Warsaw Pact. IISS estimates for NATO forces deployed in Europe have swung dramatically up and down between 833 000 and 1 094 000 men in alternate years, swings of some 25 per cent in numbers of personnel. These did not reflect real deployments and withdrawals of NATO forces but are an example of the IISS changing its counting methods. Somewhat curiously, over the same period, 1983–6, the IISS was far more certain about the size of Warsaw Pact forces than those of NATO, showing the former steadily increasing in size by some 200 000 a year until 1985–6 and then levelling off in 1986–7. In its figures for 1987–8 the IISS took the unprecedented step of acknowledging problems with the analyses of force numbers and changed its counting methods yet again. The IISS now counts forces in four categories over four geographical areas:

In Europe but outside the Soviet Union ('NATO Guidelines');
Jaruzelski (NATO Guidelines plus Denmark and Hungary)
'Atlantic to Urals';
'Global'.

The adoption of this new method of assessment now brings the IISS 'NATO Guidelines' figures into agreement with the range of numbers produced by the US, UK and international sources quoted in Table 4.2. The IISS category, 'Atlantic to Urals' (formerly called 'total ground forces') is the agreed counting area for the CFE talks and includes forces not only in East Germany, Czechoslovakia and Poland, but also Soviet forces in the Soviet Union itself up to the Ural range of mountains which run north–south through the Soviet Union 1300km east of Moscow. In the 'Atlantic to Urals' category the IISS has consistently for many years found a small numerical advantage towards NATO over the Warsaw Pact.

NATO figures are taken from official NATO publications. Despite this, NATO figures for the same years are not consistent and show huge disagreements. These differences are discussed in the main text.

exaggerated. NATO's 1984 estimate of 6 million Warsaw Pact military personnel can only be realised by counting not only Warsaw Pact forces available globally (i.e. those east as well as those west of the Urals) but also a further 1.3 million uniformed personnel such as railway and construction workers with only rudimentary military training from National Service. Thus again NATO was not comparing like with like. In this case NATO was comparing NATO's reinforced forces in Europe with the global total of Warsaw Pact forces. This was particularly misleading because some of the Warsaw Pact forces counted were deployed opposite large Chinese and Iranian forces in the eastern and southern theatres.

In NATO's 1988 figures there was a most striking reduction in the estimate of the size of the Warsaw Pact armies. The size of the Soviet forces appeared to have diminished by an astonishing 1 million soldiers since 1984. The figures were further evidence that in 1984 NATO was counting in 2 million Soviet reservists who were certainly not 'rapidly deployable', as the 1984 statistics put it. In 1988, NATO's estimate of Soviet forces still exceeded the authoritative IISS estimate by 1 million Soviet troops. It would appear that NATO was still making generous estimates of the manning levels of Soviet divisions many of which are maintained well below full strength.

The Soviet Union has released very few figures for comparison, particularly in the period before 1988, but the two sets of figures (from the previous and inconclusive Vienna MBFR talks and pre-CFE data released in early 1989), show rough parity of numbers of military personnel between East and West. This assertion is reinforced by all other sources except NATO.

Divisions

Looking at the balance of forces on a division-by-division basis, much apparently contradictory data can be reconciled once it is realised that different sources are again counting forces deployed over different geographical areas or (which often amounts to the same thing) forces at different levels of mobilisation or reinforcement. In general, all the divisional comparisons of NATO and Pact forces show NATO in a worse light than does the comparison of troops. The main reason for this is simply that most Soviet divisions are smaller than their Western counterparts (11 000 – 12 000 men, against 17 000 men) and they therefore end up with more divisions for the same number of troops.

As Table 4.3 shows, the figures released by NATO are inconsistent in some important respects with all other sources and show a much greater imbalance of forces. Rather strikingly, NATO's 1984 figures for divisions were inconsistent with its figures for numbers of military personnel.

If we take the generally accepted average troop complement of Warsaw Pact and NATO divisions 11 000–12 000 Warsaw Pact to 17 000 NATO) one can calculate, using NATO's own 1984 figures, that NATO must then have outnumbered the Warsaw Pact. NATO's figures of 88 NATO versus 115 Warsaw Pact 'reinforced by rapidly deployable' divisions convert to 1 628 000 NATO versus 1 437 500 Warsaw Pact soldiers – a small NATO numerical advantage. But, in the very same figure in a different column on the same chart of the 1984 *Force Comparisons* (p. 8, fig. 2), NATO says that it is outnumbered by 4 million to 2.6 million in 'reinforced by rapidly deployable' military personnel.

In its 1988 divisional figures (*Conventional Forces in Europe: The Facts*) NATO gave an even greater NATO: Warsaw Pact divisional imbalance and an even greater discrepancy with all other sources. There is a very simple reason for this. NATO counts all Soviet divisions, *whether or not* they are fully up to strength. But two-thirds of Soviet divisions are so-called 'category 3', at below half-strength. Such divisions would take up to six months to be ready to fight at full strength. NATO gives a clue to this in its notes to these figures, which state: 'Covers active combat and artillery divisions . . . presently manned at above 5 per cent of their full wartime strength.' What this note means is that the comparisons drawn by NATO in the accompanying pie chart are virtually meaningless. The only meaningful comparisons for threat assessment are actual physical quantities of tanks, troops and other military equipment in functioning units at given times after mobilisation or alert. This is what has been performed by most of the other sources of information to a greater or lesser degree; hence their assessment of a more even balance of forces.

Discrepancies in the NATO Figures: Why?

NATO distortions of the statistics are no accident. NATO biases the statistics in various ways to serve the purpose of the publications in which they appear. In '*Conventional Forces in Europe: The Facts*' (NATO, 25 November 1988), the purpose of the force-comparison statistics was to convince the public that NATO deserved more

Table 4.3   Forces in Europe: divisions, 1984–8

	NATO	WP	Ratio	Remarks
Author	22	25	1:1.1	forces in East and West Germany
	28	40	1:1.4	adding forces in Benelux and Czechoslovakia
	40	57	1:1.4	adding forces in Poland and NATO reinforcements
GKL 1984[5]	27	26	1:1	'in position'
	29	39	1:1.3	'available after 9 days'
	36	61	1:1.7	'available after 30 days'
UK DEs[7]	40	57	1:1.4	'current disposition' (not USSR)
	40	94	1:2.4	'current disposition' (including USSR)
IISS 84/85[8]	28	60	1:2.1	'deployed in peacetime'
	64	77	1:1.2	'immediate frontal' reinforcement
	101	110	1:1.1	'war mobilised'
IISS 87/88[8]	32	49	1:1.5	'peacetime' (NATO Guidelines Area)
	44	57	1:1.3	'war mobilised' (NATO Guidelines)
	107	101	1:0.9	'peacetime' (Atlantic to Urals)
	149	201	1:1.3	'war mobilised' (Atlantic to Urals)
NATO 82[14]	84	173	1:2.1	'rapidly deployable'
84[9]	88	115	1:1.3	'rapidly deployable'
	115	192	1:1.7	'fully reinforced'
88[11]	72	210	1:2.9	'active combat'
Warsaw Pact[15]	94	78	1:0.8	(WP include French and Spanish forces)

Table 4.3\ Notes

My figures giving rough parity of forces at NATO 22: 25 WTO divisions are made up as follows:

On the NATO side: 2 British, 3 French, 5 American and 12 West German divisions.
On the Warsaw Pact side: 19 Soviet divisions in East Germany (known as Group of Soviet Forces, Germany) and 6 East German divisions.

My figure of NATO 28:40 WTO arises from adding in 5 Soviet divisions deployed in Czechoslovakia, 10 Czech Army divisions, Danish and Canadian forces, and 2 Belgian and 2 Dutch divisions who are usually based in their home countries.

The IISS obtain a peacetime balance of NATO 32:49 Warsaw Pact by adding in four more divisions allocated to NATO (there are 3 US divisions with pre-positioned equipment for example) and a proportion of Soviet and Polish forces deployed in Poland.

My figure of NATO 40:57 WTO, identical to the smaller UK MOD figures, arises from counting in 2 more UK divisions, and US and French divisions allocated to NATO, to my original total, and on the Warsaw Pact side, all the Forces deployed in Poland: 2 Soviet divisions and 15 Polish divisions. The equivalent IISS 'war mobilised' figure is NATO 44: 57 Warsaw Pact.

After a period of some months, many more NATO and Pact reinforcements would be available and from a much wider area. The IISS figures are NATO 149:201 Warsaw Pact for forces 'Atlantic to Urals'.

NATO's estimate of its own forces by division is much smaller then the IISS figure. This is because (with the one exception of the 84 reinforced figures) they do not count any NATO reinforcements which would be available after mobilisation.

NATO counts Soviet peacetime forces as if they are at full strength when some two-thirds are normally at below half-strength. This is very misleading.

After unilateral Soviet and Warsaw Pact force cuts (six to ten divisions in the Central European region), the balance of forces deployed in the Central European region will be very even. The effect of these cuts would however gradually diminish as reinforcement progressed.

---

financial support and to irritate the Soviet Union into releasing its force estimates. The best way to achieve those objectives was to show NATO in a poor light in comparison with Warsaw Pact forces. As a result, in this publication, NATO did not mention the extremely large forces (over $2\frac{1}{2}$ million troops) which it can muster, some within two to three days. The publication *did* however count up all Soviet divisions even if they were only at 6 per cent of full strength (pp. 22–5).

In this case the lie was given by another NATO publication. In 'Enhancing Alliance Collective Security', published *only five days later* (1 December 1988), NATO actually *boasted* about the forces it could mobilise: 'mobilisation results in a personnel enhancement to the defence of over 200 per cent'; and

> Denmark moves from a standing force of 29 000 to over 100 000 in 2 or 3 days . . . likewise Norway, with a base of 38 000 in peacetime, increases to some 300 000 in 2 or 3 days, with 80 000 . . . mobilised in hours. Germany enhances its defence by mobilising over 800 000 personnel at short notice, thereby almost tripling the force normally deployed in peacetime.

and finally, 'with adequate warning the United Kingdom can triple its forces in the central region within 72 hours.'

These are the very same forces which NATO neglected to mention in its earlier publication. This was because the purpose of 'Enchancing Collective Security' was to persuade the Americans that NATO was really pulling its weight in defending Europe, thus NATO efforts had to be shown in the best light possible.

It really was an astonishing cheek for NATO to release two inconsistent force analyses in such close synchrony. But what was even more astonishing (and worrying) is that no defence correspondents (certainly in the UK media) pointed out these discrepancies. On the whole they gave out the messages NATO wanted from their press releases attached to these publications; in the one case 'Warsaw Pact superiority in every area' (*Times*, 26 November 1988) and in the other, 'Europe rebuts US accusations over NATO defence costs' (*Times*, 2 December 1988).

The 1984 force statistics tell a very similar story. The 'Force Comparisons' were written to show NATO in a poor light when compared with the Warsaw Pact and to enable NATO to justify increases in military spending over and above inflation. The Eurogroup document was designed to show the Americans just how much the Europeans contributed to defence. The booklet even has a short questionnaire with only four questions. The questions ask how the reader's copy was acquired, the reader's occupation, feedback on content, and, 'As a result of reading this booklet would you say that the European contribution to Western Defence is: much as you thought, more or less than you had realised?' Clearly, the authors wanted to see if their message was getting across.

I believe that the only reasonable conclusion that can be drawn is that the NATO figures are *deliberately* biased. I should also say that I am not saying that the drafters of the booklets in question were necessarily striving to mislead. But certainly the drafters were operating within very severe political constraints as to the type of end-analysis that would be acceptable to the diplomats of the member-countries and for transmission to the public. Certainly NATO would have looked extremely foolish if its senior politicians had prominently voiced the NATO Eurogroup statistics showing NATO outnumbering the Warsaw Pact in soldiers. Needless to say, the figures which were widely used were the ones showing NATO at the most severe disadvantage.

Tanks

Table 4.4 is a collation of estimates of tank forces available in Europe from a wide variety of sources. In 1988, the IISS sustantially downgraded its estimate of the NATO Warsaw Pact imbalance over previous years. Much light has been shed upon the situation by two recent in-depth analyses of tank forces (the Gervasi and Bradford studies) which estimate numbers of tanks available after given lengths of time.[16] These two independent analyses agree quite closely and are also consistent with IISS figures.[17] From comparisons with these sources it can be established that NATO is again not always comparing like with like. In NATO's 1984, 'rapidly reinforceable' category, NATO was comparing NATO tank forces likely to be available in ten days with Warsaw Pact forces likely to be available after *four months* mobilisation. NATO's 'reinforced' figures are NATO tanks available after four months compared with the total global holdings of Soviet and Warsaw Pact tanks (including tanks facing China, Iran and Afghanistan). NATO's 1988 figures are close to the IISS Atlantic to Urals figures once 5800 NATO tanks in storage are added in.

Table 4.4   Tank forces East and West, 1984–9

Source		NATO	WTO	Remarks
Italy[18]				
White Paper	1985	8 050	16 650	'Rapidly deployable'
UK Defence				
Estimates[7]	1984	7 800	18 000	(excludes those in the USSR)
	1985	7 800	16 840	'some in storage'
IISS[8]	83/84	13 097	37 490	Main Battle Tanks in Northern Europe
	84/85	13 716	32 100	"
	87/88	12 700	18 000	NATO Guidelines
		22 200	52 200	Atlantic to Urals
		30 500	68 300	Total holdings
Gervasi/	86			
Bradford[16]	84/88	10 350	14 590	Europe in ten days
		21 900	28 600	After four months
		32 000	67 400	Total holdings
NATO	1982a[14]	13 000	42 500	
	1984a[9]	13 470	26 900	'Rapidly reinforceable'
		17 730	46 230	'Reinforced'
	1988a[11]	16 424	51 500	
		22 224		adding NATO tanks in storage
Warsaw Pact	84[15]	12 000 to 13 000	—	
		18 000	—	(including France and Spain)
		30 000	—	(including all those in store)
	89[13]	30 690	59 470	

Table 4.4 Notes

There is a sharp discrepancy in the numbers of *Western* tanks between the UK and Italian White Papers on Defence on the one hand, and the NATO and IISS figures on the other. The difference between the UK and IISS figures amounts to about 5000 tanks – equivalent to the total number of US tanks in Europe.

Tanks actually in the Soviet Union, over 1000 miles from the front, some of which are allocated to other military tasks in the Southern and Eastern theatres require transportation by rail to get to Europe.

According to the IISS, only 33 per cent of the WTO tanks are made up of the modern T-64, T-72 and T-80, which are largely reserved for Soviet forces and which are comparable to Modern NATO tanks. The remainder, 66 per cent, are the rather old, and by Western standards almost obsolete T-54, T-55 and T-62s, deployed in large numbers with the Polish, Czech and East German armies.

Unilateral Soviet Force Cuts:
The removal of 5000 Soviet tanks is a very significant reduction and virtually wipes out the tank imbalance in Central Europe. The significance for the overall Atlantic–Urals balance is smaller because of the larger forces involved, although another 5000 are to be removed from the European theatre of the Soviet Union. Overall 5000 tanks are to be destroyed, the other 5000 to be retained in storage.

All sources do, however, agree that the Warsaw Pact has more tanks than NATO. In two weeks the imbalance is roughly 3:2 and in total stocks roughly 2:1. What does this imbalance mean?

To attempt to answer this question it is necessary to look at the relative fighting capabilities of Soviet and NATO tanks.

The first thing that has to be said is that NATO and Warsaw Pact tanks are very different. The first most striking difference is that NATO tanks are much heavier than those of the Warsaw Pact (the average weights are 49 and 37 tonnes respectively). This is due to the different design philosophies of East and West. Warsaw Pact tanks are designed for cheap mass production and are smaller, with smaller engines and have comparatively light side, top and rear armour protection, concentrating most protection at the front. The relatively low weight of Soviet tanks means that it is very difficult for the Soviet Union to add more armour to give added protection against advanced warheads such as precision-guided munitions because the additional weight would slow them down too much.

Another major difference is the age of equipment: 70 per cent of Warsaw Pact tanks first came into service before 1962 while only 55 per cent of Western tanks are of this vintage. 50 per cent of Warsaw Pact tanks are the T-34 and T-54/55 types first introduced by 1956. Only 27 per cent of Western tanks are as old as this.

Quite extraordinary reports come from American experts who have actually driven Soviet tanks captured by Israeli forces in the Middle East. The T-72 tank, for example, has such a cramped interior, that the crew of three (not four as in Western tanks) have to be less than 1.6 metres in height (5' 4") to fit in. A specialist military journal has published a photograph taken by a rather amused Western military observer of three extremely short Soviet tank crew posing outside their tank.[19] In the T-62, not only do the crew need to be as small, but being left-handed is also an advantage. This is because the loader sits on the 'wrong' side of the gun breech. The extremely cramped tank interior led one US retired Admiral to remark that the Soviet Union would be in serious trouble if they ever ran out of left-handed midgets.[20]

American and Israeli drivers, found that the T-72 tank had an extremely heavy clutch, apparently two were burned out in training an American driver. To make matters worse, getting into top gear was extremely difficult, rumour has it that Soviet drivers are issued with a small sledge-hammer to achieve this difficult task. Certainly Western drivers needed to use a 'sharp blow from a heavy hammer' to make a gear shift, continuing: 'No wonder that clutch and transmission breakdowns occur often, leaving an otherwise perfectly serviceable tank abandoned on the battlefield.' Another problem for the tank crew is that in action the gun's exhaust gases vent into the crew compartment poisoning the crew and leading to battle fatigue or exhaustion: 'tank crews have been known to abandon their mounts totally exhausted, choking from the poisonous fumes'.[21] The US Defense Intelligence Agency calculate that, on average, Soviet armoured vehicles break down every 160km, while the NATO average is a break down every 250km. If these performance figures are correct, a Soviet first thrust could not reach the Rhine, or could only do so by deploying numerous reserve echelons. This may go some way to explaining the large numbers of vehicles in the Warsaw Pact armies. They are needed for spares; three to five vehicles are needed to guarantee one on the battlefield.[22]

Crack forces such as the Group of Soviet Forces in East Germany, do not even regularly use their newest armoured forces such as the T-72 and T-80 tanks but train with T-64s or even T-54s and T-55s. In Spring, 1984 the Soviet armed forces newspaper *Red Star* (*Krasnaya*

Zvezda) took the unprecedented step of publishing the results of
snap inspections revealing serious deficiencies in training standards.[23]

Detailed comparisons of Warsaw Pact and NATO tanks' capabilities show that in observation, fire-power, mobility and armour,
Warsaw Pact tanks are inferior to their Western counterparts.[24]
Specific points are that Soviet tanks have no 'passive' night vision
(the ability to see by starlight), but rely upon infra-red searchlights
which are very visible to Western sensors; Soviet tank guns are less
accurate; Soviet tanks have crude gearboxes, clutches and brakes
together with weak engine technology (hence shorter mileage between breakdowns achieved by Warsaw Pact tanks). From October
1988, the most modern M-1 Abrams tank will be fitted with a new
uranium and steel armour, two-and-a-half times as dense as steel
which, according to Pentagon officials is 'a major advance' and will
take the Soviet Union 'almost a decade' to copy. The same Pentagon
sources claim that not only does the new armour stop all Soviet
anti-tank missiles but *all those known to be under development*.[25] If
these claims are true, the only Soviet weapons which could knock out
an attack by US M-1 tanks would be large-calibre armour-piercing
rounds, fired by artillery or heavy mortars and possibly from the guns
mounted on the most modern Soviet tanks.

The only factors in which Soviet tanks appear to be superior are
cold weather operability and detectability (Soviet tanks being smaller
than their NATO counterparts are harder to see).

It is possible to take some of these comparative factors into
account numerically and then to see what the balance of tank capabilities as opposed to simple numbers looks like.[26] First, let us assume
that war breaks out after two weeks of mobilisation and that NATO
is outnumbered by 3:2 (1.5:1). At least 20 per cent of Soviet tanks
will break down, while only 10 per cent of NATO tanks will do so.
This changes the ratio to 1.3:1. Considering the greater age and
relative inferiority of Soviet tanks but allowing for their greater
numbers we can introduce a combat efficiency factor of 1.5 in favour
of NATO, taking the overall ratio to 0.9:1, now slightly in favour of
NATO. Thus the two forces are very evenly balanced.

This is a very important finding for the CFE negotiations. If it is the
case that the tank forces of East and West have very similar fighting
capabilities at present despite the large disparities in numbers, then
should these disparities be negotiated away, NATO, because of its
superior forces would actually have an *advantage*. To redress the
imbalance the Soviet Union would need to upgrade the fighting

capabilities of their tanks significantly – or of course adopt a different defence posture such as defensive deterrence.

Should war break out after substantial reinforcement, the greater relative numbers of Soviet tanks would be offset by the fact that more of these would be the very old T-54/55 models while NATO would still be reinforcing with modern tanks. I should stress that my analysis does not include the possible impact of the new US tank armour which is too new and untested a quantity to be included at the time of writing.

Air Power

Considerations of the balance of forces in Europe often seem to ignore the existence of air forces and air power. The air forces, however, with their long-range attack potential have many important ways of influencing the outcome of any conflict:

- prevention of hostile air attack by attacking airfields;
- attacking communications and supply lines;
- providing close air support for ground forces;
- attacking command posts;
- destroying nuclear weapons on the ground.

There is a sharp difference in the types of air forces deployed by East and West. NATO air forces have a deep-strike role, primarily to fly behind enemy lines knocking out airfields. Force concentrations, bridges and communications are important but subsidiary targets. NATO thus possesses large numbers of long-range ground-attack aircraft. NATO argues that this is in fact a defensive strategy in order to slow down or halt any Soviet attack and to protect NATO ground-forces.

A large proportion of the Warsaw Pact air force, is designed to stop NATO penetrating Pact airspace, for which they require and have deployed large numbers of fighters. In many force comparisons (including NATO's) the distinctions between defensive interceptors and attack aircraft are not drawn, which leads to an apparently massive advantage in Soviet forces which is not an accurate reflection of offensive capability (NATO argues that many of the Warsaw Pact's fighter/interceptors could in war be converted relatively easily to carry bombs).

When designated *ground-attack* or *close air support* aircraft are

Table 4.5 Air power, 1988–9

NATO	WTO		
3215	3218	IISS '88/9 Atlantic–Urals	Bombers and FGA
1178	4432	IISS '88/9 Atlantic–Urals	Air-defence/Fighters
4100	2800	Warsaw Pact Jan. '89	Attack aircraft
5450	5350	Warsaw Pact Jan. '89	Combat aircraft
3477	8250	NATO Dec. '88	

FGA = fighter/ground attack.

compared, NATO and the Warsaw Pact have almost identical numbers of aircraft – around 3215 each (IISS statistics, 1988/9) (see Table 4.5). The Warsaw Pact has rather more air-defence aircraft and fighters, however (1178 to 4432). The Warsaw Pact breaks down the figures rather differently, finding another 1000 NATO attack aircraft (mostly due to counting naval-based aircraft). Nevertheless, NATO, the IISS and the Pact themselves agree that the Warsaw Pact has 7650 to 8250 aircraft of one sort or another. This is good agreement between such different sources. The real difficulty is in reconciling the various statistics for NATO'S aircraft. As usual NATO gives the smallest number of all. The IISS finds another 1000 aircraft while the Pact finds another 6000! This latter figure takes NATO's total to near the IISS figure for the global holdings of NATO warplanes. Essentially, in these statistics the Pact is counting in many US planes based in the USA and on various US battle carrier-groups operating off the coasts of Europe.

These numerical differences apart, NATO has a significant edge in training and equipment. NATO also has a significant advantage in bomb-delivery capability at a distance. For example, the US FB-111 can deliver a payload of 17 000kg at 1900km, which is one-and-a-half times, to twice as much the payload of the Soviet Tu-22 'Blinder' or the Su-24 'Fencer' and at 25 to 30 per cent longer range.

BEHIND THE SOVIET THREAT

Reports from unofficial sources within the Soviet Union and intelligence sources outside, give a very different picture of the supposedly perfectly oiled Soviet fighting-machine. One such example, *The Liberators*, written under the pseudonym of Viktor Suvurov,[27] gives a detailed account of apparently low morale in the Soviet forces brought about by excessive attention to discipline for pettifogging offences. More importantly however, he refers to details of exercises such as the Soviet crossing of the Dneiper in 1976, accomplished by a Soviet force of 5187 tanks. The exercise was repeated in detail several times, while tanks manned solely by officers crossed the river on pre-placed tracks. The task was much too complex and the display much too important to be entrusted to ordinary soldiers. Not exactly realistic war games! He also refers to nine full-strength 'court' divisions kept purely for show with no battle training whatsoever.

Such reports are difficult to check, but other authoritative (and named) sources back up some of this information. For example, certainly up to 1986 no soldier under the rank of Captain was given maps or lessons in map-reading because of excessive Soviet security and lack of confidence in the abilities of 'lower ranks'.[28] Other sources refer to the Soviet attitude to the terrain as an obstacle to be surmounted rather than to be used to advantage, and to the lack of initiative in Soviet forces.[29]

The drive for reform in the Soviet Union however, has started to improve the abilities of Soviet forces. Prominent Soviet military figures have given interviews reported in the Soviet press referring to the implementation of reforms (and cuts) in Soviet armed forces. General Moiseyev, Chief of the General Staff, in an article in *Krasnaya Zvevda* referred to the improvement of technical training. Admiral of the Fleet Vladimir Chernavin, in an interview in *Izyestiya*, emphasised that '*Perestroika* has changed the demands of the Officer Corps . . . the preference now is being given to officers capable of making innovative decisions, creative and searching people capable of objectivity and critically assessing the results of their work'.[30]

The Soviet invasion of Czechoslovakia in 1968 was keenly observed by Western intelligence:

Helicopter-borne troops were landed on the wrong mountain tops. Logistic planners apparently relied in their planning on seizing Czech fuel and supplies; but even the minimal resistance of the Czechs denied the invaders those supplies and added to the growing logistics snarl. Soviet tanks and armoured personnel carriers blithely poured into narrow bottle necks causing rush-hour-style traffic jams that would have provided tempting targets in a real war. One analyst has concluded 'under actual combat conditions, they would have lacked essential items after the first 24 hours'. And these problems confronted a Soviet force trying to occupy a nation half the size of the Federal Republic of Germany . . . with no army opposing its advance.[31]

The mobilisation of these 500 000 troops (roughly 30 divisions) took no less than six months to achieve. Not the one to three months anticipated by NATO. Prior to sending 150 000 troops into Afghanistan in 1978–80, the Soviets again required six months. Some of the units were so-called 2nd and 3rd category units (usually manned at below 75 per cent and below 50 per cent full-strength, respectively). These units proved incapable of fighting and had to be replaced by category 1 divisions.[32] Part of these problems relate to the relatively unrealistic and limited scope of Warsaw Pact military exercises in comparison to NATO. A comparison of exercises conducted in 1987 found that NATO conducted longer and larger exercises than the Warsaw Pact; roughly twice as many troop days, and one-and-a-half times the duration and size.[33] These factors mean that NATO forces are far better prepared for fighting than are their Warsaw Pact counterparts.

Another problem for the Soviet Union would be the high probability of non-cooperation or even outright opposition by some of the Warsaw Pact states. Strong evidence for the importance of this was given by large-scale Warsaw Pact exercises as early as 1984 in which the Soviet Union practised a complete reinforcement exercise without using Polish forces or facilities.[34] This was interpreted as a clear military response to the political pressures exerted by the Solidarity movement in Poland. Since the advent of *glasnost* in the Soviet Union and elections in Eastern European countries resulting in non communist party governments, it seems even less likely that the Soviet Union could count upon unquestioning support for any military action which did not seem entirely justified.

Apart from these doubts, Polish, East German and Czech armed forces are not well equipped. For example they possess the oldest tanks in the Warsaw Pact arsenals.[35]

SUMMARY AND CONCLUSIONS

In terms of the numbers of troops and numbers of divisions it cannot be correctly stated that NATO is outnumbered by the Warsaw Pact.

Certainly, phrases such as 'overwhelming imbalance' are totally inappropriate. In troop numbers, however they are counted, the Warsaw Pact and NATO are very evenly matched and NATO slightly outnumbers the Warsaw Pact.

The remaining plank of NATO's argument is that Warsaw Pact forces far outnumber NATO in numbers of tanks and artillery. Tanks are a prime concern because of their mobile and potentially offensive nature, especially as a means of invading and occupying Western Europe. Warsaw Pact forces do have larger numbers of tanks than NATO forces.

Here again, however, once differences in the combat ability, age, reliability and weight of tanks are taken into account, NATO and the Warsaw Pact are fairly evenly matched. The Pact's advantage in numbers is further offset by poor training standards, although these standards seem likely to rise as part of the Soviet forces restructuring in progress.

My analysis of NATO's own force statistics leads me to the inescapable conclusion that in some cases the NATO figures have been deliberately chosen to present the Warsaw Pact:NATO balance of forces in an unfavourable light towards NATO in an attempt to justify the defence policies of the NATO countries. In other cases, for US consumption, NATO does the reverse and tries to maximise its forces and contribution to European defence. This sometimes results in huge inconsistencies in NATO's own figures for its own forces. These internal inconsistencies and inconsistencies between individual NATO countries' estimates and independent international estimates, seriously challenge the credibility of NATO's figures.

The level of inconsistency in NATO's presentations of its own forces, let alone Warsaw Pact forces, is so large and so obvious once one knows where to look, that NATO does appear rather schizophrenic. If NATO is to avoid future severe bad publicity as conventional forces receive more attention as the CFE talks progress, NATO needs to ensure that the various committees producing force comparison figures talk to each other an attempt to reach some internal consistency.

On the rare occasions when they have been prepared to commit themselves, Soviet numbers have been somewhat more realistic than NATO ones.

The alleged supremacy of Soviet forces in Europe was the subject of some controversy within the NATO establishment itself. From 1984 to 1988, NATO was in the somewhat embarrassing position of being unable to release further force comparisons. NATO member-countries were unable to reach the necessary unanimous agreement upon the figures and form of words. Prime dissenting voices were the potentially violently opposed Greeks and Turks, but Denmark, Norway, and relatively new members, Spain and Greece, also dissent from NATO's nuclear strategy in various ways.

A clue to the arguments that go on can be seen in NATO's 1988 figures. Although individual countries' force statistics are given, the columns are not totalled (the reader is left to do this). In this way NATO avoided actually printing any numerical NATO:WP force comparisons; the only comparisons are in the red and blue pie charts which again have no numbers beside them. This was NATO's way of compromising between publishing a detailed force comparison and publishing none.[36]

The degree to which the Soviets are really changing their posture and strategy and the degree to which NATO can respond by cuts of its own, will be an important political issue for the 1990s. If the CFE talks in Vienna are successful and both sides deploy equal numbers of equipment and troops the new emphasis of analysis and argument will be upon the *capability* of the equipment deployed. Already in 1989, Northern Army Group army intelligence officers were speaking of a 'leaner but meaner' Soviet army in Europe and that the reductions in the hardware of Soviet forces in Western Europe would actually *increase* the 'efficiency, speed of manoeuvre and adaptability of the remaining forces'.[37]

Certainly equality of equipment and personnel does not mean equality of force or capability. Here the West has a significant advantage in quality of training and equipment which the Soviets would find hard (and very expensive) to match. It seems however, that the Soviets are making an opportunity out of this problem by considering an alternative, more defensive strategy, and cutting defence spending rather than embarking on an arms quality race with the West.

THE WORST CASE

Military analysts when seeking to test their defence strategies usually adopt a 'worst case' analysis, their argument being that if the strategy cannot deal with the worst possible case then one is potentially vulnerable. By its nature this type of analysis always accentuates any potential differences between two opposing forces. The danger is that as both parties take the worst case both try to out-arm the other leading to further common insecurity. This is the long-term (or strategic) problem to which worst-case analysis leads. In my view, worst-case analysis is too often used to set policy without adequate consideration of more likely (average-case) eventualities or other political considerations.

NATO and Warsaw Pact forces are technically very evenly matched *providing* NATO starts mobilising forces as soon as the Warsaw Pact. If NATO delays, Warsaw Pact forces could outnumber NATO by 3:2 and in the worst case, with a delay of two weeks, by up to 2:1. But for this to happen NATO would have either to fail to spot or to fail to react huge reinforcements in Warsaw Pact forces in East Germany and Czechoslovakia involving the movement of 35–40 Warsaw Pact divisions over hundreds of miles in a massive logistical exercise several times larger than that of the D-Day landings in Normandy. The parallel stops there however. Uniformed Western observers (Military Liaison Missions) are actually permitted to drive around certain areas of East Germany (and Soviet observers around West Germany) under the little-known Huebner–Malinin agreement dating from the Second World War and the arrangements to administer occupied Germany. Nowadays spy-planes gather intelligence and satellites monitor from space. Following the 1987 agreement at the Stockholm Conference, these rather limited measures have been greatly enhanced by the right of inspection by foreign observers when military forces of divisional size or over are moved. The CFE talks are discussing further detailed force inspection provisions including an 'open skies' agreement to licence routine aerial surveillance by NATO and Pact aircraft, taking this process even further.

The doubts about the Soviet Union's ability to mount an attack without the West having substantial warning time are echoed in a classified Pentagon report prepared in early 1989 but leaked to the US press in November 1989.[38] The study, prepared by US military intelligence and the CIA for planning the 1992–7 Pentagon budgets, concludes that the Soviet Union could not mount a 'major sustained attack' without the western intelligence community receiving 'some 33 to 44 days of warning' and that 'Soviet forces in Eastern Europe are not now postured for a standing start or short warning attack against NATO'. Neither British or West German military intelligence fully share this US confidence, however.

One can imagine three worst-case scenarios, assuming that a hostile Soviet Bloc is intent upon invading the West.

1. The Group of Soviet Forces in Germany mount a surprise attack with their full complement of 19 divisions (or much less after force reductions). At the very least these would face 12 West German divisions of larger size which they could try to avoid by attacking in the UK, Belgian or Dutch sectors. Complete surprise could be achieved only in a risky 'standing start' attack for which Soviet forces are not postured. This scenario is only possible as long as several Soviet divisions remain in eastern Germany.

2. The Soviets reinforce over a period of two to three weeks and NATO does not fully reinforce for some political reasons (such as the fear of inadvertent escalation triggered by reinforcement). In the worst case, some 60 Soviet divisions would then face about 30 Western divisions of larger size. Complete surprise could not be achieved. After a successful CFE-I treaty it would be highly unlikely that the Warsaw Pact could achieve a force ratio of more than about 45 to 30.

3. The Soviets and NATO reinforce over a period of two to three months during a protracted period of worsening international relations. About 200 Warsaw Pact divisions would face 150 NATO divisions. A CFE-I agreement would reduce both forces proportionately.

The possible military outcomes of these scenarios are examined in the next chapter together with a consideration of the influences of important factors such as the terrain, and NATO and Warsaw Pact strategy.

5 Battlefield Europe

Having assessed the balance of *numbers* of forces East and West, in Chapter 4, in this chapters look at the *capabilities* of the forces deployed in Europe and the forces that would be necessary with the current strategies to mount a successful defence of Western Europe. Throughout my analysis I will not consider the influence or effect of nuclear weapons and nuclear strategies but will concentrate upon the ability of non-nuclear forces to achieve military objectives in Central Europe. This is of central importance for defensive deterrence.

An important factor is NATO strategy. In order to meet an assumed attack from the East, NATO forces are deployed in the NATO strategy of 'forward defence'. NATO's intention is to stop or delay any attack by the Warsaw Pact as near to the border as possible.

FORWARD DEFENCE

There are political and military reasons for the choice of forward defence. In geographical terms, West Germany is a long and relatively thin country, thus Warsaw pact forces deployed in East Germany would not need to penetrate very far in an attack to take over a sizeable proportion of the country. 30 per cent of the population of the Federal Republic of Germany lives in a strip within 100km of the border. This same strip contains 25 per cent of the country's industrial capacity. Any military strategy which seems willing to 'give up' this strip even temporarily is politically unacceptable in Western Germany. This strip of land is also rather easier to defend than the rest of Germany because it is on the whole more mountainous, particularly to the south, and contains many natural obstacles to an attacking mechanised army.

For command purposes and because of the many different nationalities of troops in NATO, responsibility for the defence of the front is split up into nine sectors. One national army corps is given the task of defending each sector with the possibility of reinforcements from adjacent sectors. For overall command purposes Germany is considered split into northern and southern areas called NORTHAG and CENTAG (NORTHern and CENTral Army Groups) respectively (see Figure 5.1). Given the NATO choice of

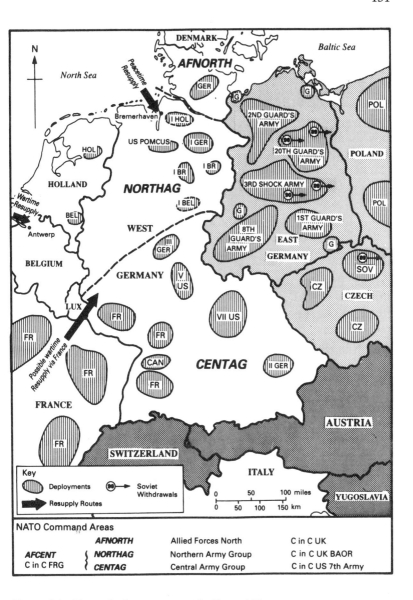

Figure 5.1   Force deployment areas in Central Europe

forward defence as its strategy and its forward deployment of forces, any war fought in central Europe would be won and lost in Germany. From this starting-point a very important factor in deciding the outcome of any military conflict is the terrain over which occupying forces would have to be moved.

In CENTAG the terrain is quite mountainous and contains numerous rivers and forests all of which pose severe obstacles to the movement of large mechanised forces. The geography of the area quite naturally limits large-scale force movements to three main channels. These are known by Western strategists as the Hof corridor, the Gottingen corridor and the Fulda Gap (see Figure 5.2).

The Hof corridor is a break in the mountains of the region formed by the Main, Naab, Saale and Ohre rivers. Advancing WTO forces would have to move through passes north and south of the Erzgebirge mountains and cross several rivers before reaching the flatter areas around Bayreuth in Bavaria, or south of Leipzig and west of Prague. Possible objectives of a WTO attack could be a southern attack on Frankfurt (200km away) or an attack leading towards Stuttgart 270km away. An advance by Western forces (VII American and II German corps) would have the rather more attractive military targets of Leipzig (140km away and on the way to Berlin) or Prague or Dresden both about 165km away.

Because of the many obstacles and the narrow channels defined by the geography of this area neither side could expect a frontal assault here to succeed. Inevitable concentrations of troops or tanks would provide sitting targets for attacks from the air.

The Gottingen corridor is a strip of land, 20–30km wide south of the Harz mountains. There are numerous forests. Advancing WTO forces would have to cross the Leine and Weser rivers before reaching flatter terrain with the military objective of capturing the heavily industrialised Ruhr 240km away. For their part Western forces (III German corps) would have to cross many rivers before reaching Leipzig 140km away. Again it seems unlikely that a major attack could be mounted solely in this region.

The Fulda gap is a relatively unobstructed path, only 100km long, between Frankfurt and East Germany, defended by V American corps. Apart from the Fulda river there are no severe obstacles to the movement of tank formations. Opposite the gap in Eastern Germany numerous rivers would block a NATO attack.

Frankfurt is an extremely important military target because of its key role in communications between north and south Germany; its

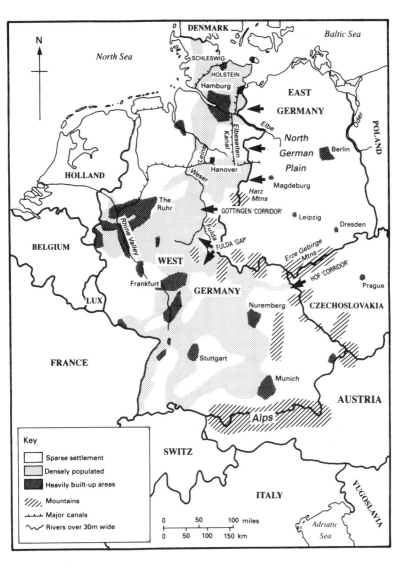

Figure 5.2 The terrain of Central Europe

capture would leave forces in southern Germany isolated. For these reasons an attack toward Frankfurt is the most threatening of the three possible avenues of attack upon NATO in the CENTAG region and a major although channelled attack could be mounted in this direction.

In NORTHAG the terrain is the relatively flat north German plain which military strategists regard as ideal for the rapid deployment and advance of tank formations in a *blitzkrieg*-type attack. (In a *blitzkrieg* – German for 'lightning attack' – highly mobile armoured formations integrated with mechanised infantry and air-support aim to penetrate defences rapidly and 'pour through' the gaps created spreading out behind enemy front-lines, avoiding centres of resistance and destroying lines of supply and communications. It is essentially an attack upon an opponent's means to wage war.)

The German plain, however, is not without obstacles to the rapid movement of masses of armour. On the western side, working from the north to south through NORTHAG; in Schleswig-Holsten there are numerous bogs, rivers and urban sprawl around Hamburg. Further south, are the Luneburger Heath, the Urgenau river, the Elbeseitenkanal, extensive urban sprawl around Hanover (the military man-made equivalent of forest) the Aller, Oker and Leine rivers and finally the Harz mountains. On the Eastern side there are numerous rivers – particularly the Elbe, Elde, Havel and Ohre. Thus the two least obstructed paths are via routes south of Hamburg, north of the Luneburger Heath, and east of Hanover.

Thus in the entire central front there are five clear avenues for invading land forces, two on the North German Plain and three to the south. Forces could also be landed from the sea in a counter-attacking or outflanking manoeuvre into the northern Netherlands, north-west Germany or Denmark from the North Sea and Baltic Sea, or into north-Eastern Germany or Poland from the Baltic Sea. Forces would also be airlifted and dropped behind enemy lines. In the north the terrain does not favour either side particularly, except that from a purely military point of view WTO forces have the attractive objective of capturing Hamburg only 50km away along the autobahn. The only city of equivalent size in East Germany is Berlin, 200km away. Further south, with the exception of the Fulda gap where the terrain favours an attack from the east, the terrain favours Western forces who could advance down river valleys into East Germany and Czechoslovakia. However, in the south, ground-forces could only move in relatively narrowly defined channels. This favours the defence because concentrations of advancing troops or tanks inevitably occur at predictable 'choke' points providing 'sitting targets' for air strikes or pre-planned long-range artillery or missile bombardment.

WHO WOULD WIN?

Trying to predict the outcome of a conventional war in central Europe is obviously a very risky enterprise. Much would depend upon the exact circumstances, timing and intentions surrounding the outbreak of the conflict, not to mention sheer luck. However, whatever the political factors deciding how a conflict might arise and factors determining and influencing its course once the military forces are engaged, military factors will primarily influence its outcome – at least in the short term.

A useful analogy is the case of the Philistine and Israeli armies in ancient Judea. Political factors had brought about the battle and military–political factors had brought about the decision to choose two champions – David and Goliath. Predicting the course of the battle would have been extremely difficult before the two armies met, especially as one might not anticipate the decision to choose champions, despite the customs of the day. Once the champions had been chosen (if one were an expert in advanced weapons systems) the outcome was quite predictable; the slow-moving Goliath presented a clear target and was outgunned and outranged by highly accurate slingshot fire. (Perhaps the ancient equivalent of the modern infantry anti-tank weapon?) The complexities and possible interactions of modern weapons systems however pose a much harder task for the modern analyst.

This is as far as the purely military analysis can take us; to give us information about the likely courses of battles in the shorter term if strengths of forces, terrain and technological factors are properly considered. There is no reliable analysis method. Only history can tell us the final outcome of the continuing conflict – although it is somewhat ironic that the area of Judaea is one of continuing conflict. Similarly we should be able to work out who would win a set of conventional battles in Europe where the battle-lines are clearly drawn and set. In the longer term the outcome is increasingly less clear as time progresses without a cease-fire or settlement because of the interplay of political and economic factors and because of the increasingly likely use of nuclear weapons and escalation to the destruction of the battlefield, the armies and European civilisation.

Can the Soviets Win?

To assess whether NATO's belief that its forces would be quickly overwhelmed in a conventional attack is correct, we have to see how the Soviet Union could deploy its forces to gain a decisive military advantage.

It is generally accepted by Eastern and Western strategists from many studies of battles, that for an attack to succeed against prepared defensive positions, a numerical advantage of forces is required. The defence has the advantage because they know the terrain and are in cover, the attackers have to expose themselves moving over unfamiliar ground under heavy fire. The only advantage possessed by the attackers is in choosing the time and place of the attack and, possibly, surprise. But with modern intelligence techniques against an adversary prepared for attack such as NATO, complete surprise is very unlikely to be achieved.

Based on the lessons of the Second World War, the Soviets estimate that the size of a decisive superiority in numbers in a given battle (not a war) ranges between 3–5 times for infantry, 6–8 times for artillery, 3–4 times for tanks and self-propelled artillery and 5–10 times for aircraft.[1] The American Army also agrees on these figures.[2]

Thus, to achieve a decisive advantage, the Soviet Union would have to covertly deploy forces 3–5 times those of NATO in a given sector in order to achieve a breakthrough.

Taking the worst of the three worst-case scenarios outlined earlier, NATO's worst case is that NATO forces delay reinforcement and that the Soviets attack at the worst possible imbalance of forces. In this, the absolute worst case, NATO forces would be outnumbered by 2:1, or 60 divisions to 30.

NATO's forces, in accordance with forward defence, would be deployed fairly evenly along the front line, making an average of four divisions per Corps sector. If the Warsaw Pact decided that to be sure they needed an advantage of 5:1 to break through in a *blitzkrieg* type attack they would need twenty divisions in that sector (possibly more to allow for the smaller Soviet divisions). Thus out of a total force of thirty divisions, they could attack along a maximum of three axes leaving other areas totally unprotected against NATO counter-attacks. Otherwise they could attack along two axes and maintain some defensive forces.

If the Warsaw Pact were prepared to take the risk of having an advantage of only 3:1 (which works out at twelve divisions per NATO sector) the maximum number of attacking axes would be four, without leaving whole sectors undefended and rather obvious gaps for NATO intelligence to spot.

Thus, if this hypothetical Soviet attack were to come, it could only come along two to four avenues of attack, mounted by twelve to twenty divisions. Needless to say, this would involve quite a massive redeployment of forces. For it to hope to succeed without being hopelessly bogged down by the terrain, such an attack would almost certainly have to be mounted through the Fulda Gap or the North German Plain in the German or British Corps sectors. The Belgian and Dutch sectors are also potentially vulnerable sectors but these forces have been allocated much narrower sectors of front and are in any case flanked by stronger UK or German forces.

NATO is well aware of the most likely avenues of attack and one would expect NATO to deploy its forces more strongly opposite them. This is in fact largely the case. The larger and most heavily equipped German and US Corps cover the Fulda gap and the Gottingen corridor. The North German Plain itself is probably the least-well-covered area. The British forces with their three divisions, half the size of the German and US divisions, cover Hanover, flanked by I German Corps and relatively light Dutch and Belgian forces. These forces, however, are backed up by US reinforcement divisions pre-positioned matériel configured to unit sets (POMCUS) divisions which would be formed out of Bremen to the rear. The two Corps based in Southern Germany, V USA and II German might well be better deployed in part at least further north. That is unless NATO has some counter-attacking role for them into Czechoslovakia or southern East Germany. It is interesting however to note that NATO's forces have not been allocated their sectors of front upon any particularly rational basis, the positions of US and UK forces represent the rough locations of Allied forces at the conclusion of The Second World War.

Our hypothetical attacker, however, has additional problems. It is all very well if one can succeed in deploying a locally overwhelming advantage in numbers, but to succeed, these forces have to be brought to bear. Obviously there are limits to how many divisions one can actually deploy against a defending force in a given space without them getting in each other's way. Military strategists refer to this as the 'force:space' ratio or the 'crossing the T' phenomenon. John Mearsheimer reports that there is broad agreement between experts from America, Germany, Israel and Britain, following observations of recent conflicts in the Middle East, upon the amount of front-line a brigade can hold – which comes out as to 7–15km (this amounts to 14–30km for a division).[3] In NORTHAG NATO has the equivalent of thirty brigades (six Dutch, thirteen German, seven British, four Belgian) along a front line of about 225km. This works out at 7km per brigade which is very near an optimum force:space ratio. If these forces are deployed in the traditional two-forward and one-in-reserve manner, the twenty forward brigades would have 11km each, leaving ten brigades in reserve.

Once the natural obstacles on the front are taken into account, NATO has about the optimum number of forces to hold the line while reinforcements are brought up. Thus, if this analysis is correct and NATO does not make any serious errors, the balance of forces becomes less important because the WTO attack would be held until reinforcements arrived.[4] Unless the WTO can win quickly, the far greater economic resources of Western Europe and the US must win out in the end. Also, contrary to the impression given in NATO documents, the greater bulk of NATO'S reinforcements does not have to come across the Atlantic Ocean from America, but comes from Germany itself. In an acute crisis, West Germany can mobilise forces of 1 250 000 in about 60 hours, including reservists and the FRG Territorial Army of some 450 000 men. The large contribution of Western German forces to NATO was in fact one of the motivating forces behind various Soviet proposals at the Vienna MBFR talks, to keep the total forces of the FGR less than half of the NATO total. The Soviets feared the possibility of a re-emergent and hostile Germany.

Analysts in the Brookings Institution have made calculations of the chances of a successful WTO attack in various stages of NATO and WTO reinforcement. Taking the case of sixty WTO divisions versus thirty NATO, William Kaufmann estimates that the WTO divisions would have a roughly 70 per cent chance of penetrating 50km or more in seven days.[5] If, however, NATO could bring up further reinforcements during this time amounting to a further seven divisions, this chance would reduce to 50 per cent (even chances). WTO forces in this case would be likely to penetrate only 27km. Interestingly, however, in the same analysis the effectiveness of barriers

along the front line are calculated. In these two cases the chances of
WTO 'success' then become 45 per cent and about 30 per cent
respectively. WTO forces would also get less far into Germany. In
this quite complex analysis all NATO and WTO forces are given
military effectiveness quotients and barriers are rated as reducing the
effectiveness of an attacking force by about 40 per cent.

These figures, whilst somewhat favourable towards the Soviet
Union, are not exactly wonderful as seen from the perspective of a
hypothetically implacably hostile Warsaw Pact. Hardly a triumphant
sweep through to the sea, more a hard fight to gain relatively limited
ground. The ISSS have described the situation (referring to military
aggression as an option in Europe) as 'a highly risky undertaking for
either side'.[6] The Brookings Institution analysis also looks at what
the Institution saw as more worrying scenarios: that of a complete
surprise attack by thirty WTO divisions which has a chance of success
of 80 per cent (assuming that the German commander makes a
tactical error and wrongly deploys three divisions), or an attack after
a long period of reinforcement taking two to three months in which
case the chances of success are again about 75 per cent (assuming 120
Warsaw Pact versus forty-five to fifty NATO divisions). This latter
analysis was unfortunately based upon a misleading assessment of the
relative balance of NATO and Warsaw Pact forces. Based upon more
realistic figures, the chances of Warsaw Pact 'success' are still about
50:50, less if some defensive barrier systems existed.

The former case – attack out of the blue – is extremely unlikely
because the chances of amassing and mobilising a thirty-division
force completely in secret seem very small. Since the Huebner–Malinin agreement of 1947 between the Allied Powers, the UK, France,
USA, and the USSR have military missions consisting of about sixty
uniformed military staff whose job it is to drive around the country-
side observing – or trying to observe, by binoculars and cameras –
troop movements and training manoeuvres in East and West Germany. The Western observers are based in Berlin, while the Soviets
are based in Bunde, Frankfurt and Baden-Baden, West Germany.
Each side provides the other with maps showing areas which are
supposedly out of bounds. These are either 'permanently restricted
areas', known as PRAs, which are mostly garrison and training areas
and cover approximately a quarter of East and West Germany and
'temporarily restricted areas', or TRAs in which temporary exercises
are taking place. Mission members engage in a sometimes highly
dangerous game of cops and robbers as each tries to sneak off into

unauthorised areas after shaking off their tail. This system of institu-
tionalised spying took a more serious turn when an American Mission member, Major Nicholson was shot dead while allegedly taking
pictures of a new Soviet tank (a T-80) in a tank shed.[7] The provisions
of the INF treaty and the forthcoming CFE agreements include many
more opportunities for East and West to monitor closely each other's
forces.

As a result of such activities, both East and West know the
positions and dispositions of forces in East and West Germany. Not
much of importance can be kept secret – the location of the Soviet
divisions in East Germany, for example.

In view of this, the feared 'Hamburg grab' in which Soviet forces
attack out of the blue and capture Hamburg, an important port giving
access to the North Sea, does not seem really feasible. The only other
possibility of an attack being mounted under cover of a large military
exercise is covered by the fact that both sides have now agreed to
notify in advance and allow snap-inspection observers at short notice
to monitor large exercises. Prior to this (voluntary) observer invita-
tion to exercises in Eastern Europe had been sparse.

Can NATO Win?

From an Eastern perspective, a very similar analysis can be performed, with the important difference that the Soviet Union assert
that there is rough parity between Soviet and Western forces.
Another important factor is a result of the geographical situation. For
an invading Western force, the nearest military objective is Berlin
130km (80 miles) from the nearest part of the border. The Polish
border is 200km (125 miles) away, while Moscow is a staggering
1000km (600 miles). An idea of just how far these distances are can
be gained by imagining the equivalent for an invading Warsaw Pac
force. Just to reach the Soviet border is equivalent to Eastern forces
reaching the Spanish border, while Moscow is as far from the border
as Madrid. There is no Western equivalent of 'the Hamburg grab'.
The fate of successive armies invading the Russian steppes is also not
encouraging.

A surprise attack by NATO would thus be suicidal, while one after
a long period of mobilisation would have no hope of 'occupying' the
Soviet Union. The only scenario which can make any sense at all is
the case of extensive unrest in East Germany, Czechoslovakia or
Poland where for some reason NATO felt unable to stay out. NATO

forces could only hope to 'liberate' limited sections of the Warsaw Pact for a limited time. Towards southern Germany however, the geography favours NATO forces somewhat. German and US forces are reasonably well-placed to make a counter-attack into southern East Germany or Czechoslovakia. In the case of political unrest in the Warsaw Pact however, invasion or 'liberation' by partly German forces might well have the effect of reuniting a divided Warsaw Pact in view of the casualties inflicted by German forces in the Second World War.

THE IMPLICATIONS OF A CONVENTIONAL ARMS REDUCTION TREATY

Two stages of arms reductions deserve attention:

1. a reduction to just below NATO present force levels;
2. reduction to approximately 50 per cent of current NATO force levels.

I shall call these CFE-I and CFE-II.

Inevitably, once the debate over *quantities* of armed equipment has been settled in the form of a binding Treaty, the focus of debate will shift to the *quality* of the armament deployed. Following my analysis of the present balance of forces, equal deployments of Warsaw Pact and NATO forces would leave NATO at a small advantage. However, by the time CFE-I could be fully implemented, many other changes to NATO and Warsaw Pact forces are to be expected.

In CFE-I the main effect will be upon Warsaw Pact forces where cuts of roughly 50 per cent or more will be required, whilst NATO requires cuts of only around 15 per cent. This implies a massive reduction of the Warsaw Pact offensive capability. However, Warsaw Pact cuts will be offset by several factors:

- The Pact will cut their oldest and most obsolete equipment and deactivate the most nominal infantry units, leaving the best forces. The remaining forces would thus be leaner and (weight for weight) 'meaner'.
- Pact training programmes are already being improved.
- Logistics problems are reduced for smaller forces thus Warsaw Pact units could be more mobile than before.

Nevertheless, with the scale of Warsaw Pact force cuts needed to reach numerical parity, all these factors will leave the Pact with a much-reduced offensive capability.

Turning to NATO, CFE-I cuts would leave NATO with the forces that it would probably end up with anyway as the combined effects of budget cuts and personnel shortages took their toll. CFE-I cuts would not by themselves force any major revision of NATO strategy, although associated political factors could.

By contrast, Warsaw Pact forces face a complete overhaul and rethink along the lines of 'reasonable defence sufficiency'.

CFE-II, 50 per cent cuts, would force a rethink of NATO strategy because for the first time NATO's forces would have to be drastically reduced. NATO argues that its present forces are necessary to cover the front adequately and that smaller forces would inevitably leave gaps which would threaten NATO's strategy of forward defence. There seem to be two options with smaller forces, either to plan for greater manoeuvrability and to abandon forward defence for a manoeuvre war in depth in Germany, or, to opt for greater dispersion in defence and defensive deterrence. At present NATO's preferred option is to plan for a war of greater manoeuvre associated with air-strikes deep into the Warsaw Pact, or even actual counter-attack into Eastern Europe. In my analysis, this option would create greater crisis instability in Europe.

A host of unpredictable political considerations and pressures are likely to play a very important role by the time a possible CFE-II agreement could be implemented, so it would be foolhardy to predict the debate so far ahead, but it seems very likely that NATO will try to keep the strategies and attitudes that it has possessed for the past 25 years intact. Concerning the military debate, the focus for argument will be upon quality and capabilities of equipment, reinforcement times and manoeuvrability.

The basic point I wish to make is that whether or not the resultant forces of East and West make for more stability after CFE-I or CFE-II will depend upon the strategies and deployments chosen. Even after 50 per cent reductions, *both* sides could conceivably be more capable of attacking the other if both adopted potentially offensive or provocative strategies or deployments. Thus after CFE-I or CFE-II the question of whether or not defensive defence is adopted is even more vital than at present to ensure that the resultant 'balance' is stable (see Appendix).

SUMMARY

The spectre of Soviet forces 'sweeping' through and overrunning NATO defences quickly or easily, is an illusion. At worst, outnumbered two to one, NATO conventional forces have a 50:50 chance of repelling attack. If NATO does reinforce in time or if NATO were to erect some defensive barriers NATO stands a good chance of repelling attack.

There is no good reason why non-nuclear forces deployed by NATO should not halt a non-nuclear attack by Soviet forces – particularly if NATO were to opt for more defensive options, such as tank barriers or exploding buried pipelines in key areas.[8] The geography of central Europe naturally limits attacks to five main avenues from the east or west, making the task of the defence easier. The much wider procurement and deployment of precision-guided munitions would also offset numerical inbalances in armoured forces. Using 'defence multipliers' deployed in place of the present emphasis upon 'force multipliers' would, however, mean adopting a different way of thinking among the NATO Allies, particularly in the aggressive tradition of US forces. Such steps would mean that NATO would have a very high likelihood of succeeding in its defence without having to take the risk of threatening to use nuclear weapons early on in a non-nuclear conflict and thus precipitating all Europe and, almost inevitably, the USA and USSR into a nuclear holocaust. Other possible options for NATO are the redeployment of the stronger German and US forces opposite the weakest areas, specifically a redeployment of some US forces from the Fulda and southern German region to the Dutch, Belgian and Danish sectors.

So the bottom line, quite at odds with NATO's assessment, is that the existing capability of NATO forces is quite comparable with the Warsaw Pact. Although the forces roughly balance, the situation is not one of overall stability because of the potentially highly offensive nature of some elements of both NATO and the Warsaw Pact's weaponry and strategies. In a seeming contradiction in terms, the balance is equal but unstable (see Appendix).

The next chapter examines military options towards the deliberate creation of a different kind of imbalance – one where the forces of defence on one side outnumber the capabilities of offence on the other and the creation of a stable balance of forces.

6 Non-Nuclear Defence: Basic Principles

One can list the key requirements for a viable defensive strategy:

1. to engender stability in both the short and long term, i.e.:
   (a) in a tactical-military sense in a crisis, and
   (b) in the longer term – by enhancing military and political conditions which lessen the likelihood of the outbreak of war;
2. to withstand all feasible hostile conventional attacks, i.e. concentrated blitzkrieg or broad frontal attacks.

There is a most pressing need to prevent crises escalating to war. Some weapons systems at present deployed and strategies currently in force in NATO and the Warsaw Pact, are either designed to be highly offensive or to have a highly offensive capability and thus create a perception of imminent attack in a crisis, which (at some critical and unknown level of international tension) would escalate a crisis further. Examples of such offensive capabilities in the WTO and NATO are combined mechanised and armoured forces such as the Soviet Operational Manoeuvre Group (OMG) which mirror, to some extent, the US Air-Land Battle concept of combined air and land operations with built-in conventional, chemical and (in East and West) nuclear use. NATO possesses weapons systems such as Tornado with a primary role of attacking Pact airfields deep inside Warsaw Pact territory. Such an attack is most advantageous very early on in any conflict.

Part of the reason for the possession of mobile armoured forces possessed by NATO and the Warsaw Pact armies is historical. Such weapons deployments hark back to the Second World War. NATO forces are modelled on the forces which fought their way into occupied Europe, establishing bridgeheads and gradually retaking lost territory. The Soviet and Warsaw Pact forces are modelled upon those which finally threw back the German Army in the Eastern Front at the very gates of Moscow and which fought a long and bitter campaign to retake Soviet territory and more besides. Ideally NATO will choose to fight in a forward zone of West Germany with a series of counter-attacks to outflank and throw back invading forces. Unof-

144

ficial NATO sources assert that NATO would attempt to fight forward into a wider zone of manoeuvre in East Germany if this seemed feasible, while official NATO sources deny that their forces would ever try to fight beyond peacetime boundaries. Warsaw Pact forces have a more offensive style and would attempt to use West Germany as a zone of manoeuvre. Cross-border manoeuvres also have the advantage of forcing any 'tactical' nuclear use by a defender upon home territory.

With existing force deployments, both sides are presenting each other with high-value military targets in the shape of tank depots, nuclear launchers and military airfields. If these forces are vulnerable to attack and if they could be knocked out then the conditions are right for surprise-attack options to be built in to NATO and Pact planning. Certainly in computer simulations of conflict in Europe, NATO planners have always found that conflict rapidly escalates to nuclear strikes with both sides trying to 'get in first'.

In order to create greater crisis-stability, military systems are required which are either not such valuable and vulnerable military assets in themselves that they inherently pressure the military towards preemptive use in a crisis before they are themselves hit, or systems which are inherently less offensive in capability. To avoid the dangers of preemption means that weapons systems chosen must either be well-protected against attack or must not inherently present good high-value military targets in the first place. It is not easy to define what, if anything, is meant by a non-offensive or less offensive weapon. There is some contradiction in terms between the concepts of 'weapon' and being 'non-offensive'. However one can envisage weapons systems with limited firing range or limited mobility. Weapons can also be pulled back from front lines, in tank-free zones or corridors for example. A purely defensive option such as impenetrable fortifications or barriers only exists in the realms of science fiction at present. A problem for a more defensive system is to retain an ability to retake lost territory without retaining an offensive posture. In an 'ideal', purely defensive system, concentrations of hostile forces would somehow have to be met without concentrating defending forces in potentially offensive formations. Vitally, the system must still be operable under attack, which means that command, control, communications and intelligence (C3I) must be robust and not vulnerable to disruption or 'decapitation' strikes. The implications of all these criteria favour cheap, numerous and dispersed systems with decentralised and dispersed communications.

Some words of caution: the implementation of defensive measures alone will not lead a potential adversary to see one's own forces in any less threatening light but quite the reverse. This is because an increase in defensive capability alone is equivalent to a forced reduction in the offensive or counter-attacking capability of one's opponent's forces.

DEFENSIVE DEFENCE

Both the Warsaw Pact and NATO regard a counter-attacking or counter-offensive capability as vital for their professedly defensive policies. NATO or Warsaw Pact 'purely defensive' modifications alone could thus have a destabilising effect upon a sometimes fragile political relationship and actually decrease security rather than increasing it. To avoid such problems and to achieve greater security and stability, measures to enhance the defence must be linked to reductions in offensive capability. Such ideas are sometimes called 'non-offensive' or 'defensive' defence. The Soviet term is 'reasonable' or 'sufficient' defence. I will use the term 'defensive defence' here.

Some proposals for approaches similar to defensive defence have been in circulation for some time, but have only recently gained increasing acceptance, and then in rather specialised military and academic circles.

As early as 1952–4 Colonel Bogislav von Bonin, then the head of the equivalent of the German Ministry of Defence, suggested a defensive zone some 50–70km deep with numerous small well-camouflaged fortifications distributed in depth and with numerous anti-tank guns and plenty of mines.[1] Von Bonin was ostracised as a dissident shortly after his proposal. The issue was picked up by Sir Basil Liddell Hart in the early 1960s. He suggested that such a scheme should be manned by civilian militia along Swiss lines backed up by conventional regular armoured forces. Colonel E. A. Burgess (now General Sir Edward Burgess, deputy to General Rogers in 1985) also worked on this idea.[2] In 1976 onwards the military researcher, Horst Afheldt, inspired by Guy Brossollet,[3] a French army officer, developed the concept of 'area defence'. This system was presented in a number of variants; some covering the entire area of West Germany by dispersed 'techno-commandos' in units of four to five men in numerous reinforced camouflaged positions, armed with modern anti-tank missiles and backed up by precision-guided munitions delivered from dispersed but fixed MLRS-type artillery rocket-launchers of 40km range providing coordinated fire.[4]

Most recently the German Study Group on Alternative Security Policy (SAS) has conducted a series of computer simulations of various defensive models.[5] The SAS model currently under scrutiny consists of two defensive zones of 36km depth behind a 14km fire zone, integrated with mobile armoured forces which cannot operate outside the support logistic network provided by the dispersed networks. The SAS also pays attention to the role of the air forces and navies of NATO; often ignored in such discussions.

Before going into more detail some fairly graphic metaphors are useful to help to fix in one's mind some of the proposals for defensive or non-offensive defence.

The various meshed or networked, defence-in-depth models (e.g. Afheldt's – see Boxes 6.1 and 6.2) can be likened to a net or sticky spider's web which slows up and wears down an attacker who eventually grinds to a halt, sooner or later, 'stuck' somewhere in West Germany. When the mesh is seen as a layer in front of armoured forces, the mesh is rather like a shield through which only some enemy spears (OMGs or larger concentrated thrusts) penetrate. The heads of these spears are then 'chopped off' by the 'sword'of the armoured forces behind. The armoured forces can also regroup to 'evict' intruders from the web. In the most developed models (such as SAS) where the armoured forces are partially integrated into the mesh, the armoured forces can be seen as the 'spider in the web'.[6] The spider is undoubtedly offensive, especially supported by its strong and sticky web, but it does not pose so great a threat of attack outside its web, where it would have to be more self-sufficient. The key point is that the *overall system* is designed to appear, and to be, defensive.

The concept of 'defensive' defence has some very important advantages over conventional approaches to defence. Conventional defence strategies take an essentially competitive approach to defence, matching force with force. An inherent military assumption is that attack (and certainly counter-attack) is often the best form of defence. This may be true in tactical terms and once a conflict is actually in progress but it is not clear that this is the best strategy in the strategic long term. In a period when hostilities are not actually in

---

Box 6.1   The Afheldt Mesh Model[7]

Afheldt's matrix defence system consists of three main sections which are all highly dispersed: light infantry (techno-commandos), rocket-launchers and communications.

In a sector of the net 45 x 26km there would be some 2400 soldiers dispersed in command groups of five soldiers; over a hundred concealed stores; 150–180 anti-tank systems; 200–300 obstacles, 20 000 anti-tank mines and some 3000 rockets and mortars.

An infantry section of twenty five men would occupy 10–15km². Four company sections, each consisting of thirty men equipped with anti-tank missiles, mortars and rocket-launchers together with sapper, medical and command detachments would cover a combat sector of 50–80km². A battalion would be made up of four companies (600 men) and covers 250–350km². A brigade would be made up of four battalions.

In total, fifty brigades (about 135 000 troops) are envisaged in a mesh covering the entire German border. 13 000 are at the edges, the remainder are inside the network.

Calculations have been performed for the Fulda [Gap] region and an attack by a concentrated force attacking across a front of 26 km. Afheldt and Eckart calculate that hostile forces would suffer losses of 50 per cent and penetrate 45km in three days. As the Rhine is 230km distant, an echeloned attacking force of some six Soviet divisions would take 15 days to reach the banks of the Rhine, by this, the shortest route from East Germany, and would arrive with a strength of only three rather badly mauled divisions. Hardly a blitzkrieg, more a slow and costly battle to reach the Rhine.

Note: Horst Afheldt works at the Max Planck Institute, Starnberg, FRG.

---

progress, the maintenance of excessively offensive military strategies and capabilities is destabilising (much of the debate centres upon how much offensive or counter-attacking capability is enough).

A problem arises in that as one increases one's offensive capability, so can one's opponent, leading to an arms race and the increased likelihood of the eventual outbreak of hostilities. Unless one's opponent can be completely wiped out so that no further arms competition can ever restart, war only causes a temporary hiatus in the offensive capability race. After recovery of the vanquished party the competition in arms can resume or (as after the Second World War) new sides form out of the previous victors to continue a different competition ultimately leading to war. If a defensive strategy, capable of withstanding an offensive aggressor, can be developed and

---

Box 6.2   The German Bundeswehr University

The German Armed Forces computer has been used to run various simulations of proposed alternative defence strategies for the West German frontier.

Fifteen different types of defensive systems have been investigated in a program which not only simulates a battle fought with a full range of modern weapons systems and contemporary and hypothetical armoured infantry and tank battalions of the West German Army together with consecutively attacking Soviet motor rifle divisions but which can also be programmed for different defensive strategies. The BASIS program calculates the probability of a breakthrough or a successful defence and also calculates defensive efficiency in terms of the force ratios of attack and defence before and after battle. Calculations were also made of the relative costs of different systems in relation to their effectiveness in military terms.

The results basically support the notion of defensive defence in the sense that it supplements today's all-armour active defence. Important conclusions were that defenders must have a suitable mixture of weapons types to avoid problems created as the visibility of the battlefield deteriorates from possibly 1000–5000m down to as little as 350m because of smoke and debris and often poor weather conditions.

So-called 'emerging technology' (longer-range complex systems) was found to be non-cost-effective whereas precision-guided munitions (based upon existing types) and large-calibre recoil-less rifle and machine cannon were found to be particularly useful in poor visibility.[8,9,10]

---

accepted – and this is a big 'if' – this strategy would cut through the pernicious cycle of armament and rearmament. Increases in the offensive capability of one party would then be met by increases in the defensive capability of the other. As long as this response is seen as non-offensive in character, one driving force towards further armament by the aggressor is removed. Should the potential aggressor choose to copy the defender weapon for weapon and system for system one would then create an arms race in reverse, until both sides were totally impregnable to any hostile attack by the other.

Key Elements of Defensive Defence

Some (of the many) key elements of feasible systems can be identified as follows: dispersal, deliberate limitations of mobility of mobile forces, cooperative pull-back of forces and demilitarised zones, specialisation of defensive forces, mobility of fire, greater involvement of reserve forces, networked or 'mesh' systems, simple yet high-technology sensing, and communication systems based upon passive sensing methods and robotic remote sensing.

Dispersal is a key element because any defensive system, which by virtue of its defensive stance will not attack preemptively, must not present high-value targets for a possible first-strike of an aggressor. Dispersal is necessary at such a level that there are effectively 'no targets', or that there are so many small and randomly dispersed targets along with numerous decoys that attack from the air, by artillery or even with 'tactical' use of nuclear or chemical weapons will not be militarily decisive.

Limitation of mobility is necessary to ensure that the overall strategy is demonstrably defensive and that any retained mobile armoured forces are not capable of initial attack. They need, however, to retain sufficient mobility and range to defend and to mount a decisive counter-attack to regain lost territory.

Specialisation of defensive forces enables greater cost-effectiveness to be achieved – particularly if different NATO partners can agree to take on slightly different but complementary roles for their national forces. The attacker also faces forces uniquely adapted and with equipment and weaponry ideally suited to their terrain and conditions thus maximising the natural advantage of the defender in familiar territory. Mobility of fire replaces (some) of the mobility lost by the limitation of the mobility of forces.

Reserve forces and reinforcement methods based upon small units allied to towns and hamlets enable reinforcement to be achieved more quickly than reinforcement based upon large unit sets (as currently practised in NATO).[11] Reinforcement can also be achieved without crisis escalation because reinforcement does not imply preparation to attack.

Networked or meshed defensive systems enable the system to function as a whole whilst still retaining the vital element of dispersal. A meshed communications system based upon fibre-optics cables is intrinsically 'hardened' against nuclear electromagnetic pulse. Modern mobile dispersed communications systems also have built-in multiple redundancy. Thus if part of the system is destroyed the rest still works, albeit at a slower rate. Communications are now routinely made simultaneously via many often exotic communications channels (such as reflections off meteor showers – meteor-burst transmission) to ensure intelligibility.[12]

Passive sensing means that the system waits, watches and listens silently and covertly. It emits no signals for possible detection and targeting of hostile attack.

Robotic remote sensing ensures that troops themselves do not need to be exposed to the intensely hostile and dangerous environment of an active defence system under attack and near the front line where hostilities will be most intense.

Dispersed Defence versus Concentrated Attack

A central problem for a more dispersed defensive system such as defensive defence, is to enable sufficient force to be brought to bear upon a small area where a hostile force concentration is attempting a breakthrough.

As an example of the scale of the potential hostile target, an invading Pact division would constitute some 3500 vehicles (800 tanks plus logistics and armoured personnel carriers). These forces would have to deploy over an area of some 250km² across a front of some 10km and upon about 230km of useable roads, representing a massive amount of traffic. The tanks alone would fill the roads at a density of one every 500m.

To knock this force out requires that some 60 per cent of these vehicles are disabled – some 2100 successful hits – which works out at about 4 hits per square kilometre (with a defending force density of 2 soldiers per square kilometre – see box 6.1 – this works out at two hits per soldier). It is unrealistic to expect even the bravest and most highly trained troops on the ground to achieve such a success rate at this most thinly dispersed level (the figure of two soldiers per square kilometre corresponds to NATO's existing force levels dispersed over a depth of more than 150km). One also has to consider that a dispersed system could be repeatedly attacked in the same sector to weaken and wear it down gradually.

The task can only start to look feasible by the deployment of additional 'autonomous' firepower such as mines at say 20 per square kilometre by additional mines laid from the air from Tornado dispensers or helicopters. A single 'intelligent' mine can cover quite a wide area by listening for the sounds of a tank and then deploying its own deadly submunitions when it detects a target. Further support would be provided from sectors not directly under attack by means of MLRS PGM dispensing systems. At a range of 40km, even a narrowly channelled attack could be subject to fire from at least thirty

MLRS systems capable of delivering 360 rockets containing nearly 1 million bomblets *in one salvo* (this calculation assumes NATO's full planned deployment of 581 MLRS spread evenly across the front together with the purchase of 567 500 rockets – one MLRS can deploy several thousand submunitions). To make this firepower effective the important role for the dispersed infantry would be to stay out of sight but to act as the 'eyes and ears' for defensive fire and minelaying by air. In the forward areas even this role could and possibly should be taken over by remote sensing means on the ground and in the air.

The massive MLRS firepower would be very difficult to suppress by artillery fire, particularly if a more diffuse dispersal mode for MLRS-type rockets was used. The only option left for a determined aggressor would be for infantry to laboriously clear a path for armoured forces who would then have to gradually flush out dispersed forces in prepared defensive positions. This would slow the attack to such a degree that mobile armoured forces behind would have ample time to re-deploy ready to repel any breakthrough.

COSTS OF OFFENCE AND DEFENCE

A more defensive strategy can only work if the military economics make defensive strategies more cost-effective. If an equivalent defensive measure to a given offensive capability costs twice as much as the offensive option, then the defensive option is a non-starter. The key element of the new weapons technologies, however, is that weapons systems are now being designed and produced which are many times cheaper than the offensive systems that they are designed to destroy. Thus the military–economic pendulum has swung firmly towards the defence in the conventional sphere. Another key element is that new networked intelligence and communications systems enable processing to be performed by a dispersed, mobile network which by increasing the number of targets improves resistance to decapitation or preemption strikes. Only destruction of the entire dispersed system guarantees its demise. Table 6.1 shows the unit-cost of different types of military equipment. Some cost comparisons can be drawn directly from Table 6.1. For example:

- One fighter costs approximately half a strike-aircraft capable of a deep-strike role.

Table 6.1   Unit costs of military equipment ($)

Anti-aircraft missiles		
Stinger	50 000	shoulder-fired
Hawk	500 000	
Patriot	1 000 000	
Helicopters		
Chinook CH-47D	5 000 000	
Black Hawk UH-60	7 000 000	
Super Cobra AH-1W	7 000 000	
Super Stallion CH-53E	18 000 000	
Abrams M1A1	2 500 000	
Missiles		
Tomahawk	1 500 000	nuclear capable
Harpoon	1 500 000	anti-submarine weapon
Torpedo	1 000 000	
Ships		
Cruiser	900 000 000	
Destroyer	700 000 000	
Submarine		
Submarine	750 000 000	carries cruise missiles
(SSN-688 Los Angeles)		
Aircraft		
F-15E (Eagle)	42 000 000	deep-strike
F-16 (Fighting Falcon)	20 000 000	multi-role combat
Tornado	29 000 000	multi-role/strike
Air-to-air missiles		
AIM-9M (Sidewinder)	63 000	
AMRAAM	570 000	
Ground-based weapons		
MLRS	6 200	
M1A1 Tank	2 500 000	

Source: As note 13.
Notes: For the more complex weapons systems, costs have to be added for weapons training and support staff. For Tornado or the F-15 aircraft this amounts to at least $6m per plane.

- One tank costs 400 times one MLRS missile (containing 28 anti-tank mines).
- One sophisticated aircraft costs 100 times one anti-aircraft missile capable of shooting it down (Tornado/F-15 including pilot training costs: Hawk missile).
- One helicopter costs 140 times the ground-to-air missile capable of shooting it down (Black Hawk: Stinger).

These types of cost-ratios make the military economics of defensive defence look very promising. For the price of 100 Tornado aircraft (10 per cent of production) one could buy about 2200 Leopard II tanks (or Soviet T-80s?) or some 550 000 (!) MLRS Phase I Rockets. The prime threat perceived in the West is massive tank attack, yet for the price of just one M1A1 tank one could purchase more than 400 MLRS rockets capable of deploying 11 200 AT2 anti-tank mines. Even if only one in a thousand mines destroyed a tank, for the price of one tank one could knock out ten enemy tanks. The MLRS Phase III, should be far more effective than this. The MLRS system at 40km range not only outranges tank artillery but outguns it in accuracy and lethal effect.

Such comparisons are somewhat simplistic, because to make a sound military judgement one has to assess the capability of the defensive systems to survive in a hostile environment and their likely percentage-kill success. Also, it has to be acknowledged that the tank is an efficient, accurate means of dispensing fire in a hostile battlefield environment. But, even taking such factors into account, the odds in simple cost-effectiveness terms, with latest generation PGM systems, are heavily stacked against potentially vulnerable and very costly concentrations of resource such as tanks and aircraft. It should be noted that as much as a single tank represents an expensive concentration of resources, a company of ten to twenty tanks represents even more of a concentration of increasingly vulnerable military resources.

If the choice is made to opt for more defensive weapons, small reductions in offensive capability can pay for large increases in defensive capability. There is a trade-off, possibly in terms of reduced mobility or flexibility, but in cost terms alone the procurement of defensive weapons technology is a cheaper option than that currently pursued by NATO.

7 Non-nuclear Defence: A System for Europe

Having dealt with some basic concepts, it is necessary to progress further and to look at real or possible defensive systems, based from the outset upon existing forces and the physical realities of central Europe. Following the necessary key elements of defensive defence outlined before, what we are talking about is an in-depth dispersed defensive system capable of withstanding hostile attack from concentrated combined forces of heavy and light armour with helicopter, artillery, motor-rifle and infantry support. I shall argue the case through to a complete system.

A good deal of work has been done in the Federal Republic of Germany upon various possible non-offensive or non-provocative defensive systems. Although the many proposals have significant differences there is considerable common ground between them. I will focus upon a system based upon layers of defensive zones. The system which I describe could be adopted by NATO or the Warsaw Pact after substantial reorganisation and retraining.

What I describe here is a system for West Germany facing towards the Warsaw Pact. The same concepts could be applied for Warsaw Pact forces facing the West. Looking ahead towards an uncertain future, one could envisage such a system being used to stabilise a neutral Germany or in a neutral or partly demilitarised zone across the two Germanies.

THE DEFENCE ZONES

It is important to grasp that the defensive zones defined are not merely conceptual areas where certain military strategies would be implemented. Each area represents an actively different zone in military terms both physically and organisationally. A very important aspect is the networked nature of the dispersed system. Although small units would be separated in space they would be highly inter-linked by a multiply redundant communications and intelligence system. This would require the installation of a network of underground fibre-optic communications links in a grid from the sensor

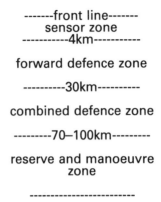

Figure 7.1   The defence zones for defensive defence

zone to the rear, and between individual foxholes in the first two zones. The density of communications links would correlate with the density and numbers of the forces planned to be deployed. There would still be a place for mobile and dispersed communications systems such as RITA and Ptarmigan, but fibre-optic links are inherently cheap and robust and avoid the need for expensive, heavy, sophisticated communications units vulnerable to electro-magnetic pulse and hostile fire.

The First Two Defensive Zones

The first two zones in the defensive defence system – the trip-wire and front defence zones – are very important and highlight what appears to be a severe deficiency in NATO strategy. NATO already has 'screening' zones of similar depth to the defensive defence zones, but in defensive defence there is a new and highly important accent upon anti-tank mines and other defences.

It seems absolutely incredible that NATO expecting an attack from tanks 'sweeping' across the North German plain, have constructed no obstacles to delay them. John Keegan, defence editor of the *Daily Telegraph* and formerly at Britain's Royal Military College, Sandhurst, has written 'It is an almost bizarre hiatus in the NATO defence system that no fortifications have been constructed on its fronts'.[1]

Large permanent Maginot-style fortifications are not very cost-effective because of their vulnerability to modern artillery fire. A more cost-effective approach is to build many small, camouflaged positions distributed randomly in advantageous sites and in some depth behind the border. Another fairly simple way of creating obstacles 'on demand' as it were, in advance of invading forces, is to bury many empty tubes underneath major routes with arrangements for filling them with explosive fuel-gas mixtures to suddenly create anti-tank obstacles.[2] These can be laid with the same type of equipment as is used for laying gas mains. Strips and zones of specialist mines can also be quickly laid from the air using dispenser systems.

William Kaufmann, a consultant to the Brookings Foreign Policy Studies Program has calculated that the erection of a system of obstacles and barriers would reduce the effectiveness of an offensive force by as much as 40 per cent. They 'would [also] reduce to essentially zero the probability that the enemy could achieve even a temporary advance with a smash-and-grab attack. Indeed, using 17 allied divisions supplemented by barriers, NATO should be able to halt even a concentrated attack by 30 Pact divisions'.[3] Further calculations show that with 60 Warsaw Pact divisions facing only 30 NATO divisions, such a system would reduce the chances of Pact forces penetrating 50km in seven days, from 70 per cent to 45 per cent.

Thus dispersed defensive obstacle and barrier systems should be a key element of the forward defence zone of a defensive defence system. To construct such a system little more than earth-moving equipment and concrete are required. Estimates of the cost of such a programme are in the range of $1million per kilometre, amounting to some $500–1000 million for key areas of NATO's defence.

This is equivalent to the cost of roughly thirty-five Tornado aircraft (the German Bundeswehr alone have ordered 300 Tornado, and overall orders stand at around 1000 aircraft) yet the results for NATO defence far outstrip the most optimistic assessment of thirty Tornado upon a conflict. At a Pact reduction in effectiveness of 40 per cent, barriers would be equivalent to a reduction of 24 to 48 Pact divisions or the equivalent of another twelve to twenty NATO divisions. It is also worth noting that the Warsaw Pact has considerable defensive minefields and fortified positions. NATO sources recognise that these installations would impede the Pact attack itself and some minefields would have to be cleared to allow massive Soviet attack.[4]

A major problem for defensive defence is to equip and train soldiers spread out over the terrain in such a way that they can physically and – perhaps equally importantly – psychologically, withstand attack from concentrated forces. Obviously, troops near to the front line itself are the most vulnerable to attack and least supported by their colleagues and supporting forces behind. Such forces would have to be extremely brave to fight in such circumstances. The worst part of this problem is avoided by creating the forward-most 'sensor' or 'trip-wire' zone a few kilometres deep, populated not by troops (or by very few in lightly armoured, highly mobile reconnaissance vehicles much as in current NATO deployments) but by sensors and 'smart' mines with supporting MLRS-type rocketry behind and watched over by remotely piloted vehicles above. Any hostile incursions by armoured forces would invite accurate lethal fire from smart mines and advanced munitions dispensed by MLRS or other dispersed rocket-launchers with target-area allocation provided by passive sound and heat sensors and small remotely piloted 'spies in the skies' carrying multispectral cameras and beaming the information directly to dispersed rocket launchers.[5] Pre-targeted 'fire' zones would be prepared to enable conventional artillery to strike accurately at concentrations of armoured forces.

Behind the initial fire zone the defensive mesh proper starts. Some proposals suggest a dispersed infantry deployment in units of two to three men and platoons of twenty to thirty, with at least five pre-prepared and expedient camouflaged foxholes for each small unit of two or three. These forces would be organised in anti-aircraft and anti-tank units with PGMs and mortars and supported by longer-range fire from advanced PGM-dispensers such as MLRS and artillery fire. Units would operate in territory with which they were intimately familiar and where smart mines and potential barrier systems such as buried exploding pipes underground would be utilised to block, clog up and channel attack into pre-prepared 'fire zones' for back-up fire.

As a general principle, the density of troops on the ground would increase the further back they were from the front line. The further back the lower the possibility of successful longer-range attack by hostile artillery or aircraft. Longer-range hostile fire defines a zone some 30km deep as an initial 'front-defence' zone in which no mobile high-value units (such as heavy armoured divisions) should be deployed and also a zone of most diffuse dispersal. The option is still open to deploy light mobile forces taking advantage of the excellent road system of West Germany. Many traditional analysts of NATO strategy acknowledge that there would be a highly useful role for mobile light infantry to play in NATO's defence structure.[6] NATO commanders are aware of some of these possibilities. In recent NATO exercises, light infantry detachments waited until tanks actually ran over their concealed positions before firing at the relatively unprotected rears of the departing tanks.[7]

The Combined Defence Zone

Behind the forward defence zone, calculations indicate that a further zone some 40–100km deep is necessary (depending on the assumptions) to stop a concentrated armoured thrust along Soviet operational manoeuvre group (OMG) and in which some armoured forces could be deployed. I shall call this a 'combined defence' zone.

In the combined defence zone behind the forward defence zone armoured forces are deployed in such a way as to pose a low offensive threat to a possibly paranoid opponent. Mobile armoured forces are needed to counter possible penetrations of the forward zones at unknown points, but being deployed behind the forward defence zone are not configured for preemptive attack. NATO's armoured forces are already deployed in this way, however, with the increased defensive capabilities of the forward zones the size of the armoured forces could be reduced from present levels. Another difference is the planned logistic support.

In current NATO strategy, armoured forces are supported by large numbers of fuel tankers and other support vehicles which are in themselves vulnerable targets and a considerable logistic problem which limits the mobility of the forces they are supporting. In the combined defence zone, a dispersed fuel support network in the form of numerous small fuel depots would support the armoured forces interlinked with dispersed, mobile light infantry armed with modern anti-aircraft and anti-tank weapons. There is already in fact a dispersed network of diesel fuel – every farm has its own supply tanks. One could envisage grants being made available for farmers wishing to install larger tanks to enhance this existing resource. Another option, popular with the armoured forces, is to add extra 'strap-on' fuel tanks in the form of standard $4\frac{1}{2}$ gallon cans. If some of these options were utilised, existing mobile but highly vulnerable logistic support in the form of large fuel-bowsers could be reduced in quantity. Within the supportive mesh or web, the armoured forces would be far more mobile and less vulnerable by virtue of their reduced logistic 'tail'. In this way, isolated tank companies would still have some – albeit limited – military utility, because they could not 'be separated' from logistic support as long as any fuel was left. The dispersed fuel supply would also be less vulnerable to attack or overrunning by invading armoured forces. Armoured forces deployed in such a defensive mesh would increase stability in a crisis because they would not pose an imminent threat of attack. Also, an attacker would not be provided with high-value targets in the form of tank concentrations near to the front line and would know that any attack would be first channelled, and once channelled, attacked by combined air, infantry and armoured assaults.

Behind this zone, the final defensive zone would be a reserve and manoeuvre zone, to hold reserves and to guard against attack behind the lines either from the sea or by air-lifted rapid-deployment forces. NATO has long argued the case for reserve forces to fulfil this mission.

The defence system would not seek to halt an attack near to the front but to bog down, tie up and eventually halt any advance. The strategy would seek to destroy invading forces in a piecemeal fashion and in such a way that attack was channelled and blocked from achieving swift and mobile penetration of NATO lines. In this way time would be bought for diplomacy to begin to work again and to enable reinforcement and regrouping for counter-attack.

SPECIALISATION

Specialisation of defensive forces is another important aspect of the defensive system. The West German front is by no means uniform terrain. It contains forests, marshes and extensive urban areas. A study undertaken by US Defense Science Board of the Department of Defense specifically addressed the question of the defence of urban areas (which are initially – and somewhat theoretically – excluded from NATO's 'first-use' of nuclear weapons plans). The study found that urban areas not only have 'a high degree of inherent survivability' but that 'this inherent capability can be enhanced if troops are properly trained in such tactics'.[8] The study found that the urban areas of West Germany could be 'internetted'. 'Internetting' means the use of small villages and hamlets as bases for a defensive network of forces linked by a communications system. Some experts calculate that as much as 60 per cent of the area of the Federal German Republic could be defended in such a way,[9] and that internetting would considerably enhance NATO's defence against first-echelon forces. The importance of internetting is that while experience has shown that heavy armoured forces or OMGs for that matter can *move* through difficult terrain, they cannot *fight* in it. It is for this reason that standard blitzkrieg or Soviet OMG strategy is to avoid towns, cities or strong opposition and is to find 'cracks' in the defence. Otherwise the element of surprise can be quickly lost and an opponent regaining balance can isolate hostile-force incursions. This is a major weakness in Soviet strategy.

In the defence one can envisage troops with equipment such as hovercraft or other specialised vehicles taking advantage of West Germany's areas of difficult terrain such as marsh and peat bog (the Luneburger Heide, for example, south of Hamburg in NORTHAG) to act as relatively safe havens from tanks and from which to launch attacks on armoured forces.

The US Defense Science Board Report also found that a mobilisation structure allied to small towns and hamlets along the lines of the Swedish model was both less expensive and more rapid than the current NATO reinforcement methods. This is one example from a source not noted for advocating alternative defence concepts.

Air Forces

At present NATO's primary air mission is bombing behind enemy lines to destroy key targets (bridges, airfields, etc.). This role cannot be supported in a non-offensive defence system because it is very offensive and also there is a very high 'value' in striking first which is destabilising in a crisis. In defensive defence the primary role of the air force would be air defence and ground support, particularly mine-laying from the air, the latter a role for which the new dispenser systems on Tornado are well suited. This is not to say that if one were choosing an airborne weapons platform for defensive defence that one would chose Tornado – far from it. But at least the existing aircraft could perform a useful defensive role until in the much longer term a cheaper alternative could be phased in. Leaked air intelligence reports also indicate that the deep-strike role is in any case one which will be very costly in terms of pilots and aircraft. Apparently, for every enemy aircraft destroyed on the ground by NATO air attacks, NATO is highly likely to lose one of its own aircraft because of effective Pact air defences.[10] This high 'attrition' rate is envisaged even without very sophisticated air-defence systems such as those possessed by the Western Alliance. Much air defence, particularly for low-level aircraft, can now be dealt with by precision-guided missiles, not to mention the simple but effective expedient of firing all machine-guns into the air to hit any overflying low-level aircraft (as was utilised in the Falklands–Malvinas conflict). Low-flying aircraft are very vulnerable to such measures. It is interesting that the same intelligence report to which I have referred, predicts that in a defensive role, NATO would destroy four to five hostile aircraft for every one NATO aircraft lost – quite a favourable ratio for NATO. Such figures and the capabilities of the latest generation anti-aircraft systems strongly suggest that a deep-strike role is in any case seriously in question as a viable military option. In a defensive defence system the role of the air force would be primarily interception, maintaining air superiority over one's own territory as a defence for ground forces and support of ground forces by means of mine-laying and munition dispersal in front of or over hostile force incursions. The air defence forces themselves would be highly dispersed, as is now the practice among Swedish forces where basing is highly dispersed in small units and operations are carried out using the road system for temporary airstrips.[11] Vertical or Short take-off and landing aircraft such as the Harrier would be most effective in this role. As now practised in NATO, airfields must be located well back from the front line because the dispersed defensive defence system must provide 'no targets' for worthwhile air attack near to the front. Defensive defence, however, would imply a significant change of role for the bulk of NATO's air forces and higher levels of dispersal. Increased rearward basing of air forces would also be desirable. One goal of the CFE talks could be to negotiate an E–W pull-back of main air bases.

Naval Forces

Turning to Naval forces, a great deal could be achieved by specialisation within NATO. One possibility would be to give the nations bordering the Baltic the task of defending this area and leaving the North Sea and the Atlantic approaches to the UK and the USA. This would work out much cheaper because it would eliminate much duplication in Naval design for different roles at present undertaken by most European countries. In accordance with the strategy of non-offensive defence, were the Danes and the Dutch to 'freeze' the Baltic approaches with the widespread utilisation of mines, US naval battle-groups would be unable to enter the Baltic Sea as much as Soviet forces would be unable to leave. This would act as a brake on escalation of the conflict at sea and on outflanking amphibious operations.

Some of the ideas of defensive defence can be applied to naval operations, particularly by Western navies who have a major advantage over their Soviet counterparts. The Soviet navy has to emerge from its ports through relatively restricted sea-passages which are extensively monitored by NATO sea-bed sensors (the Greenland–Iceland–UK [GIUK] 'gap' for example). If NATO were to plan for the far more extensive use of mines, particularly across such gaps, sea-lane mobility would be much reduced. This would be a stabilising strategy as it would engender caution and delay rather than a quick and violent clash of surface fleets culminating in exchanges of tactical nuclear weapons which seems most likely at present. Some modern mines are the sea-based technological equivalent of land-based PGMs and can sit on the sea-bed or tethered beneath the surface waiting to dispense numerous lethal munitions to surface ships within range. Such munitions can be delivered underwater or launched from beneath the sea into the air to fly low and fast to their targets. By a very small re-allocation of funds from large surface ships towards more defensive procurement, NATO could purchase great numbers of 'smart' mines ready for deployment in the Baltic and in the Northern Atlantic in a crisis. A detailed description of possible modifications to naval forces and strategy, however, is beyond the scope of this book.

COSTS AND RESOURCES

Finding the finance and resources for any defence policy is a fundamental requirement. NATO's conventional forces budget currently faces two severe problems: equipment-cost inflation and personnel shortage.

NATO member-countries are under strong domestic budgetary pressure to keep military spending under control, despite ritual reaffirmations of intent to spend 3 per cent over and above inflation.[12] Such statements have been honoured by few NATO countries in the past and seem very unlikely to be honoured in the future. Even the UK, a staunch supporter of NATO, has cut defence spending in real terms continually since 1985.[13]

There are two main areas of military spending: equipment and troop pay. Little can be done to reduce troop costs without reducing the number of troops, while equipment continues to rise in cost at a rate well above inflation. There are no signs of a reversal of this trend; quite the contrary. The cost-inflation of complex military hardware such as combat aircraft is such that price extrapolations show that by some time in the twenty-first century, NATO countries would be able to afford only one plane or only one advanced frigate. Clearly things would never get this far, but something has to give; budgets simply cannot accommodate such inflation levels.

The second major problem facing NATO, particularly West Germany is demographic. As the average age of the population increases after the post-war 'baby-boom' years, the numbers of young men and women of suitable age for the armed forces is decreasing dramatically.

Non-offensive defence would require increased spending upon dispersed barriers, dispersed air-force basing, increased numbers in types of mines and PGMs, increased ammunition and fuel stocks and reorganisation. These costs could be met without any additional financial burden – and with money to spare for other purposes by diverting funds earmarked for a range of planned NATO arms programmes, by reorganisation of US and European forces, by troop reductions or various combinations of these options.

Estimates of the costs of non-offensive defence are up to £2bn for barriers (pipe-burying and some small strong points over 500–1000km in key areas), maybe £4bn for reorganisation, and £2bn on additional ammunition, fuel stocks and precision-guided munitions. Say £10 000m in total, including additional dispersed-communications networks. This figure compares well with such studies as the European Security Study (ESECS)[14] and other estimates,[15, 16] which calculate sums of £15–20bn for new NATO high-technology defences in the old mould.

Focusing upon large items of expenditure, NATO is currently planning to spend £30bn on the European Fighter Aircraft (EFA) (The UK contribution to this project is £10 000m); the German–UK–Italian Tornado aircraft has cost a similar amount and can now be purchased for £24m per aircraft.

NATO is spending £100m on project definition alone on the NATO Frigate which will probably cost in the region of £150–300m per boat with overall project costs in the £20 000–30 000m range. This is planned to be the largest NATO collaborative project ever (although the UK pulled out in 1989). The NATO modular stand-off weapon had a budget of over £200m (most of the European collaborators have pulled out of this, too – but there are numerous other stand-off weapon projects underway in Europe and the USA with substantial budgets). The UK alone has spent £5000m on one tor-

)edo project (Tigerfish). The nuclear Trident programme will cost
he UK some £9000m (freezing warhead numbers at the Polaris levels
:ould save about £2000m). Such projects are not necessary for
1on-offensive defence and – amongst other examples which could be
'ound in almost all NATO member-countries – are prime examples
)f the type of projects which could be cut. Cuts could also be made in
:ank and aircraft replacement programmes.

The EFA is a very good example of a project that would not be
financed in non-offensive defence. The EFA would represent an
astonishing concentration of limited resources: £30bn on only 800
aircraft. If this project were cancelled, savings of at least £10bn could
be obtained by concentrating upon updating existing aircraft designs
such as the Northrop F-20 for example, an option that has been
suggested by the German SAS group. This alone could finance
non-offensive defence but only over a period of 10–15 years, the
likely spending timetable of the EFA. In NATO as a whole, sums of
the order of an additional £10bn could be diverted, from a plethora of
more complex weapon-system projects over a similar period, if the
political will existed (overall, the sum of £20bn, twice the amount
needed, represents less than 10 per cent of the NATO countries'
combined military spending for one year – including that of the
USA). Thus in the longer term the finance for conventional defence
enhancements could be found.

It is important to note that providing conventional defence enhancements are phased in over ten to fifteen years, even without any
successful CFE negotiations, there would be no additional burden on
defence spending. In fact defence budgets would be reduced.

NATO defence spending levels are set to be reduced following
CFE-I, albeit by relatively limited amounts (say ten to fifteen per
cent). Such cuts would be easier to implement if defensive defence
were to be adopted, as many expensive military programmes such as
described above would be scrapped.

The CFE negotiations will only substantially affect NATO's military spending levels if the negotiations can successfully reach a
second stage (CFE-II) and negotiate cuts of about fifty per cent. Here
again the phased implementation of defensive defence over a ten to
fifteen year period would facilitate cuts whilst maintaining defensive
stability and provide a conceptual framework for prioritising and
restructuring NATO's defence.

RESTRUCTURING DEFENCE

Consideration of the issue of non-offensive defence highlights some anomalies in the way the Allies organise their defence. This is particularly the case in the present economic climate where both the USA and Europe are looking for ways to cut military expenditure without endangering security. Yet the methods by which the Allies achieve savings or threaten to do so are either relatively economically insignificant or disproportionately damaging to the Western defence capability. What I am saying is that the Allies are spending their existing money on defence very inefficiently and that large savings could be made whilst actually *increasing* NATO's defensive capabilities. To be specific:

1. NATO underfunds unglamorous areas such as fuel and ammunition stocking (which consumes less than 5 per cent of the budget) whilst continuing to fund huge spending programmes on large weapons systems such as the EFA and NATO's Frigate.
2. NATO fields roughly 1 million regular soldiers in peacetime. In Europe, with military conscription there is a large untapped pool of recently trained potential reservists who could, with a minimal amount of organisation form up to twenty-one additional reserve divisions (some 350 000 troops).[17]
3. The USA fields four divisions in Europe and has the ability to increase this number by airlift to twelve divisions in about 10 days. Further US reinforcements amounting to some additional 500 000 troops would then come across the Atlantic by sea on the so-called 'sea-bridge' over the next three months. This sea bridge is extremely expensive in resources, requiring the maintenance of numerous US and European convoy vessels, frigates and battle carrier-groups to escort hundreds of ships across the Atlantic. There is a far cheaper alternative which has been suggested by Dr S. Canby, a defence analyst. If the US land forces' primary mission was to provide defensive cover whilst the Europeans mobilised their existing large reserve forces with the additional possible reserve formations suggested above, the 'sea-bridge' would no longer be necessary. Naval forces are extremely expensive and the US could save some $40bn. Such suggestions have also been discussed by the US Institutes of Resource and Security Studies and Peace and International Security respectively.[18]
4. *Air forces*: A large proportion of European military equipment

spending and research and development costs goes on air forces: both tactical fighters and ground-strike aircraft. However, the US have large numbers of aircraft in all these categories. If the US were to deploy 500 additional US fighters to Europe (about this number are not allocated for any specific US roles,[19]), the Europeans could save about £10bn by reducing their contribution.

. The USA could save an additional $50bn by:

(a) reducing USAF staffing levels (in personnel per plane the USAF use six times as many as the Swedish and four times as many as the Israeli Air Force. Both these countries have highly efficient air forces);

(b) replacing US Navy personnel on a block basis rather than individually;

(c) increasing the enlisted service period from 3–4 years to 6–10 years. This could save 20 billion dollars in reduced training and retirement costs.[20]

. Finally, defence specialisation. In the longer term, increased defence specialisation would mean additional savings. With Denmark and West Germany taking responsibility for mine-laying and the Baltic approaches, and the UK, Belgium, The Netherlands and the USA responsible for the North Sea and North Atlantic, the West Germans could make savings in naval forces for diversion to NOD. By this time additional factors could also mean large savings. A conventional arms reduction agreement in Europe for example.

This type of financial exercise leads one to consider seriously the motives of the Americans in threatening cuts in US troops in Europe when this might actually save very little (if anything) because of additional barracking and dislocation costs which would be incurred when the forces were moved back to the USA. Presumably the naval lobby is too powerful for Congress to suggest structurally-more-sensible cuts in naval forces. The threat of US troop cuts may also be more useful in pressurising the Europeans to spend more on defence.

SUMMARY

Having established that non-offensive defence could be paid for whilst reducing military budgets over a 10–15-year period, the question is, exactly what type of system should Europe plump for? How

far should Europe move towards completely non-offensive defence'
How much is actually necessary?

Some possible options can be envisaged, all predicated upon the
requirement for substantial de-nuclearisation of NATO strategy:

1. Restructuring of NATO's strategy towards non-offensive defence
   dispersed, small strong-points to be built in identified weake
   spots in NATO's front; underground pipes laid for exploding
   barriers; military procurement for airfield attack weapons to be
   diverted to advanced aerial mine-dispenser systems; cancellation
   of any outstanding orders for Tornado; replacement cut-backs
   and cancellation of the EFA.
2. As above, with the additional conversion of some NATO unit
   (particularly German units) to a network defence system some
   30km deep with mobile light infantry backed by armoured force
   deployed behind in a combined defence zone. Increased rearward
   basing of main air bases.
3. A complete restructuring of NATO defence strategy to a network
   of interlinked defence zones 100km deep.

The first option, although it moves towards non-offensive defence
does not go far enough and would not necessarily increase the
technical chances of successful defence against concentrated attack
A network defence is needed to absorb and deflect such attack, and a
network some 30km deep is the minimum needed with modern
weapons to enhance the chances of the defence.

The third option could only come about over a time-scale of 10–15
years, taking us into the twenty-first century. It would imply a very
radical restructuring of Western defence policy. It could, however, fit
in with any radical restructuring of Warsaw Pact forces.

This leaves the second option, a denuclearised NATO with a
defensive network zone about 30km deep backed up by a combined
defence zone 40–70km deep. This would still leave the vast bulk of
NATO's forces and armament unaffected initially, but would imply
gradual changes over several years as more defensive systems and
strategies replaced offensive ones. It would also fit in with calls which
have been made for a general demilitarised zone to straddle the
East–West border with no forward deployments of heavy armoured
forces.

This option for defensive defence could be brought about partly a
a result of a second stage of the Vienna CFE talks, provided that

defensive defence can be built into the arms control process. The most important role for the arms negotiations would be to negotiate reductions in offensive forces and strategies. The defensive enhancements of defensive defence could help such negotiated reductions by creating a non-provocative military insurance against cheating or reneging on any treaty provisions.

To reiterate, the defensive net would *not* be expected to *stop* attack but to delay and channel it and to prevent the seizure of territory by an aggressor by the mere act of passing through it. The remote-sensing elements of the net would act as sophisticated 'eyes and ears' for the defence waiting behind. If hostile forces passed through quickly, they would leave their supply lines vulnerable and the rear open to piecemeal attack from dispersed forces hidden across the landscape. By defending in greater depth, NATO would choose the time and places to counter-attack with armoured forces in situations advantageous to NATO. Small cuts in offensive air–ground capability could pay for defences which would have an equivalent value of ten to twenty additional NATO divisions, whilst small cuts in tank forces could pay for anti-tank weapons far in excess of the value of the armament lost.

Whatever the choice of defensive strategy, the restructuring of the US and European contributions to defence deserves very serious consideration. If the USA and Europe consider that the defence of Europe is sufficiently important, NATO should consider changing the role of US, German and UK forces in Germany to an explicit covering force for a more extensive mobilisation and utilisation of reserve forces. The USA could save very substantial amounts, far above those of troop cuts in Europe by cuts to the US Naval Atlantic sea-bridge.

If defensive restructuring along these lines together with the East–West negotiating process can lead to substantial cuts in forces in Europe, around £75bn could be saved in personnel and equipment costs (50 per cent cuts could save 30 per cent of spending). The problem would not be how to defend Europe but what to do with all the surplus equipment, soldiers and civilian workers.

If cuts of 50 per cent of forces and savings of 30 per cent of defence budgets were made over 8 or 9 years with a target-date of 1998–9, this would be equivalent to holding defence spending to 4 per cent below inflation over the 9-year period (assuming average inflation of 5 per cent).

Thus, there is an affordable alternative. The next chapter deals

with the political practicalities and pitfalls which would have to be
overcome before such change might occur.

'THE SPECTRES HAUNTING NATO' REVISITED

Let us now re-examine how NATO would fare in its two worst-case
military scenarios, although it has to be said from the outset that one
of the main advantages of defensive deterrence is intended to be the
avoidance of situations where hostilities break out or crises escalate
out of control, thus the whole scenarios are less likely to occur at all.

The removals of Soviet forces from Eastern Europe make surprise
attack at the German border virtually impossible. However, the
concept of surprise attack provides an excellent test for defensive
deterrence at this and other Eastern European borders.

The extracts which follow are taken from the scenarios which
introduce Part III of this volume.

1   Blitzing NATO

It is Christmas Eve, and NATO forces are standing down. Although East–West tensions are high, the Soviet Union and its allies
have not mobilised for war. But at 2300 hours, troops of the Soviet
Third Shock Army move out of their garrison near Magdeburg,
East Germany. Under cover of darkness, they head west through
secret passages in their own minefields.

It would be very difficult for Soviet troops to mobilise successfully in
secret without alerting NATO. If an exercise was used as cover,
observers under the Stockholm agreement would observe any ir-
regularities and in any case NATO would take precautionary alert
measures. In defensive defence, such a high alert state would have no
possibly-hostile implications towards the Warsaw Pact and would not
pose a conceivable threat of preemptive strike against Pact prime
targets.

*   *   *

The first detachments reach the West German border at midnight
and plunge across without warning, raising the alarm at NATO
headquarters.

Because of the dispersed nature of the defence system and sensor network, the alarm would not only be raised but the course of any incursion tracked. Further in, the lead-force would be unable to escape tracking and hostile fire as it was tracked from hidden dispersed NATO defensive positions.

*   *   *

The main body follows only one hour later. To the north and south, other Warsaw Pact armies slash into NATO's defences at almost the same moment. Spearheading the Third Shock Army is a division-size raiding party, known as an 'operational manoeuvre group' (OMG). This mobile force attacks of opportunity, but whenever it runs into stiff opposition, it disengages and drives deeper into West Germany to disrupt NATO defences.

Before one hour had elapsed NATO regular forces dispersed in advance of possible invasion routes would have filled and primed buried explosive pipes for tank obstacles. Tornado jets would be ready to lay minefields from the air. The OMG would find it impossible to 'disengage'. The now completely 'internetted' West German terrain would offer no easy routes of passage and a move in any direction, particularly 'deep into West Germany' would meet stiff opposition. The OMG would find itself deflected if avoiding direct battle into increasingly difficult and marginal terrain. Its lines of communication and supply to the rear would be cut.

*   *   *

Meanwhile, Soviet war-planes, paratroopers and missiles tipped with non-nuclear warheads, are striking NATO targets even farther behind the lines, including airfields, missile-launchers, supply depots and communication centres.

The new defence posture would present no centralised supply depots, airfields would be operating in a dispersed mode and aircraft operating from stretches of autobahn. Command and control would be dispersed and not reliant upon the survival of a few deep bunkers. There would be no nuclear launchers to hit.

*   *   *

Behind the raiding parties, the Third Shock Army moves on.
By 0200 hours on Christmas morning it reaches Brunswick and
bypasses the city. By 0400 hours it enters the outskirts of Hanover
50 miles inside West Germany. That city is bypassed too, as the
Third Shock Army races towards the Rhine. The main bodies of
each Soviet army likewise, thrust through the cracks in NATO's
defences, with the aim of bringing about a collapse of the NATO
political structure within a matter of days.

Calculations indicate that the invading forces could not penetrate this
far, nor could they simply bypass cities, as roads would by now be
impassable. There would be no 'cracks' in NATO's defences to go
through.

*   *   *

The British Army on the Rhine, the BAOR, charged with defending the Brunswick–Hanover sector, manages to get most of its
troops out of the camps by 0400 hours. In neighbouring sectors
American, West German and other Allied forces also respond
quickly. NATO, however, needs at least 48 hours to achieve full
mobilisation.

NATO would not require full mobilisation in 48 hours because the
attack would be slowed. In any case mobilisation based upon small
units would be achieved more quickly than at present. Forces would
be based in position near the front, not behind their intended defence
areas.

*   *   *

Their surprised conventional forces in disarray, NATO's political
leaders must soon consider the next fateful step – the use of nuclear
weapons. But the advancing Soviet columns are already deep
inside West Germany; nuclear strikes against them would endanger countless NATO troops and German civilians. And many
of the airfields and missile sites from which a nuclear barrage
would be launched, have been damaged or occupied by Soviet
attackers. In the end, NATO's leaders cannot agree using nuclear
weapons. The Soviets are left in a commanding position for the
conventional war which follows. The West, outnumbered and

outgunned on the ground, has lost without firing a single nuclear shot.

NATO would be much less vulnerable to surprise as the forward defence and sensor zone would always be at a relatively high state of readiness. NATO would not need to consider the use of nuclear strikes against any Warsaw Pact incursions. Any such incursions would be isolated from their logistical support and defeated or evicted by armoured forces operating in close conjunction with the dispersed network of anti-tank forces and the spreading of mines from the air.

2. Attack after Reinforcement

East–West tensions have been high for four months, and NATO and Warsaw Pact forces are reinforced and in a high state of alert. Soviet Navy surface ships and submarines are deployed in large numbers out of Murmansk in northern Russia. A Soviet attack is expected, but despite continual military exercises and training near border areas, and continuing bad relations, an attack does not come.

Finally, the attack comes. NATO forces, although nearly fully reinforced, are gradually driven back by the sheer weight of over 100 Soviet divisions at full combat power against a NATO force of less than half this size. NATO forces hold in most places, but in others, concentrations of Soviet forces break through behind NATO's thin forward line of defence, disrupting supplies and communications. Reserve Soviet divisions pour through the gaps.

NATO forces would not be significantly outnumbered by Warsaw Pact forces. Also, by the judicious use of 'defence multipliers' such as barriers, the balance of offence and defence would be roughly equal and NATO would not be driven back. Rather, the situation would be similar to that in the First World War: stalemate. In the longer term the greater economic power of the USA and Europe combined would prevail over the Eastern Bloc. NATO would no longer have a 'thin forward line of defence'.

*   *   *

NATO is losing and commanders seek permission to use their nuclear weapons before they are overrun or destroyed by air-strikes.

For some the permission comes too late, but when it does, Soviet forces fire first, destroying NATO's ground-based nuclear forces on the ground.

The Soviet forces reach the Rhine and halt. The American, British and French consider using their strategic nuclear weapons in silos and submarines, but do not do so, knowing that their nuclear strike upon the Soviet capital and other Soviet cities will undoubtedly bring about a savage nuclear retribution on Paris, London or Washington, and the destruction of their countries too. They have no choice but to negotiate. Germany is now no longer a threat to the Soviet Union. Germany's army, the *Bundeswehr*, has been destroyed fighting to the death. The remnants of the Allied forces regroup in Holland, Belgium and France, licking their wounds. The political map of Europe has once more been altered by war and Germany is devastated yet again.

There would be no high-value military nuclear targets to hit from the air and any high-value targets behind the lines could not be 'overrun'. Land commanders would not need to seek nuclear release permission and this mechanism for nuclear escalation would have been removed. If the Soviet Union were to threaten the 'limited' use of nuclear weapons they would face the threat of nuclear retaliation by strategic nuclear weapons which could themselves have as one option a 'limited' nuclear response. Any threat of strategic nuclear use would have the counter-threat of strategic response. There would be a nuclear stand-off which would be stabilised by the removal of strategies for nuclear war-fighting. It is also most likely that if NATO had removed all land-based nuclear weapons then a similar removal would have been negotiated with the Soviet Union in which case the spectre of limited nuclear war would be further reduced.

Part IV
The Transition

There is nothing more difficult to take in hand, more perilous to conduct, or more uncertain in its success, than to take the lead in the introduction of a new order of things . . . the innovator has for enemies all those who have done well under the old conditions, and lukewarm defenders in those who may do well in the new . . . opponents who have the laws on their side and . . . the incredulity of men who do not readily believe in new things until they have a long experience of them.

Niccolo Machiavelli, *The Prince*, AD 1513[1]

8 The New Defence

In this chapter, first, I clarify the reforms to nuclear forces needed in defensive deterrence. Second, I attempt to answer various possible objections to alternative security concepts such as defensive deterrence. Third, I present a series of arguments which I feel make a powerful case for the adoption of an alternative security policy. In my view, defensive deterrence is potentially a closer fit to the defence and security concerns of Central Western European public opinion than NATO strategy. Defensive deterrence is also potentially a closer fit to new ideas for the forces of the Soviet Union which are now being discussed at high level in the Warsaw Pact and by senior Soviet policy-makers.

DEFENSIVE DETERRENCE: HOW MUCH DE-NUCLEARISATION?

I have argued that NATO's strategy has highly dangerous and destabilising nuclear 'war-fighting' elements and that nuclear weapons cannot bolster or buttress conventional forces, they undermine them. The idea of 'limited' nuclear war is also a nonsense, both in terms of its devastation and the likelihood of escalation. This leaves only one potential role for nuclear weapons in defensive deterrence, that of strategic deterrence, and in the case of actual nuclear attack, nuclear retaliation. In the latter case, deterrence would have failed and the motive would be revenge 'from the grave' as it were.

In defensive deterrence, shorter-range 'tactical', 'battlefield' (howitzer rounds and short-range missiles such as Lance) and 'theatre' nuclear weapons (cruise, Pershing-II, bombs on strike air-craft) have no role and are redundant. The war-fighting role of these weapons would be replaced by conventional forces with greater defensive capabilities than before. NATO would no longer, as it does now, threaten to use nuclear weapons against non-nuclear Warsaw Pact attack in its so-called 'first-use' strategy.

The INF agreement has already removed the land-based 'theatre' weapons, (Soviet SS-20 and US cruise and Pershing-II). What remains are over 5000 nuclear shells and missiles (NATO has 2400 or so) and up to 4000 nuclear bombs on nuclear-strike aircraft (NATO has about 1700). These remaining nuclear weapons are all highly vulnerable to nuclear attack and thus cannot form a reliable second-strike capability (the ability to be used in retaliation after a nuclear attack). Most are also highly vulnerable to conventional attack. The shorter-range weapons are by necessity deployed in West Germany where they provide high-value targets for air attack. In the case of the short-range artillery they are intensely destructive to the country using them and would cause more damage to the defender on home territory than the aggressor. The air-launched weapons are deployed from fixed, well-known and highly vulnerable air-bases. Nuclear drop bombs deployed from air-bases well back from the East–West border could be considered for use as a late-use deterrent but could not be relied upon after nuclear attack.

Thus for defensive deterrence to be fully adopted would mean the removal from Europe of all short- and intermediate-range nuclear warheads deployed on land-based missiles, artillery shells and air-borne bombs and missiles. Surface naval fleets in the European theatre would also have to relinquish a nuclear land-attack role.

Overall such reductions amount to the removal or destruction of about 14 000 relatively small nuclear warheads East and West; about ten times the number removed in the INF agreement and similar to the numbers of larger strategic warheads under negotiation in the START negotiations.

The complete acceptance of defensive deterrence, whilst implying large nuclear adjustments, would not mean that all nuclear weapons would be removed from the European area. These removals while very substantial, indeed unprecedented, in themselves would still leave very substantial nuclear forces remaining: some 20 000 US and Soviet strategic warheads, several hundred more French, and British warheads deployed in submarines.

DEFENSIVE DETERRENCE: ANSWERING THE OBJECTIONS

One can identify three types of objection to defensive deterrence:

- basic objections to the concept as a whole;
- objections to the reforms in conventional forces proposed;
- objections to the proposed reforms in nuclear forces.

I deal with these in turn.

Objections to the *Concept* of Defensive Deterrence

The chief objections relate to the assertion that defensive deterrence would undermine the NATO Alliance in various ways. That it would undermine:

(i) conventional burden-sharing such as reinforcement;
(ii) the integrated command structure;
(iii) defence project cooperation;
(iv) the posture of the USA, UK, etc.

The first three assertions are based on a hypothesis that one or more countries would adopt defensive deterrence, and 'withdraw into their own shells', 'shunning [reinforcement or defence cooperation] obligations'.[2] I am not suggesting this. I argue that NATO as a whole should adopt defensive deterrence. Certainly unilateral adoption of defensive defence by, say, West Germany and Denmark would create severe problems for NATO as a whole if, say, the USA and UK did not agree. Their forces deployed in Germany would then have a quite incompatible strategy with the West Germans. However, concerted action by NATO as a whole towards defensive deterrence would be another matter entirely. In this case NATO would have an improved reinforcement capability and increased cooperation.

The fourth point is possibly the most serious in that defensive deterrence does fundamentally challenge the posture of the USA and the UK in Europe. This, however, is exactly the idea – to challenge and change this posture. I argue that the capability for 'force projection' in Europe is over-emphasised to the extent of being a liability. I believe that any desire by the USA to 'project' force into Eastern Europe is dangerous, much as similar attempts by the Soviet Union into Western Europe have been seen as threatening. The whole point of defensive deterrence is to limit offensive force projection whilst increasing defensive force capability. Defensive deterrence still retains tank-forces and a limited deep-strike capability. NATO could also have a rapid intervention force of a size insufficient to affect the European East–West security system significantly, but sufficient to react to possible regional threats, say in the Middle East.

Surely if defensive deterrence can safely defend Western Europe then the objection to NATO's change in posture amounts to one facing all radical ideas; the problem of gaining acceptance. No radical ideas would get off the page into reality if the fact that they challenged basic assumptions and postures was acknowledged as an overwhelming problem. Never the less, the perceptions attached to defensive deterrence are important for the chances of its acceptance or success, and care must be taken, for example, to avoid presenting defensive deterrence as anti-Americanism. I deal with this point in more detail later when I discuss the US contribution to NATO. It is crucial that NATO as a whole adopts defensive deterrence – I do not believe that the fragmentation of NATO into neutralist countries would contribute to European security unless it was accompanied by a parallel process in the Eastern Bloc.

Another fundamental criticism is that the proponents of defensive deterrence have a fundamental misunderstanding of the causes of war and that they over-emphasise the importance of technical factors. The argument runs that no war is *caused* by weapons systems predisposed to preemption but that the causes of war are always the result of political decision, although technical factors play a part in this decision. This argument is similar to the one which argues that arms races do not cause wars: they are effects of the same cause that creates the war.

But if there is a choice between two systems, one of which does not build in preemption and the need to take horrendous political decisions in minutes about whether or not to release nuclear weapons, and one which does, surely one should choose the system which avoids preemption?

Also, in a crisis, decisions can often move quickly out of the strictly political arena into an arena of the military where pre-delegated authority and predetermined strike options can powerfully pressure and channel supposedly purely 'political' decision-making. Military models also typically underestimate likely civilian casualties, leading to the presentation of a false picture to a 'political' decision-maker of the human costs of various options.

Whatever the original 'cause' of war, one should attempt to create systems of maximum dynamic stability, so that whatever the 'cause' of the conflict in the first place, the system does not have a tendency to become unstable.

Finally, defensive deterrence *is* aimed at the political causes of war and aims to enhance the political means of avoiding it by engendering good international relations and facilitating arms agreements.

Does Defensive Deterrence Go Far Enough?

There is one type of potential criticism, this time from those in favour of nuclear reductions, that defensive deterrence does not go far enough, in not asking for complete de-nuclearisation, or that it does not address possibilities for the UK or other NATO countries outside of a NATO context.

Concerning the 'acceptance' of minimum nuclear deterrence in defensive deterrence, I regard this as the most realistic political goal for the present time, until or unless international relations start to be conducted and enforced in an internationally accepted legal and moral framework. At present, in my view, international relations are based upon the politics of power and generally anarchic relations, albeit tempered by other considerations.

Unpalatable though I find it, I believe that *some* small number of nuclear weapons can have a deterrent value. In this reality, complete nuclear disarmament has to remain a very distant and uncertain goal. If deep cuts in nuclear and conventional forces are achieved, then it will be the time to reconsider more idealistic directions and goals specifically. Until then I believe that it is vital to make proposals that are politically possible within five to ten years on what will undoubtedly be a long, dangerous and arduous path towards greater security and stability. Very substantial reductions in nuclear weaponry are also needed to get anywhere near minimum deterrence levels of, say, a few hundred nuclear warheads in the possession of the USA and USSR (it has even been suggested that the United Nations should be ultimately the only possessor of this kind of number of nuclear weapons).

The consideration of substantial nuclear reductions by the United States and the Soviet Union raises questions about the arsenals of the smaller nuclear (or potentially nuclear) powers: Britain, France, China, Israel, South Africa and others.

Focussing on the French and British nuclear arsenals, these two countries are engaged in nuclear rearmament programmes involving very substantial increases in the numbers of their nuclear warheads. These programmes are increasingly anachronistic in a world where the two nuclear superpowers are now considering cuts in the START talks and where waves of strong anti-nuclear sentiment are widely prevalent on the European continent.

The unilateral removal of nuclear weapons is no longer on the UK political agenda since the Labour Party policy review. In a pragmatic sense, complete unilateralism never was on the agenda because of the lack of sufficient public support. Whether or not this remains the case will depend on any long-term opinion shifts resulting from the impact and duration of the sweeping changes in Eastern Europe. The most pragmatic path for a UK Labour Government would seem to be a judicious mixture of multilateral and unilateral (or independent) actions.

The UK as a nuclear power could wield substantial influence by challenging the NATO strategy of nuclear flexible response and by committing its nuclear forces into the relevant arms negotiations. Some independent NATO cuts of nuclear forces would also be quite appropriate to help to create a reciprocal process of nuclear disarmament with the Soviet Union.

Turning to the NATO context, I have deliberately not considered neutrality or non-alignment for Britain or other countries in NATO. With the possible exception of German neutrality, I do not consider these as realistic options in a world dominated by two major military superpowers and with a third, China, waiting in the wings.

As much as the world is now more interdependent, then military interdependence follows. I believe that if gradual demilitarisation is to come about it should proceed throughout politically opposing blocs as other trans-bloc economic and political alliances are forged. Neutrality, however, could still be an option for some countries, perhaps as a demilitarised buffer between opposing factions. Germany could be an interesting case in point, as long as it was very strictly monitored by both East and West.

Defensive deterrence could in this instance provide a suitable military framework to stabilise both East and West Germany or in some kind of East-West German buffer zone.

Such possibilities are however beyond the scope of this book. I am more concerned with pragmatically trying to seize the opportunity for reforms of NATO and the Warsaw Pact presented in recent trends and developments.

Problems with the US Contribution to NATO

US military spending in 1988 was $290bn, of which about $170bn was spent on forces in or allocated for use in Europe. This money made up over half of NATO's military spending, providing three militarily differentiable contributions to NATO:

1. 325 000 troops and associated conventional land, sea and air forces;
2. potential nuclear war-fighting nuclear weapons: nuclear artillery shells, short-range missiles and drop-bombs;
3. what is known as the strategic 'umbrella' – a promise to respond at some unspecified level of conflict in Europe with long-range (strategic) nuclear strikes upon the Soviet heartland.

The strategic nuclear 'umbrella' is rather a misnomer because if nuclear 'rain' does ever fall it can at best guarantee more of the same upon the Soviet Union. The term strategic nuclear 'threat' is far more accurate but has much less reassuring resonances.

Until early 1989 the USA made various threatening noises at various times about reducing the US contribution to NATO and with different justifications – in relation to the possibility of a unilateralist Labour administration in the UK; and in connection with allegedly low military contributions to NATO by the nations of Europe.[3] The latter has been a perennial theme as the Americans start to consider steps to cut their huge budget deficit. In Spring 1989, President Bush decided to make an opportunity of Congressional pressure to cut US troop numbers in Europe by proposing such cuts as a part of a package of NATO force cut proposals prior to the opening of the Vienna CFE talks. US military budget and troop cuts are now an accepted part of the European political landscape. The only uncertainties are questions of actual numbers and the timing.

Whether additional threats of US troop withdrawals would be specifically linked to European proposals to institute defensive deterrence is not clear. It would seem that the answer would relate to the way such proposals were seen by the Americans, whether as a tide of anti-Americanism or a lack of European commitment to their own defence, when additional US withdrawals would seem quite a real possibility, or if defensive deterrence was presented as a way of getting best value-for-money in NATO defence, in which case the USA would find the threat of additional troop withdrawals very much harder to justify.

The real questions, however, are what is in the best interest of the USA, and how will this be expressed as a result of internal politics in the USA? The Republican White House seems keen to keep US forces in Europe but the Democrat Congress will force through cuts in military spending and a gradual reduction in the budget deficit. But as I have already outlined in Chapter 7, there are many better ways of cutting US military expenditure than purely by removing troops from Europe. These other measures would however cause Congress problems with the powerful military lobby, associated various military projects and armed forces jobs spread liberally across the USA.

In my analysis, it is simply not in the US self-interest to dissociate itself from the defence of Europe. First, as long as the USA sees the Soviet Union as a potential aggressor it clearly makes military sense for the USA to have a policy of forward-basing US forces as near to the Soviet border as possible and as far from the USA as possible. This means Europe, amongst other places. Second, in Europe there is a powerful advantage in helping to maintain a friendly buffer of powerful states to assist in this operation. The USA and Europe have many common interests and objectives. This type of strategy can be seen operating in South Korea, Japan and other countries bordering the Soviet Union.

Right now, and as long as *perestroika* seems to have any chance of success, the US Administration is beginning to see that it is in its best interest to seek to influence events in the Warsaw Pact by giving monetary assistance but keeping some control over the purse-strings. This is a very powerful reason for the USA to maintain an influential position in European politics.

For all these reasons I do not think that a complete US withdrawal from Europe is a remote possibility. The only scenario in which I can see this happening is if Soviet forces also pulled right back out of Europe. But even then the USA would want to store military equipment and retain a reinforcement capability to match that of the Soviet Union.

It is unfortunate that the USA is still insisting, along with the UK, upon the maintenance of nuclear forces in Europe. As I have already argued, these forces are unnecessary and destabilising. It is in fact difficult to see how it really benefits the USA to keep the short-range weapons in Europe particularly with the strength of political opposition in West Germany, Holland and Belgium. The most obvious reason – and the least palatable from a European standpoint – is that the USA wants to retain 'limited' nuclear war in Europe as a possible option in the US Single Integrated Operational Plan (SIOP) – the US targeting options in war. Unlikely as a possibility of keeping nuclear war 'limited' to Europe may be, in the eyes of the nuclear strategists who pore over the SIOP, the retention of even a slim possibility of war limitation slightly decreases the total risk of direct nuclear strike upon the USA itself and is thus beneficial. Whether this is the correct interpretation or not, this type of interpretation is already being made in West Germany and will further focus public opposition to shorter-range nuclear weapons.

Twenty-Three Objections to Defensive Deterrence

Here I list several possible objections (some drawn from Gates, 'Non-Offensive Defence: A Strategic Contradiction?'[4] and some from Baylis in 'Britain, NATO and Nuclear Weapons'[5]) together with some refutations and answers; many points are dealt with at greater length in 'The Case for Defensive Deterrence' which follows:

1. *Defensive deterrence is vulnerable to nuclear or chemical attack.*
   So is any defence. Defensive deterrence is designed to be less vulnerable than existing defence by building increased dispersion of forces. Some of the systems used, such as 'smart' mines, are invulnerable to such attack, while the maintenance crews of fighter-bombers needed in current NATO strategy are highly vulnerable. This role would be reduced and conducted from further back behind the front line.

2. *Defensive deterrence is vulnerable to concentrated, repeated, or air attack.*
   Reserve and mobile forces would compensate for this, as would also the drastically improved defensive firepower provided by air-sown mines and the increased numbers of anti-tank weapons. Detailed calculations show that this problem can be overcome by a suitable mix of defensive forces. Concentrated tank attack actually provides a very good target for attack by smart missiles and mines sown in its path by redesignated Tornado bombers.

3. *Military reserves are not consistent with the concept of non-offensive defence.*
   This is a problem of the critic, not of the proponent. Defensive deterrence would use reserves to reinforce its non-provocative strategy. Mobilisation of reserves would no longer imply an offensive threat.

4. *Needs too much cooperation and burden-sharing for NATO to manage.*
   A real problem, but defensive deterrence is intended to reduce

the overall burden of defence upon NATO. Defence specialisation, whilst needing greater cooperation would simplify some countries' defence tasks. Defence cooperation and burden-sharing is in any case already a problem in existing NATO strategy.

5. *Defensive defence would lead to job losses: fewer tanks mean fewer jobs.*

Absolutely not the case: it is a fallacy that defence spending creates more jobs in the economy. Defence spending creates fewer jobs than can be created by equivalent spending in other sectors. This point is dealt with at greater length below.

6. *Too technical: countermeasures will undermine defensive deterrence.*

My emphasis is upon relatively simple weaponry – far simpler than the increasingly expensive, highly complex weapons systems upon which NATO increasingly depends. The retention of a mix of defensive forces also insures against any one mistake in defence procurement. Certainly one needs to avoid putting all one's defensive 'eggs' in one basket.

7. *Neglect of intentions and perceptions: assumes that Warsaw Pact is predictable.*

Defensive defence is aimed precisely at the perceptions of the Warsaw Pact, which obviously are not entirely predictable, but all the signs are that defensive deterrence would answer many Pact security concerns. They seem in fact to be making the initial moves to adopting it themselves.

8. *Defensive deterrence is too inflexible.*

Defensive defence is certainly *less* flexible. I argue that this reduced flexibility is still more than adequate for defence and is necessary to avoid the potential 'flexibility' of overt aggression.

9. *Allows aggressor to calculate costs too exactly.*

Yes, but this is no problem because the aggressor can only get a very unfavourable answer. The much vaunted 'uncertainty' built into current NATO strategy is as much a liability as a deterrent. Often it seems that NATO itself would not know what it could or might do in any given circumstance. But it is very cheeky of NATO to present, as they often do, their uncertainty, particularly concerning nuclear use, as an advantage.

10. *Gives attacker too much initiative.*

The attacker has more initiative but also a markedly reduced ability to exploit this.

11. *Defensive defence would cost too much.*

Gates even suggests that defensive deterrence would necessitate *buying* a defensive strip of land 18km deep along the 800km of the German border. I have shown how reductions in some complex and expensive systems could pay for the necessary increases in defensive capability. The idea of actually buying a strip of land is laughable. I am certainly not suggesting this any more than that NATO should purchase the entire land area of the FRG for defensive purposes!

12. *The Warsaw Pact countries would be an effective sanctuary for hostile forces.*
Not entirely. The first 40km depth would still be vulnerable to MLRS. NATO would still possess Tornado and other strike-aircraft with a deliberately reduced deep-strike capability. If large-scale force movements occurred at greater depth, the best way to deal with such forces would be as they deployed towards Western Europe and not before. Air forces would be met by increased numbers of anti-air missiles which are already, according to NATO internal assessments, threatening the whole concept of deep-air-strike by aircraft.

13. *Defensive deterrence would not deter.*
Surely it would as long as it was clear that it was workable.

14. *Defensive deterrence would expose territory to the ravages of war.*
Existing NATO non-nuclear strategy would do so just as much, however much the ritual phrases of 'forward defence' are repeated. Nuclear use would devastate and poison the FRG far more than any conceivable conventional war could do in defensive deterrence or any other strategy.

15. *The combatant – non-combatant distinction would be blurred.*
Nuclear weapons have already totally blurred this distinction, making us all hostages to the nuclear threat. In conventional war the possible increased role for civilian based forces would be a matter of individual choice.

16. *Defensive defence would provoke a Soviet build-up of offensive force to compensate.*
If this occurred it would be cripplingly expensive for the Soviet Union as offensive forces are more expensive than defensive ones. At present such a response is not within the bounds of reality and quite the reverse is happening and seems likely to continue because of the Soviet Union's very severe economic problems.

17. *Purely non-nuclear defence cannot work.*
I agree, Defensive defence allows for the retention of a minimum

nuclear deterrent or some retention of a nuclear threat capability.

18. *Territorial defence is too weak.*
    Defensive deterrence is not a form of territorial defence but is designed to be a NATO-wide strategy.

19. *Some forward strike capabilities must be retained.*
    They are.

20. *Troops charged with fighting tanks without tank support will be unable to sustain morale and will give up.*
    Towards the rear, troops would have tank support. At the front, troops would have greater foxhole protection than at present and better anti-tank weapons than now. They would also have large-scale fire-power to call upon, plus air back-up. NATO is already practising the techniques needed for this type of warfare and only the best troops would be deployed to the more forward defensive zones.

21. *The move away from forward defence will be unacceptable to the West Germans.*
    Not so much now, it would seem. The rise of the Green party and the general hostility to any military activities in Germany provides a window of opportunity for defensive defence designed to prevent any nuclear weapons being detonated on German soil and West Germany would certainly not use them first.

22. *A US withdrawal will be provoked weakening NATO's conventional forces.*
    As I have already argued, this is not in the USA's own best interests. In any case if the CFE talks are successful European forces could easily provide the reduced forces then required to face a dramatically reduced Soviet threat capability.

23. *The concept is irrelevant to the possibility of a German Confederation or a re-unification of Germany.*
    It is not. In fact, defensive deterrence would be an ideal way for the British, American, French and Russian authorities to stabilise Germany in a new strategy entirely appropriate for the 1990s.

Objections to Nuclear Reductions and Removals

The main objections are:

(i) NATO/US resistance to nuclear reductions;

(ii) French and British resistance to nuclear reductions;

(iii) the problem of nuclear 'blackmail';
(iv) arguments in favour of flexible response.

I describe the first three problems at length in the three sections which follow. NATO, US, French and UK resistance is essentially institutional and political. In my view this type of institutional resistance is the most severe of any obstacle facing the concept of defensive deterrence. It is worth highlighting that this problem is not that defensive deterrence is not a good idea, it is primarily that it is too different a security idea to be easily accepted or even initially recognised as a possible alternative by NATO as a bloc. In my view therefore, change requires either the mobilisation of political pressure to force change, or a gradual shift in the perceptions of key decision-makers over a period of time towards defensive deterrence. Despite these admittedly very severe obstacles, they are only to be expected in reaction to the radical idea of defensive deterrence. I do not believe that they are insurmountable.

The problem of nuclear 'blackmail' is answered in my proposal by the retention of some Euro-strategic nuclear weapons; see the section entitled 'A Eurobomb?' below.

I have already dealt at length with flexible response in Chapter 1, and I will not repeat these arguments. I will, however, answer some additional arguments raised by NATO spokesmen from time to time.

The NATO alliance is very resistant to *any* change and is a major obstacle to change in the direction of defensive deterrence. NATO, post-INF, and with the possibility of further nuclear reductions in the START negotiations, is still a nuclear alliance wedded to nuclear strategies. As the overwhelming number of NATO's nuclear weapons are under US command, a major influence in this attitude is the USA.

It seems likely that NATO, whilst actually reducing the numbers of its short-range nuclear arsenal (by removing 1000 nuclear howitzer shells), will continue to secretly develop a whole new generation of longer-range but still short-range nuclear weapons. A new nuclear howitzer shell and a short-range air-launched cruise missile are in the pipeline.[6] The UK, France and West Germany have also discussed specific plans to deploy additional nuclear weapons in the medium-range air-launched category not covered by INF (the INF Treaty covers only medium-range missiles actually *launched* from the ground). The original term used for such new weapons was 'compensating measures' (to 'compensate' for INF).[7] Because of unfavourable publicity and charges that this was not in the spirit of the INF

Treaty and might even threaten its ratification, the new words now in vogue are 'modernisation' or 'buttressing'.[8] And most recently 'kept up to date where necessary', a deliberately ambiguous phrase chosen by NATO drafters about which German Chancellor Kohl said it was 'for the "theologians" to speculate' as to its 'correct' meaning.[9] The phrase deliberately leaves open the questions of exactly what 'up to date' or 'necessary' mean. It is a clever way of papering over differences between NATO member-countries.

Post-INF there has been some polarisation of attitudes to proposals for further nuclear reduction in NATO member-countries. Post-INF, the UK and US administrations are strongly opposed to reductions in the remaining land-based nuclear weapons in Europe (short-range missiles and artillery) while the West German administration is deeply split on the issue. In the wake of Warsaw Pact unilateral force cuts, the UK and USA are supporting the removal of some 1000 old NATO artillery shells, providing that the Lance missile 'modernisation' (actually a replacement with a new missile of longer range) goes ahead at some time in the future (presently defined as 1992). Again, what exactly the NATO communiqué actually means has been a hotly contested issue and the NATO drafters have again brilliantly performed their job, writing a document which is 'all things to all men' – so everyone can be happy (or alternatively everybody can be unhappy if they take another country's interpretation which conflicts with theirs).

The UK government at first publicly opposed the INF Treaty, but reversed its position after strong US pressure and when INF seemed inevitable anyway. General Alexander Haig spoke of 'unprecedented levels of arm-twisting of European leaders'.[10]

The German government originally opposed the INF Treaty arguing that it would remove 'their' nuclear deterrent in the shape of Pershing-IA missiles in Germany fitted with US warheads (under the post-war 1954 Treaty of Brussels the Germans are forbidden to possess or deploy nuclear weapons). In a seeming reversal of position after the signing of the INF Treaty, and after opposing the removal of the Pershing-IAs, the German administration demanded *further* nuclear reductions – specifically, the removal of the remaining US short-range land-based nuclear weapons. With the removal of their 'deterrent' the Germans now argued that the risk of 'limited' US–Soviet nuclear war in Germany was far higher. In any such conflict, most of the nuclear artillery shells, if used, would be detonated in Germany itself, because their range is 30km or less. These weapons, however, have not been on the US–Soviet post-INF agenda because the USA (and the UK) have regarded these weapons as 'not negotiable' (the Soviets would like them included, possibly another reason for Western reluctance). Senior Western negotiators merely refer to the fact that 'it would lead to the denuclearisation of Europe' as if this were an argument in itself. The delay or cancellation of NATO short-range nuclear modernisation, however, is likely to remain a very live issue.

In France there is strong cross-party support for the independent French nuclear deterrent. This is based both on land and at sea. Along with the British, the French are very resistant to the idea that they may be asked to reduce their strategic nuclear weapons in a possible START-II negotiation or even in START-I. The British and French may thus be a substantial block to the START negotiating process at some stage.

NATO representatives and leaders often raise the idea that NATO simply could not cope with 'denuclearisation' and would 'unravel' or break-up. As much as this is a genuine fear it reveals a dangerous inflexibility in NATO. It is a clear political weakness for NATO to link its unity to some highly dangerous nuclear weapons systems in the face of a viable alternative such as defensive deterrence. Such fears are overstated and in part represent attempts by NATO leaders to maintain things as they are by threatening the worst. But NATO already has several nuclear 'dissident' members and has not broken up. The Norwegian Government has served notice that it will press for a fundamental change in NATO nuclear deterrent strategy. The Dutch Government plans to unilaterally reduce the number of 'nuclear tasks' allotted to it by NATO.[11] Denmark and Spain (a new NATO member) already refuse to allow nuclear deployments in peacetime. What is more to the point is that NATO's nuclear doctrine would be very likely to change if one of the three largest NATO factions – West Germany, the UK or the USA – were to dissent and become wedded to defensive deterrence. If this is what is meant by 'unravelling', the sooner the process starts the better.

Finally, NATO presents some basic arguments for the retention of nuclear weapons:

1. the Soviets have a range of nuclear weapons therefore NATO must have a similar range and similar numbers;
2. the need to offset conventional inferiority;
3. to force Soviet conventional forces to disperse;

4. nuclear deterrence,
5. coupling: linking the US strategic deterrent to Europe, as an expression of US commitment to Europe.

The first argument is really more an expression of a gut feeling than an argument. To deter, one needs both the capability of unacceptable retaliation and the political will to do it. Such a capability does not demand a complete range of nuclear weapons – a relatively small number of strategic warheads is quite sufficient. Most of NATO's weapons are in fact the result of other factors such as inter-service rivalry (if the navy has a nuclear weapon then the other two services have to have them) and fairly esoteric theories of nuclear war-fighting and limited nuclear war which I have already described.

NATO's professed desire for nuclear equivalence is also at odds with its stance on short-range nuclear weapons where it professes to be substantially outnumbered by Soviet systems. If NATO is genuinely concerned with a Soviet superiority in shorter-range Soviet nuclear weapons then why not agree to reduce them to zero on both sides as the Soviets (and West Germans) say they want? INF has surely shown how such an agreement could be negotiated and verified successfully.

I have already comprehensively covered the question of NATO's alleged conventional inferiority. First, the imbalance is overstated by NATO and provides no safely exploitable militarily advantage for the Soviet Union; second, defensive deterrence provides a means to offset any alleged conventional imbalance more safely than with nuclear weapons.

Concerning dispersal of Soviet forces brought about by nuclear weapons, concentrations of Warsaw Pact forces would now be very vulnerable to MLRS with a third-generation tank killing capability similar to that of nuclear weapons themselves.

I have already covered the question of nuclear 'blackmail'. NATO asserts that the threat of 'strategic' retaliation against a possible Soviet limited nuclear attack is not credible, thus NATO needs the capability of retaliation at a level just higher but still controllably higher than any Soviet nuclear aggression. This is the strategy of escalation dominance. As I explained in Chapter 1, I do not believe that this strategy could possibly work and that almost *any* nuclear use is highly likely to precipitate general nuclear war. Thus the 'requirement' for a completely graduated range of nuclear responses is based on false premises.

Finally, the need for coupling to the strategic forces of the USA does not require US short- or intermediate-range nuclear weapons in Europe: the presence of US troops is quite sufficient.

A 'Eurobomb'?
The 'Eurobomb' is the name sometimes given to the concept of an identifiably European strategic minimum deterrent – that is, one of last resort.

There are three conceivable ways in which such a deterrent can be constructed, the first two of which in my list below are already in place in Europe. Each raises different problems:

1. The US strategic nuclear deterrent. The potential problem is that in the absence of shorter-range 'non-strategic' US nuclear weapons in Europe, how is the deterrent to be guaranteed? In other words: why should the USA risk Washington for Hamburg or Berlin?
2. The British and French deterrents. How are these linked to the defence of Europe and West Germany in defensive deterrence? Would the French and British risk Paris or London for Hamburg or Berlin?
3. The Europeans provide a Eurobomb collectively. Who is to pay and how is payment to be made? How can the Germans be involved (they are not allowed to build or fire nuclear weapons)? How would the decision to fire be taken?

To answer the first suggestion, that of the retention of the US deterrent; as long as the Americans deploy almost 1 million service personnel and families in Europe, this has to be the most concrete reason possible why the Americans link their strategic nuclear weapons to war in Europe. What American President could survive the overrunning and occupation of Europe along with the loss or capture of US forces?

Concerning the second possibility: British and French nuclear weapons, whilst it is highly likely that British and French nuclear weapons would be targeted upon the USSR in the latter stages of the devastation of Europe by nuclear means, this is not particularly reassuring for West Germany which would at this time be already devastated. Thus any threat of nuclear use intended to deter attack, would have to be hypothetically triggered early on by the invasion of Germany to deter such an event in the first place. Presumably, any UK strategic nuclear use could occur at the earliest after the destruction of the British Army on the Rhine, failing the German test.

One possibility which would avoid the German problem, could arise from a continuation of gradual moves already initiated towards increased Franco-German cooperation at a nuclear level. The Gaullist approach to French defence, 'fortress France' has now been replaced by a consensus among all French political parties, with the exception of the Communists, to support French plans to throw their military forces into the support of the Germans at the start of any conflict. Plans have been revealed for a joint Franco-German defence pact which would form an effective nuclear deterrent for joint Franco-German forces commanded by a supreme French commander and with the exclusive right of nuclear release retained by the French President.[12] French political figures now talk of the Eastern defensive boundary of France being situated at the Eastern boundary of West Germany. These statements also fit in with new French nuclear weaponry which now has sufficient range to hit East Germany from silos in France and no longer has to threaten to destroy tracts of West Germany in order to defend France. Three motivations behind this modification to previous French strategy are:

1. to fight any war as far from France's borders as possible;
2. an acknowledgement from the experience of the Second World War, that because of the terrain France would be much harder to defend than Germany;
3. a desire to avoid German neutralism or pacificism leading to vulnerability on the northern French border.

The third and final possibility for a Eurobomb, would be a nuclear submarine with a mixed nationality NATO crew, with French and British officers. The use of such a weapons system could be linked practically to Germany by the existence of UK and French troops in Germany. Various possibilities exist for the nuclear launch system itself. Only a ballistic missile could guarantee hitting and obliterating Moscow because of the Soviet 'Galosh' anti-ballistic missile (ABM) system. If the inherently much cheaper option of cruise weapons were to be chosen, other major Soviet cities such as Leningrad, Kiev or Minsk could be targeted. Cruise-type weapons can also be fired from normal-sized torpedo tubes, thus considerable savings could be made by using existing nuclear-powered hunter-killer submarines. I do not think that this alternative has a remote chance of happening – nor is it desirable.

There seem to be huge problems in the path of the creation of any specific Eurobomb. In my view, the NATO objective should be to maintain the presence US conventional forces in Europe as linkage to US nuclear forces whilst pressing the British and French to commit their weapons into the START negotiating process along with US strategic forces.

It is simply not necessary to have any cast-iron guarantee of nuclear use or nuclear linkage. The Washington or London for Berlin arguments are simplistic. As long as some strategic nuclear weapons are possessed by the UK, France and the USA, or even *just* by the USA the consequences of misjudging the risk of nuclear retaliation in Europe are simply so high as to make any nuclear adventurism by the Soviet Union quite unthinkable. In the years to come it seems increasingly likely that the UK and France will seek to retain nuclear weapons using the 'other nuclear powers and threats' argument. In this case, the dangers of nuclear proliferation are likely to increase leading possibly to a 'local' nuclear war in the Middle East for example.

Considering all of these factors, the present drastic increase in the nuclear delivery capability of French and UK nuclear weapons systems is unnecessary and undesirable. The UK does not need four submarines carrying 128 independently targetable warheads each, to deter the Soviet Union, the USA, or anyone else. This is overkill by a factor of about ten times in my view. The best that can be said is that the over-capacity should encourage the UK and France to put themselves in the START arms reduction negotiations and to press for drastic reductions.

It should also be noted that all talk of a European deterrent underlines the utter irrelevance and insanity of over 90 per cent of both the Soviet and American arsenals in deterrent terms. A strategic deterrent for Europe would 'only' comprise some hundred or so warheads yet would have the capability of utterly devastating the fifty largest Soviet cities and devastating human life and economic activity in the Soviet Union.

THE CASE FOR DEFENSIVE DETERRENCE

Defensive deterrence has a potentially large constituency of suppor
across Europe. I shall now present a series of arguments which could
be used to get the case across. For those who want it in one sentence
the arguments can be summarised by saying that defensive deter
rence would be 'safer, cheaper and "greener"'.

1 Defensive Deterrence Responds to Public Security Concerns

Public attitudes to defence and security define a persistent problem
for NATO and a significant opportunity for defensive deterrence
Public opinion surveys taken in Europe consistently show support fo
NATO, support for a nuclear deterrent in countries which have one
already, but opposition to foreign nuclear weapons.[13] In Europe, thi
last-mentioned, NATO's perennial problem, means substantial op
position to US weapons and particularly to the idea of nuclea
war-fighting or 'limited' nuclear war in Europe.

Close analysis of many opinion polls taken in the UK, German
and Italy, show that people are, on the one hand, comforted by the
idea of having a nuclear capability under their own national control
but, on the other, are concerned by the idea of possibly becoming
caught up in a war between the Americans and the Russians, par
ticularly if they want to fight it in Europe. The desire for a nuclea
capability of some kind is strongly linked to existence of Sovie
nuclear weapons. Support for a nuclear capability is likely to prevai
in the already nuclear-armed UK and France as long as the Soviet
have *any* nuclear weapons.

The majority of people in Europe already accept that tactical and
battlefield nuclear weapons cannot be used to fight a war or to win
anything because they are simply too destructive, thus this element o
defensive deterrence already has substantial support.

Changes to NATO's forces to make them more capable of defence
is a complementary principle to the withdrawals of nuclear war
fighting weapons. The increased defensive capabilities of conven
tional forces in defensive deterrence would further undermine insti
tutional resistance to these nuclear removals and reductions.

The retention of last-resort nuclear deterrence in defensive deter
rence would ensure the support of the large sectors of public opinior
who desire a nuclear deterrent of some sort (as opposed to desiring a
war-fighting nuclear weapon). A nuclear deterrent also provides a

ery concrete answer to the fear of nuclear blackmail.

A growing European public concern, particularly in the Federal Republic of Germany and the UK, is the annoyance and danger of very low-flying NATO jets. Defensive deterrence would enable this type of activity to be sharply curtailed because the aircraft concerned would be progressively redeployed to a mine-laying role not requiring such extensive periods of low flying over hostile territory.

Barriers

The value of defensive barriers and fortified positions is something which can be understood by anyone. The usual argument put forward as to why there cannot be any, is that it would be seen as a symbol of the division of Germany. Another argument is the supposed failure of the French Maginot Line in the Second World War. Concerning the division of Germany, West Germany has already constructed many artificial barriers without too much outcry. They are known as urban sprawl and provide plentiful cover for defending forces and formidable obstacles to massed tank formations. The real problem with such obstacles, however, is that people live in them, although many would cease to do so rather abruptly in the case of war. Other 'natural' obstacles which slow or stop tanks are rivers, lakes, marshes, soft ground, steep defiles and woods. West Germany already has several such obstacles but an inventive German defence minister would sponsor the planting of new forests and woods across key invasion channels, and networks of small copses as cover for defending helicopters, light armour and infantry. This policy could even be used as an additional lever in the current 'acid rain' dispute between the UK and Europe over the destruction of German forests. A UK administration keen to promote NATO would not wish to be seen to be diminishing security by toxic sulphur-dioxide emissions. Recreation lakes and even artificial hills for ski-jumps could also be built to act as tank traps or strong points. It seems difficult to believe that such an active landscaping policy with all the obvious benefits to the population at large would not be popular. The Federal German Government has in fact already made small steps in this direction. German farmers in key areas can obtain grants when they are engaged in building drainage ditches as long as the ditches are at least 3m wide and 2m deep. These are the minimum dimensions for the ditch to form a substantial tank obstacle. Another piece of ancient German legislation requires that all German cellars with windows must have them positioned so that a gun can be operated from them

The Maginot Line argument is easily answered. First, the lin
stopped at Belgium and did not protect the most vulnerable flank c
France. The line was thus outflanked. Second, the defence ha
insufficient depth and insufficient mobile forces deployed behind it t
'mop up' breakthroughs.

The actual type of barrier system I propose would not in any sens
divide Germany. The barrier or defence-multiplier network would b
invisible as one drove through it as it would consist of small disperse
dug-outs, underground pipes and existing copses and villages. In wa
the system would need to rely upon its invisibility for its success an
would only become visible to an aggressor very late as undergroun
pipes exploded and accurate concentrated fire devastated attackin
forces.

3 Defensive Defence would Reduce Soviet Perceptions of Threat

A Soviet fear is that a greater political role for West Germany i
NATO could, in less favourable circumstances, lead to a new re
surgent, powerful and aggressive Fourth Reich. Germany is rapidl
becoming a major economic force. In twelve years, at the predicte
rates of growth of national economies, the FRG alone would hav
outstripped the Soviet economy and rank third in the world after th
USA and Japan. Extrapolations for an economically unified Ge
many show a similar or even stronger position. The Soviets remem
ber the bitter fighting in the Eastern Front in the Second World Wa
an attack which was mounted by a Germany which had been sup
posedly disarmed between the wars. The Soviets, looking at th
present-day Germany, see the largest and best-equipped army i
NATO.

A defensive option leading to an increased role for West German
– particularly the deployment of more German forces to key areas c
the front such as the North German Plain and the Fulda Gap fror
southern Germany – could be politically destabilising because of th
Soviet perception of a stronger German presence in these sectors
This problem could be sidestepped if German forces were to form th
backbone of the network defence-in-depth elements of a new Eurc
pean defence strategy. This would have the very desirable effect c
actually increasing the European defensive capability in key attac
avenues while diminishing a prime Soviet fear and a strong moti
ation or justification for large Soviet forces in East Germany. Th

iermans are natural contenders for network defence because de-
enders can be deployed in familiar home territory which it is their
pecial responsibility to defend and where they would have the best
pportunity to develop the necessary defensive-network infrastruc-
ure based upon an intimate knowledge of their area.

The Soviets would Take a NATO Strategy of Defensive Deterrence Very Seriously

1 their search for a new strategy of defensive sufficiency, much
oviet analysis has focused upon great battles of the 1941–5 Great
atriotic War – the fight against Hitler's invading Panzer divisions.
ne of the decisive battles of the Second World War was the battle of
1e Kursk bulge on the Eastern Front in the Summer of 1943 which
nally broke the German Eastern offensive. The Soviet strategy was
ased upon defence in depth (some 150km deep) comprising tank
aps, coordinated fire zones, fortifications and dug-in positions for
very Soviet tank and artillery piece. These defences were backed by
1obile forces poised for counter-attack. It is important to note
owever that the overall Soviet strategy in this battle was defensive.
ad the Nazis declined to attack the Soviet defences, the Soviets
ould have been unable to throw them back. The battle was a case of
1e attacker losing by reason of being forced to expose his forces to
ghly unfavourable local combat conditions despite very concen-
ated German attacks across very narrow sectors of front.[14] This is
recisely how defensive defence aims to defeat an attack.

Defensive Deterrence Could Be Adopted by the Soviet Union

is in the Soviet Union with its highly centralised system of control
at it has been shown that change can occur most quickly. Mikhail
orbachev has sufficient flexibility of approach to consider radical
2w approaches to defence and foreign policy. There is no objective
2ason why the Soviet Union or more particularly, Soviet forces in
ast Germany should themselves not adopt defensive deterrence.
he aim is clearly defensive, which is the stated aim of the Warsaw
act as it is of NATO. Also the Soviet goals of the control of
ermany and the fostering of good relations with the West would be
1hanced. The initial Warsaw Pact concept was 'sufficient' defence,
hich did not necessarily build-in non-provocative structural modifi-
ations to military strategy – see the Budapest Declaration of the

Warsaw Pact in July 1986, for example.[15] In his speech to the United Nations Assembly on 7 December 1988, Mikhail Gorbachev clarified the Soviet view somewhat. Along with his announcement of a two year programme of cuts in Soviet armed forces in Europe, he stated

> All Soviet divisions . . . in the territory of our allies are being reorganised. Their structure will be different from what it is now after a major cut-back in their tanks it will become clearly defensive.[16]

This reorganisation, along with numerous Soviet force withdrawals should be complete by the end of 1991 at which time it will be possible to assess the new posture of Soviet and Warsaw Pact forces in Europe

Speaking more generally about Soviet forces, Gorbachev spoke of 'maintain[ing] our country's defence capability at a level of reasonable and reliable sufficiency', which is similar wording to 'reasonable sufficiency'. He also spoke of a project to draw up plans to convert two or three defence plants to civilian production during 1989.[17]

The Soviet Union is geographically better situated than the West to adopt the concept of defensive zones. The Soviets already have ample defensive depth (in the sense of separation from the West) in the shape of East Germany, Czechoslovakia and Poland. A Warsaw Pact system of defensive defence could afford to have much deeper zones than in the West which would in turn mean a deeper withdrawal of mobile armoured forces. Opposition should however be expected from East Germany, Poland and Czechoslovakia which would obviously not wish to become merely a forward defence zone for the Soviet Union. Another problem is the Soviet lag in precision guided munition technology which at present means that the best Soviet anti-tank weapon is probably another tank.

6 Defensive Defence: The Strategy for the 1990s

Defensive defence is a modern, realistic approach to defence in an age where, because of nuclear weapons, overt war is simply too dangerous to fight. Defensive defence would break free of the strait jacket in the military mind in Europe which has prevailed in Europe since the Second World War and which, in my view, would lead eventually to a Third World War. Defensive defence would put conventional defence firmly back in the political arena, where the im would be primarily to avoid war, to avoid creating the perception of the feasibility of swift victory, and if war came, to slow it down, log it up, and to delay to the very last the use of nuclear weapons.

Clausewitz in his famous dictum described war as an 'extension' of politics by other means. Non-offensive defence takes this dictum to its logical conclusion by making the political objectives of a defence policy the priority, and by modifying the military strategy accordingly. In the modern age when war is too dangerous to start and any idea of winning has to be abandoned because of the existence of nuclear weapons, the primary requirement of a defence strategy must be to avoid fighting in the first place and if hostilities were to occur to avoid escalation and a quick violent war at all costs.

Defensive Deterrence Could Be More Democratic

With the abolition of the need for politically unacceptable nuclear war-fighting strategies, strategy could be debated more in the open and be more responsive to public security concerns. Decision-making could become more open and accountable without the present over-dependence on nuclear weapons and strategies. Any politician seeking to bring in defensive deterrence would gain much popular support by a commitment to open decision-making and a Freedom of Information Act based on the American system.

For continental European armies, defensive defence could partially integrate the defence of an area into the community. After training, soldiers assigned to a particular area or role in the defensive net would retain these specific skills and knowledge relating to their geographical area or role. By such increased specialisation by geographical area and specific defence role, each soldier in his or her task would have an advantage over invaders unfamiliar with the terrain and who did not know where the dispersed, camouflaged dug-out positions and communications networks were. One hopes that this approach would help to ensure not only the understanding, but also the support, of the defensive strategy by the general public, thus creating a more truly democratic defence. This would be a distinct advantage over the present situation where the armed forces are generally quite separate from the people they are there to protect, and public understanding of their particular strategy and role is usually very limited, and in the case of battlefield nuclear weapons, positively hostile. There might also be an increased potential role for women soldiers which would neatly help to solve Germany's

manpower shortage in the 1990s (although there is a problem with the
German constitution which does not permit women front-line soldiers).
Although with CFE cuts this 'problem' will be solved anyway.

8 Defensive Deterrence Could Enhance the Arms Control Process

At present, there is a new impetus to new negotiations in Europe
discussing conventional force limitations. Both East and West find
difficulties in negotiating reductions in some of their military capabilities, tanks, bombers, personnel and so on, because they see these
as compensating for the offensive capabilities of their opponent.
Defensive defence would however enable negotiating trade-offs to be
made between offensive and defensive capabilities. Thus reduction
in tanks could be negotiated, while, as a safeguard, an increased
anti-tank capability was brought in. This would facilitate reduction
in more offensive weaponry and encourage structural changes in
armed forces leading to increased security. This is a very important
point. Arms reductions do not necessarily increase security. A more
fundamental requirement is *to increase the stability of the total East-
West conflict system*, together with reductions (see the Appendix for a
more academic treatment of this subject). Defensive deterrence
would be a catalyst for changes of this nature and would be the first
example of military technical innovation *enhancing* the arms control
process rather than bypassing it. By tagging on to the arms control
process which already has substantial momentum and credibility
defensive deterrence could quickly become an important issue and
would be a powerful mechanism for influencing change. Specific
measures suggested for NATO in defensive deterrence, such as a
more defensive role for Tornado and diversion of resources to more
defensive measures, would also be useful bargaining counters for
NATO in negotiating reductions in Soviet tank forces. I give an
agenda for change in my final summary and conclusions.

9 Defensive Deterrence Would Not Breach the Geneva Conventions

Defensive deterrence would be more humane and not be in flagrant
breach of the Geneva Conventions as the use of nuclear weapons in
anger would be. By sensible choice of weapons, some of the needless
casualties caused by modern conventional weapons could be avoided
(quite apart from reducing the likelihood of the use of nuclear

weapons). One good example which often causes public concern, is that of minefields and the accidental injuries caused after a conflict. The latest mines can be set to disarm themselves automatically after a pre-set time. This also makes the defenders' task easier: only they would know when a minefield had become inactive. One make of mine, after its active time expires, disarms itself and then 'surrenders' by sending up a white marker. It can then be re-set and re-used if required. Not only does this avoid needless civilian casualties, but also substantial savings can be made in time clearing unwanted minefields and by multiple re-use.

0   Defensive Deterrence is a Lower-Risk Strategy

One could argue that in the absence of nuclear weapons, West Germany would be open to devastation by conventional means and that the absence of a forward-defence policy would leave large tracts of German territory near to the front open to such devastation. This is, however, an unfortunate fact of life and defence. There *is* no absolute defence and risks have to be balanced one against the other. In any analysis, the worst-case consequences of even the most savage conventional war (excluding chemical and biological weapons) would have far less severe consequences than even a relatively 'limited' nuclear exchange in Europe. In my analysis non-offensive defence would reduce the *overall* risk of war significantly not only because the likely consequences would be limited to the sub-nuclear as long as possible, but also that the *likelihood* of war would be reduced now and for the future below the present levels.

A key point is that the risk of nuclear escalation would be drastically reduced and the new nuclear posture would be entirely consistent with the negotiation of drastic cuts in nuclear arsenals worldwide.

1   Defensive Defence Could Create Jobs

It is not the case that a diversion of the effort of the military-industrial sector to greater production of precision-guided munitions would mean reduced profits or job losses. Quite the reverse. Because of the larger quantities of far cheaper PGMs required, high-volume product runs would mean sharply reduced manufacturing costs and increased industrial productivity. The diversion of resources would also be less capital-intensive and more labour-intensive creating additional jobs

overall. Outside the arms industry, considerable numbers of job:
would be created over a period of 10–15 years in construction an(
light engineering for projects reguired for the defensive network.

The diversion of defence expenditure to other sectors of th(
economy would, pound for pound, create additional employmen:
and furthermore help to create structural employment based on :
real need not the distortion of the economy by defence spending
Defence spending is an inefficient mechanism for direct job creatio:
because of the capital-intensive nature of defence work compare(
with many other sectors and the unrealistically high prices ofte:
charged for military equipment. In the UK defence budget no les
than *50 per cent* of equipment costs (£3–4bn in 1988) may arise fron
unforeseen cost overruns.[18] This makes the jobs supported by thi
military production 50 per cent more expensive than the more con:
petitive private sector.

An extensive programme of research is still required to investigat(
the best ways of creating greater product diversification in the mili
tary sector and thus greater job security.

One possible mechanism would be to impose a tax on militar:
profits to fund research into diversification along the lines of th(
Swedish model and possibly to insist upon a minimum proportion o
non-military production in all companies obtaining defence con
tracts.

12 Defensive Defence is Good Value for Money

An important but simple point in favour of the less complex new
technology weapons which makes a powerful argument, is that the
cost a fraction of that of the complex high-technology systems such a
modern fighters, bombers and main battle tanks which they ar
intended to destroy. Such systems are becoming an expensive liabilit
on the modern battlefield. Rather than continually resisting change
NATO and the Warsaw Pact could advantageously make a virtue o
innovation and in the process increase defensivity and stability.

Small reductions in offensive capability can pay for large and mor
militarily useful increases in defensive capability. Tornado is a goo
example.

Between them, and counting aircraft still on order, the UK and th
Federal Republic of Germany will have 585 Tornado aircraft. A mer
10 per cent reduction in these forces would release approximatel

£1000 million (such a reduction could be achieved by cancelling some aircraft on order and cutting the replacement programme – however, as orders are progressively filled, savings from Tornado will be increasingly hard to find). This would be sufficient to build sufficient dispersed defensive obstacles and buried pipes along 1000km, sufficient to cover key potential invasion routes. At a reduction in Pact invasion capability of 40 per cent, calculated by the Brookings Institute, this network would be worth the equivalent of twenty-four to forty-eight Soviet divisions or twelve to twenty NATO divisions – a value which would far outstrip the most optimistic assessment of the likely impact upon the battle of the 58 planes removed. In fact many of these planes are only needed because NATO expects to lose so many in its hazardous deep-strikes behind Pact lines. In the face of such arguments, one has to ask whether NATO is seriously interested in getting best value for money or whether it is because Air Force lobbies are so powerful that they can obtain such huge financing for so costly an effect. Such financial contrasts display a phenomenon which is militarism for the sake of militarism, not the achievement of military objectives by the most effective means. 60-ton tanks and £24m aircraft are very good for status and prestige. Launched (like Tornado) to the accompaniment of classical music and swirling laser special effects, they may also be very good for arms manufacturers profits, but they may not be very good for fighting a modern war against smart munitions. That such options are chosen, when simple, cheap but not very 'sexy' measures are not, is a sign of a malaise in NATO, linked to the military-industrial complex which has been dubbed 'baroque'. A major advantage of defensive deterrence would be that it would challenge NATO's decadent military procurement and purchasing policy.

13 Short-range Nuclear Weapons are Obsolete

The USA has ordered 400 000 multiple-launch rocket system (MLRS) rockets for deployment in Europe at a cost of $4000m for 276 launchers. The lethality of one MLRS twelve-rocket salvo (with a Phase III warhead packing) will be comparable in its effect upon a tank battallion with that of a nuclear 'tactical' warhead. Taking twelve MLRS rockets as equivalent to one neutron shell, the equivalent nuclear fire-power of these MLRS rockets is no less than 33 000 nuclear-enhanced radiation (neutron) warheads. The UK- and

German-planned additions to the MLRS inventory (some 167 500 rockets on 305 launchers) will add a further 14 000 'equivalent' neutron shells. These numbers make NATO's 2000 or so shorter-range nuclear howitzer shells seem quite irrelevant in terms of their military 'usefulness'. And MLRS is being deployed with scarcely a murmur of hostile public opinion, in sharp contrast to nuclear deployments. MLRS, if ever used in anger, would also cause much less 'collateral' damage – i.e. kill far fewer civilians, and would certainly cause no radiation. In the face of such arguments, NATO's remaining justifications for the continued deployment of shorter-range nuclear weapons in Europe are vanishingly slender and could become increasingly seen as such by the public at large if the argument was publicly exploited.

Regrettably, all the indications are that NATO intends to use the MLRS-launcher as the vehicle for its next generation of short-range nuclear weapons. If this takes place, it will have two very adverse consequences:

1. all MLRS would have to be counted as nuclear weapons, immensely complicating arms control;
2. the potential defensive conventional use for MLRS and any chance of public support would be lost.

14 Diverting Human and Material Resources to Productive Ends

The NATO–Warsaw-Pact confrontation represents a major diversion of the world's resources away from peaceful and productive enterprises. The combination of restructuring towards defence and cuts in the scale of the East–West confrontation could liberate $200 000 000 000 ($200bn) (30 per cent savings from 50 per cent force cuts – see Chapter 7), or even more out of the combined $700 000 000 000 ($700bn) military budgets of NATO and the Warsaw Pact. Large though these sums of money are, the resources which would be freed would be far more than money – 2–3 million people (ex-military personnel), 20 per cent of scientists and engineers (40 per cent currently work on military and related research and development) and immense material consumption and industrial capacity.

This represents a massive potential for domestic industrial regeneration. Economists are increasingly making the link between high military spending and poor economic and industrial performance.[19] There is also a very clear and strong international dimension. If

NATO and the Warsaw Pact can reduce their military spending in this way whilst still adequately defending themselves and regenerating their economies then so can everyone else.

There is another intriguing possibility. The World Watch Institute has prepared a 'Hypothetical Budget for a Ten-Year Global Effort of Sustainable Development'.[20] It would require an annual budget of $140bn (20 per cent of current US, NATO and Warsaw Pact annual military expenditure) to fund six interconnected programmes:

1. tree planting and topsoil protection;
2. forest replanting to help to reduce the present atmospheric build-up of carbon dioxide – a major contributor to the greenhouse effect;
3. a programme to slow population growth in developing countries so as to improve development prospects;
4. energy efficiency programme to reduce carbon-dioxide emissions and to reduce dependence upon oil and coal;
5. renewable energy research programme to complement the energy efficiency programme;
6. debt relief: Third World countries often have to spend crippling sums on debt repayments.

Add similar spending upon domestic economic regeneration and social spending, and one has a programme with something for everyone. It would benefit both the more developed and the developing countries. The First world would benefit from the new markets opened up by the regeneration of the Third World economies as the burden of debt, population growth and environmental damage was gradually lifted. Reafforestation, energy efficiency and renewable energy programmes would benefit everyone by slowing and ultimately reversing global warming. More trees would absorb more carbon dioxide and renewable energy would reduce the production of carbon dioxide by the inefficient burning of coal and gas in power stations, industry, homes and offices. Spending in the domestic sectors would have obvious direct benefits.

It is difficult to dismiss the programme as Utopian and idealist because it is so sensible and so tuned to the needs of the world we live in today. It is also in harmony with a growing environmental movement which increasingly sees the links between the protection of the environment, nuclear weapons and the scale of military spending. Such a programme clearly needs refinement and discussion but it has the potential to obtain a high degree of public support judging by the growing public awareness of global environmental problems and the large sums donated by individuals to appeals to avert starvation in the Third World.

The political potential of such a programme can also be judged by a new espousal of 'green' issues by the Conservative UK Government. As yet UK governmental support is largely limited to rhetoric and does not address problems such as the Third World debt crisis and population pressure. Never the less there does appear to be a growing international tide towards consideration of these issues and prospects and possibilities in arms control could provide the remaining part of the unsolved equation – the money.

9 Agenda for AD 2000

What follows is an agenda for East and West which I consider to be a consistent, positive approach towards practical realistic improvements in security for the next millennium. The agenda suggests how security could be greatly enhanced and arms spending drastically cut as reforms towards defensive deterrence complement the revitalised arms control process.

A period of 5–10 years seems a realistic time in which to press for and to anticipate substantive change bearing in mind the inertia of NATO and the Warsaw Pact military systems. Major weapons systems programmes take 10 years to come to fruition; money has to be diverted from existing replacement programmes; military manuals need rewriting; retraining and reorganisation has to take place.

Probably even more importantly than this there has to be a change in long-established modes of thinking.

The agenda largely involves a much more positive approach to nuclear and non-nuclear arms control and certain direct actions which are not currently the subject of negotiations. The adoption of some measures has already been called for by the Soviet Union which carries the implied benefit, if agreed by the West, of achieving multilateral action without the need for protracted negotiations.

In the UK, the espousal of the programme would require either a significant change in approach to security issues in the present Conservative Government or a change of Government to Labour (and still some changes of approach in the latter case).

Both are possibilities. President Reagan is a recent example of a Right-wing politician who in his latter days of office chose to adopt quite a positive approach to some aspects of defence and disarmament with the dual goals of going down in history as a peacemaker and diverting attention from domestic political problems.

If a Labour Government were to be elected after 1992, Labour would face a host of priorities amongst which defence could take a relatively low profile. This would be a mistake in my view because it would miss a great opportunity to free much finance for the domestic spending on which a new Labour Government would wish to embark. It is also vital that a programme of defensive deterrence be taken up wholeheartedly and not purely as a compromise between nuclear deterrence and conventional defence. Labour has often fallen into the trap of proposing cuts in nuclear forces while promising to spend more on conventional forces. This is a fundamental mistake, and quite unnecessary in defensive deterrence.

There is a clear opportunity for the peace movement, particularly large-membership organisations such as CND (now suffering some contraction), providing that they can adopt a more politically pragmatic approach and espouse defensive deterrence. The strength of the campaign opposing cruise and Pershing-II missile deployments in the early 1980s was due to the adoption of clear, short-term objectives. Now, in the early 1990s, defensive deterrence can provide a framework for the espousal of clear short-term campaign objectives, this time linking into the new initiatives in arms control. Intelligent external public scrutiny of the arms control agenda, combined with political pressure, has a very real chance of achieving positive results.

ACTIONS WHICH SHOULD BE TAKEN WITHOUT DELAY

Conventional Forces

1. The negotiation of a draft first-stage CFE agreement.
2. Meetings between NATO and Warsaw Pact military to discuss and to clarify military doctrines.
3. Continued phased withdrawals of Soviet forces from Eastern Europe (I suggest at a rate sufficient to achieve numerical force parity with NATO by the year 2000 should negotiations fail). The destruction or disposal of tanks or their conversion to prime movers for construction projects to take place in conditions where official and unofficial Western observers can verify the process.
4. The UK and West Germany to cancel outstanding Tornado orders and planned replacement programmes towards a goal of a 10 per cent reduction in the numbers of Tornado (greater cuts could be possible within the CFE process).
5. NATO to redesignate 50 per cent of Tornado to aerial mine-laying operations.
6. Negotiations to be called between NATO and the Western European Union (WEU) with the objective of establishing how a more rearward basing of main operating bases (airfields) could be achieved (French and British bases could have a key role to play, hence the suggested involvement of the WEU forum).

7. Main battle-tank orders and replacement programmes to be restructured with the goal of achieving 10 per cent cuts in armoured forces (unless progress in the CFE Talks results in a need for greater cuts).
8. The UK to cease all military research and development without European collaboration except for very small projects. A collaboration goal of at least two other European partners to be sought for all projects.
9. All equipment procurement to be negotiated on a fixed contract price basis with time-overrun penalty clauses.
0. A NATO collaborative project to be set up to write force goals for a NATO system of defensive defence in West Germany. As part of this process, all planned NATO military equipment procurement programmes to be reassessed so as to appraise their applicability in a possible future system of defensive deterrence. The role of national defence specialisation within NATO to be assessed.
1. The European Fighter Aircraft project to be scrapped or substantially cut back.
2. Procurement of anti-tank and anti-aircraft missiles and sophisticated aerially sowable anti-tank mines to be stepped up as savings from the other cuts come on-stream.
3. NATO grants and military aid to be made available for programmes of tree planting and protection, and an active landscaping programme (ski slopes, artificial lakes for water-sports and nature reserves, preservation of swampland areas and so on) across key sectors of the German front.

ub-strategic Nuclear Weapons

4. Cancellation of all work and spending upon 'modernisation' of all sub-strategic nuclear weapons. Specifically: ground- and sea-launched nuclear weapons with ranges shorter than 5000km (this includes the ATACMS for the MLRS). Cancellation of all work upon air-launched nuclear weapons where the combined air-combat radius and missile radius is less than 2500km (this includes practically all the known air-launched missile programmes with the exception of the stealth cruise). The UK not to accept the SRAM and the UK deployment of US air-launched nuclear weapons. Britain to urge the US to start negotiations upon the reduction or removal of short-range nuclear weapons (SNF). The

so-called 'Third Zero' (the Soviets have already called for such talks). An initial negotiating goal for discussion could be the reduction to about 100 weapons each, in parallel with the CFE talks followed by the complete elimination of these weapons after CFE.

Strategic Nuclear Weapons

15. The UK and France to facilitate the START-I negotiation process by freezing their independently targetable warhead numbers at their 1980 levels. The UK could achieve this by limiting the Trident submarine fleet to three rather than four submarines and the blanking-off of thirteen of the sixteen missile tubes, or with a lower warhead packing per missile. This measure would at least acknowledge the force of the arguments made by many smaller nations considering the acquisition of nuclear weapons. Basically, the UK position is that no new countries should obtain nuclear weapons whilst it is all right for the UK to maintain and increase its own. This is widely seen as a hypocritical position particularly as the UK is a signatory to the Non-Proliferation Treaty which contains a clause affirming a goal of complete and general nuclear disarmament.

16. The UK to open talks with the French, Chinese and other smaller nuclear powers with a view to facilitating a second-stage (START-II) agreement (further cuts of 50 per cent), at which time the smaller nuclear powers cannot expect to remain aloof from the arms-cuts formula and should act to enhance it. The UK should also press the US to accept the narrow interpretation of the Anti-Ballistic Missile Treaty (this is important to avoid an arms race in space).

17. The setting up of a Strategic Arms Initiative for Disposal (SAID) to study means of safe and verifiable dismantling, disposal or monitored storage of weapons-grade material. This is needed for START to be successful.

Nuclear Testing

18. The French to cease the environmentally hazardous nuclear testing in the South Pacific immediately.

19. The Soviet Union to restart a unilateral halt to underground

nuclear testing with the goal of negotiating a worldwide complete test-ban treaty.

20. Britain to declare its support for a test-ban treaty and support for talks to discuss a complete halt to the production of weapons-grade nuclear-fissile material at some future date.

21. Britain to support the amendments proposed in the Test-Ban Treaty Amendment Conference (basically the non-nuclear countries which have signed this Treaty along with the UK, France, the USSR and the US, have only agreed not to develop and test nuclear weapons providing the nuclear powers disarm). This Treaty represents a major international agreement which can pressure towards nuclear reductions.

ACTIONS WHICH MAY BE POSSIBLE AFTER CFE-I

In this time-frame I assume that NATO and the Warsaw Pact have negotiated force parity in the CFE talks. I also assume that some progress has been made in the START negotiations.

Conventional Forces

22. Further talks to be undertaken or the CFE talks to be extended to a second phase (CFE-II?) with the goal of achieving 50 per cent cuts in conventional forces in Europe (that is, 10 000 tanks, and possibly some 700 000 soldiers and 3000 aircraft each for example)

23. A UN Commission to be set up consisting of NATO, Non-Governmental Organisations and Third World Countries to formulate a world development programme utilising 25 per cent of the savings in military expenditure or a 'no-strings' commitment of a minimum of 1 per cent of GNP per NATO and Warsaw Pact country (the latter as already passed by UN Resolution but not fulfilled by many countries).

24. NATO and the Warsaw Pact to progressively implement a strategy of defensive deterrence. Specifically the establishment of a 'tank-free' corridor across central Germany; the pull-back of forward-based aircraft, ammunition, fuel, and bridge-crossing equipment, conversion of some infantry divisions to light infantry and tank divisions to mechanised divisions, the adoption of

defence-role specialisation by certain NATO countries.

25. NATO to allocate 75 per cent of its aircraft to ground-force support operations such as ground and sea mine-laying.

Sub-strategic and Strategic Nuclear Weapons

26. By this time there should be an agenda for the phased reduction, possibly to zero, of short-range nuclear weapons from Europe.

Strategic Nuclear Weapons

27. The continuation of talks to achieve a further reduction of 50 per cent (START-II) including French, UK, Chinese and (possibly) other nuclear powers' forces (Israel, South Africa, India, etc.?).

GENERAL CONSIDERATIONS

It is important that the new unification of the European Community (EC) does not lead to the strengthening of Western Europe as an economic bloc at the expense of Eastern Europe.

It may be economically impractical for Hungary or Poland to join the European Community for some time but economic mechanisms should be sought to enable such moves as soon as a good measure of economic and political stability seems reasonably assured.

It is important that any economic aid to the Soviet Union and Warsaw Pact linked to economic reform packages does not repeat the sorry history of the provision of debt to the Third World – that is, crippling debt and an inappropriate development. Ideally, the Soviet Union should develop its own strategies for reform. A US-style capitalist economy may be entirely inappropriate, while socialist cooperative economic models which have been used with much success in Italy and in Spain may be more relevant.

Dr Sakharov warned of the inherent danger in the Soviet Union of centralisation of power without adequate constitutional checks and balances. The massacre of 4 June 1989 in Tiananamen Square in Beijing, China, was a salutary reminder of the great danger of the fundamentally undemocratic nature of the centralisation of power. Ethnic unrest in the Soviet Socialist Republics contains the same dangers of a reactionary backlash in the Soviet Union. But for all this it would be monumental folly not to press ahead at the maximum speed for defence cuts and military reforms.

10 Conclusions

I have tried to focus on one fundamental question: what type and level of military forces will best secure long-term security in Europe? The best answer I have has three parts:

- both NATO and the Warsaw Pact must cease to deploy sub-strategic nuclear weapons in Europe;
- conventional forces must be mutually cut to at least half of the numbers currently deployed by NATO;
- a new defensive strategy must be adopted.

If President George Bush is sincere about 'changing the military landscape of Europe' and Mikhail Gorbachev equally sincere about creating a 'common European home' this is the minimum that is necessary.

Without substantial cuts in conventional forces the NATO countries will not be able to make any substantial cuts in defence spending of the type needed to have any major economic benefit.

Without cuts in sub-strategic nuclear weapons, any severe crisis will contain the seeds of escalation to the destruction of Europe, America and the Soviet Union.

Without adopting defensive deterrence, or something like it, East and West (particularly NATO) will not be able to cut their forces in a way which will assure greater stability and security.

There is one, final, important question. In Agenda for AD2000, I have indicated a 5–10 year timetable for the reforms which I am proposing, assuming that the political will exists and pressure for change continues. How likely is such change to come about?

I think there are reasons for optimism. Much of the pressure for NATO and Warsaw Pact reform over the last few years, has been linked to the warming of East–West relations. But it seems likely that NATO and the Warsaw Pact will continue to experience pressure for change whatever the state of relations. In NATO when East–West relations are good and the threat from the East fades, the burden of everyday military exercises and training – low-flying jets, tanks exercising over farmland and in forests – reluctantly accepted in a Cold War, becomes unacceptable. These are very significant factors in West Germany and an increasing issue in the UK, both key

NATO-members. If relations are poor, as in the Cold War of the early 1980s, NATO's policy of nuclear deployment whilst negotiating for nuclear arms control, is seen as unnecessary escalation of tension and brinkmanship in a world where numbers of nuclear weapons are already excessive.

In the Soviet Union and in the countries of eastern Europe, there is an overriding pressure to cut military spending for economic reconstruction.

The idea of defensive deterrence allows a further important conceptual shift. It is now no longer possible for NATO or the Warsaw Pact to argue that there is no alternative. There is. If NATO and the Warsaw Pact had already instituted a system of defensive deterrence, a sudden decline in East–West relations would no longer pose the immediate fear of imminent invasion or nuclear escalation in a crisis. These possibilities would have been built out of the system.

With defensive deterrence added to the melting-pot of a restructuring Europe, it is now possible to consider a vision of Europe where, just as the possibility of armed conflict between Britain and France, or France and Germany, no longer seems a possibility, the idea of East–West European conflict is increasingly remote. A vision in which the present levels of armed forces in Europe – even half current levels – seem irrelevant, obsolescent or positively counterproductive to European security needs.

Si Pacem Vis, Para Aequilibrium
If you want peace build a stable balance
An appropriate saying for the third millennium

(Thanks to Trevor Davies for the Latin translation)

Appendix: The Topology of Crisis Stability and the Arms Control Process

Reductions in arms, even balanced reductions in arms, do not necessarily increase crisis stability. The important criterion is whether or not either side (considering two possible combatants or 'sides') can gain any decisive advantage by attacking or firing first. It they can, the system tends to instability in a crisis.

Topology is a branch of mathematics which deals with geometrical and spatial relationships. Here I have tried to use topology to represent two potential aggressors (A and B) and thus to draw up a model for crisis stability or instability and to see how various arms control or defensive reform measures such as defensive defence may affect the situation.

In Figure A.1, if either A or B attacks first the attacker gains a large initial advantage (for example, if A attacks, the strength of B reduces very quickly in comparison with A's losses). How the progress of the conflict develops is shown by following either of the two lines for A or B attacking first. The

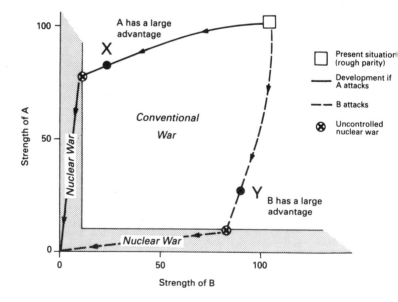

Figure A.1   An unstable system

218

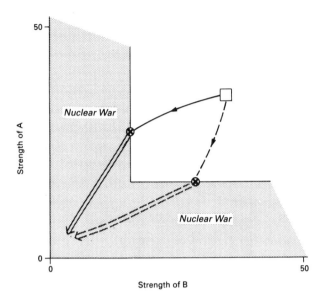

Figure A.2 An unstable system after some conventional disarmament

system is unstable if either *A* or *B* thinks that he might be able to get away without a nuclear war – if the war stopped at *X* or *Y* for example. If the war does 'go nuclear' then both *A* and *B* reduce to zero and there are no victors.

If both sides partially disarm conventionally, the situation is no safer – see Figure A.2.

Let us now consider an initially stable system. In Figure A.3, *A* attacking first makes initial losses which are quickly regained. Thus the system is stable for a conventional conflict before the point at which the lines cross over. Past the cross-over point *X*, *B* might try to resort to nuclear use, in which case neither wins.

Point *X* marks the situation after some conventional disarmament. Now the attacker always gains an advantage in a conventional conflict. The system has thus become conventionally unstable after disarmament. The nuclear 'threshold' is also closer – that is it would be crossed after less conventional conflict.

Finally, a system of defensive defence (Figure A.4). Now neither *A* nor *B* gains any advantage in attacking first. In the longer term, both sides tend towards a conventional stalemate. Most importantly, after conventional *offensive* reductions, the defence still retains the advantage and there is still no advantage for either *A* or *B* in attacking first.

In topological terms defensive defence has changed the shape of the *AB* defence–offence surface so that the defence is tactically superior, whilst in the longer term no decisive advantage can be obtained for either side.

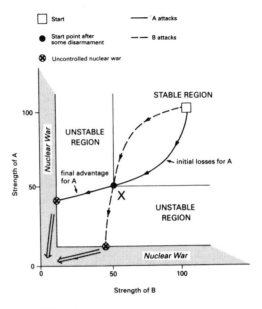

Figure A.3   An initially stable system

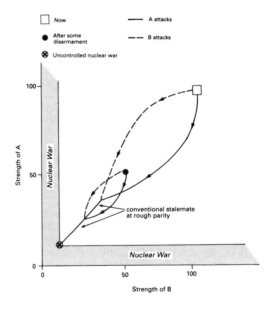

Figure A.4   A system of defensive defence

Notes and References

Introduction

1. 'When historians review 1988, they may well see it as the year in which the Cold War ended', *Strategic Survey 1988–89* (London: IISS, 1988); to 'end the epoch of wars, confrontations and regional conflicts', General Secretary M. Gorbachev; 'a kinder and gentler world', President George Bush; 'We're not in a Cold War now', Prime Minister M. Thatcher; these last three quoted by Safer World Project, *Agenda for Action*, August 1989.
2. Mandate for Negotiation on Conventional Armed Forces in Europe, Vienna, 9 January 1989.
3. *Effects of Nuclear War on Health and Health Services* (Geneva: World Health Organisation, 1988) 2nd edn, summary, p. 23; Annex 2, P. J. Crutzen, *Climatic Effects of Nuclear War*, pp. 65–82; Annex 4B, B. Levi and F. von Hippel, *Limited Attacks on the United States and the Soviet Union*, pp. 101–20; Annex 4C, A. Ottolenghi, *Limited Nuclear War in Europe*, pp. 121–32. (J. Rotblat, ed., Annex 4).
4. Mandate for Negotiation on Conventional Armed Forces in Europe.
5. *Report of the Secretary of Defense to the Congress: Fiscal Year 1989*, (Washington, DC; Government Printing Office) p. 242.
6. *Report of the Secretary of Defense to the Congress: Fiscal Years 1988 and 1989*, also Freeman, *Written Answer*, 3 February 1988 (London: Hansard, Cmnd. 669).
7. General Secretary M. Gorbachev, Address to United Nations Assembly, Official Text, 7 December 1989. Also see M. Gorbachev, *Perestroika: Our Hopes for Our Country and Our World* (London: Collins, 1987).

1 Problems with Nuclear Strategies

1. General J. R. Galvin (SACEUR) 'The Continuing Value of Flexible Response and Forward Defence', *RUSI Journal*, Summer 1988, pp. 5–9.
2. P. J. Bracken, *The Command and Control of Nuclear Forces* (New Haven: Yale University Press, 1983) see particularly ch. 5, 'The Special Problems of War in Europe'; R. Ned Lebow, *Nuclear Crisis Management: A Dangerous Illusion* (New York: Cornell University Press, 1987); A. B. Carter, J. D. Steinbruner and C. A. Zraket (eds) *Managing Nuclear Operations* (Washington, DC: Brookings, 1987); D. Ball, *Controlling Theatre Nuclear War* (Canberra: Australian National University, 1987) working paper no 138.
3. IISS, *The Military Balance, 1987–88* (London: IISS, 1987); *Jane's Defence Weekly*, 26 September 1987, p. 648; T. B. Cochran, W. M. Arkin and M. M. Hoenig, *Nuclear Weapons Databook, Vol. I* (Cambridge, Massachusetts: Ballinger, 1984).
4. *SCOPE-ENUWAR Report* (Washington, DC: Scientific Committee on

Problems of the Environment – Environmental Consequences of Nuclear War, 1985 and subsequent updates); also P. J. Crutzen in *WHO Report*, 2nd edn, Ref. 1, Introduction.

5. P. Pringle and W. Arkin, *SIOP: Nuclear War from the Inside* (London: Sphere, 1983) pp. 17 and 170–1.
6. B. G. Blair, 'Alerting in Crisis and Conventional War', ch. 3 of Carter, Steinbruner and Zraket (eds) *Managing Nuclear Operations*, pp. 75–120.
7. R. K. Betts, *Surprise Attack: Lessons for Defense Planning* (Washington, DC: Brookings, 1982) p. 86.
8. M. Walker, 'US downgrades Russian threat' quoting classified US report, *Guardian*, 30 November 1989.
9. S. D. Sagan, 'Nuclear Alerts and Crisis Management', *International Security* (Spring 1985) vol. 9, pp. 122–5.
10. Private NATO briefing, 17–18 April 1986, NATO SHAPE HQ, Mons and Brussels, Belgium.
11. S. Gregory, 'Nuclear Command and Control in NATO', Ph.D. thesis, University of Bradford, UK, Section 1.4, unpublished.
12. 'Wir Europaer sollen uns opfern', 'We Europeans had to be sacrified' *Der Spiegel*, nr 17, 24 April 1989; 'Die Raketen Krise Kriegsspiele der Amerikaner', 'American wargame missile crisis', *Der Spiegel*, no 18, 18 May 1989.
13. O. Greene, P. Lewis, private communications following briefings at NATO SHAPE HQ, Autumn 1987, Winter 1988.
14. T. Gervasi, *Soviet Military Power: The Annotated and Corrected Version of the Pentagon's Guide* (London: Sidgwick & Jackson, 1988).
15. Field Manual no 100–5; HQ, Department of the Army, Washington, DC, 1982; 'The Air–Land Battle and Corps 86 TRADOC Pamphlet 525–5' (Fort Monroe, Virginia:: US Army Training and Doctrine Command, 1986) (the TRADOC pamphlet was originally dated 1981, but has a Foreword by General D. A. Starry, dated 1986).
16. B. F. Schemmer, 'No NATO C3I Check-out Counter', *Armed Forces Journal International*, December 1982, p. 92.
17. Field Manual 100–5, p. (i) Preface.
18. TRADOC pamphlet 525–5 (see note 15 above) p. 14.
19. Field Manual 100–5 (see note 14 above) Sections 7–12.
20. *Conventional–Nuclear Operations, Reference Book 100–30, vol. I* (Fort Leavenworth, Kansas: US Army and General Staff College, 6 August 1976) p. 99.
21. Ibid, p. 103.
22. WHO Report, 2nd edn. (see Introduction, note 3, above) pp. 23–4.
23. See note 11.
24. The Air–Land Battle and Corps 86 TRADOC 525–5 (see note 15 above) pp. 14–15.
25. L. V. Sigal, in J. D. Steinbruner and L. V. Sigal (eds) *Alliance Security NATO and the No-First-Use Question* (Washington, DC: Brookings 1983) p. 111.
26. D. Starry (General, US Army Commanding) testimony before House Armed Service Committee, March 1983.
27. Cochran, Arkin and Hoenig, *Nuclear Weapons Databook, Vol. I*, p. 111

28. US Congress, Committee on Armed Services, *Hearings on Appropriations for the Fiscal Year 1980* (Washington, DC: Government Printing Office, 1979) p. 841.
29. Vice Admiral R. F. Schoultz, cited in Blair, 'Alerting in Crisis and Conventional War'.
30. Ibid, p. 95.
31. D. Ball, 'Nuclear War at Sea', *International Security*, Winter 1985/6, p. 23.
32. Ibid, p. 26.
33. Ibid, pp. 4–5.
34. *New York Times*, 6 July 1975.
35. D. Fouquet, 'Superpowers "Moving Towards Maritime Unilateralism"', *Jane's Defence Weekly*, 3 June 1989, p. 1036–7; M. Delaere, 'Will SLCMs be Next in East–West Missile Cuts?', *Jane's Defence Weekly*, 29 July 1989, p. 160.
36. See Delaere, 'Will SLCMs be Next in East–West Missile Cuts?'.
37. General B. Rogers, capitulation 'within days not weeks', *International Herald Tribune*, 26 October 1984; Congressman J. Courter, 'capitulation to conventional attack within 12 to 18 days', *Military Review*, June 1987, p. 7; General F. Kitson, 'it would cost NATO a lot more money than it spends at present to make sure of seven days', *Warfare as a Whole* (London: Faber & Faber, 1987) pp. 15–18 (this quote p. 15); 'High risk for NATO after 7–10 days', Congress Budget Office, *US Ground Forces: Design and Cost Alternatives for NATO and non-NATO Contingencies* (Washington, DC: Government Printing Office, 1980); General Wolfgang von Altenburg, Head of NATO's Military Committee, 'NATO could not sustain a conventional war for more than a few days', quoted in *Jane's Defence Weekly*, 6 June 1987.
38. *New York Times*, 30 October 1984, p. 3.
39. W. Pincus, reporting on House of Representatives Committee on Defense, *Washington Post*, 21 July 1982; US Congress, Senate Committee on Armed Services, *DoD Authorization for Fiscal Year 1983* (Washington, DC: US Government Printing Office, 1984) Part 7, p. 4334.
40. 'Important plans should be capable of being implemented within a period of 7 days and their most vital elements within 48 hours, because events could move so rapidly towards war that no longer warning period could be relied upon', Home Office, *Emergency Planning Guidance to Local Authorities*, Section 2.5, 'Planning Assumptions' (London: HMSO, 1985).
41. R. H. Ullman, 'The Covert French Connection', *Foreign Policy*, no 75, Summer 1989, pp. 3–33.
42. T. Catterall, 'War Game "Idiocy" Fires Kohl Reserve', *Observer*, 30 April 1989.

2 The Armed Bureaucracy

1. *Report of the Secretary of Defense to the Congress*, Fiscal Year 1989, (Washington, DC: Government Printing Office, 1988); *Jane's Defence Weekly*, 12 December 1987, p. 1342.

2. *Financial Times*, 2 April 1985.
3. C. Holshek and B. F. Schemmer, *Armed Forces Journal International*, December 1983, p. 38; also D. M. Abshire, 'A Resources Strategy for NATO', *NATO's 16 Nations*, October 1985, pp. 62–71.
4. *Atlantic News*, 10 June 1989, p. 1.
5. Debate in US Senate, 21 June 1984.
6. Ibid, Senator John Towers.
7. A. Gooch, *Daily Telegraph*, 31 May 1989; J. Steele, *Guardian*, 31 May 1989.
8. *Wall Street Journal*, 14 June 1984.
9. *SIPRI Yearbooks*, 1983, 1984.
10. As note 7 above.
11. Report of the Defense Burdensharing Panel, Committee on Armed Services, US House of Representatives, August 1988.
12. *Atlantic News*, 17 October 1984, p. 2; I. Kemp, 'NATO: Disarming Itself?', *Jane's Defence Weekly*, 13 May 1989, p. 857.
13. *Flight International*, vol. 123, 15 January 1983, p. 109.
14. Holshek and Schemmer, *Armed Forces Journal International*, December 1983, p. 92; *Jane's Defence Weekly*, 3 October 1987, p. 754.
15. *Atlantic News*, no 1571, 11 November 1983.
16. *Atlantic News*, 19 April 1985.
17. B. F. Schemmer, 'NATO's New Strategy: Defend Forward But STRIKE DEEP', *Armed Forces Journal International*, November 1982, pp. 52–68.
18. *Guardian*, December 1987.

3 Pandora's Arsenal

1. North Atlantic Assembly, Military Committee, Interim Report of the Subcommittee on Conventional Defence in Europe, Brussels, November 1984, p. 22; Defence Planning Committee, in *NATO Communiqués 1984*, Brussels 1984; 'NATO Selects Emerging Technology', *Aviation Week and Space Technology*, 16 April 1984.
2. J. Courter quoting General B. Rogers, NATO SACEUR, in *Military Review*, June 1987, p. 6.
3. 'ERA penetrating HOT 2 warhead on schedule', *Jane's Defence Weekly*, 24 September 1988, p. 729.
4. 'EWP – a success story unfolded', *Jane's Defence Weekly*, 24 September 1988, p. 731.
5. N. Cook, 'Boeing develops helicopter killer', *Jane's Defence Weekly*, 22 April 1989, p. 702.
6. For an early review see R. Sherman, 'MLRS: The Soldiers System' *NATO's Fifteen Nations* (Special edn) January 1980, pp. 145–51; also, General B. W. Rogers, '"Strike Deep": A New Concept for NATO' *Military Technology*, May 1983, pp. 38–50; M. Hewish, 'Attacking Targets beyond the FEBA: NATO needs new weapons', *International Defense Review*, August 1984, pp. 1053–66; C. Foss, 'European MLRS Deliveries in 1990', *Jane's Defence Weekly*, 25 June 1988, p. 1311; *Military Technology*, special supplement to vol. xiii, September 1988, 46pp.

7. S. Budiansky *et al.*, 'One Shot One Kill: A new era of smart weapons', *US News and World Report*, 16 March 1987, pp. 28–35.
8. C. F. Foss, 'European MLRS deliveries in 1989', *Jane's Defence Weekly*, 25 June 1988, p. 1311.
9. *Armed Forces Journal*, November 1982, p. 61; see also *International Defense Review*, August 1984 p. 1063.
10. *Report of the Secretary of Defense to the Congress: Fiscal Year 1988* (Washington, DC: US Government Printing Office) p. 160.
11. *Armed Forces Journal*, November 1982, p. 63; see also T. J. Jackson, 'Precision Guided Munitions for the US Artillery', *Military Technology*, December 1985, pp. 44–54.
12. K. Watmann, 'Follow On Forces Attack (FOFA) and Emerging Technologies', *Military Technology*, no 2, 1986, pp. 28–35; also see J. Courter, Note 2, and B. Rogers, Note 6.
13. 'NATO's New Strategy: Defend Forward but STRIKE DEEP', *Armed Forces International*, November 1982, p. 55.
14. *Armed Forces Journal*, November 1982, p. 62.
15. M. Urban, 'RAF's £890m bomb "might not work"', *Independent*, 16 December 1988.
16. 'RAF go-ahead for anti-radar drone', *Jane's Defence Weekly*, 4 March 1989, p. 351.
17. *Report of the Secretary of Defense to the Congress, Fiscal Year 1988* (Washington, DC: US Government Printing Office) p. 162.
18. 'UK anti-shelter decision in April', *Jane's Defence Weekly*, 22 October 1988, p. 986.
19. D. Plesch, 'NATO's New Nuclear Weapons', BASIC Report 88–1, January 1988, BASIC, London, p. 14. Also Report 90.2, 1990.
20. *Report of the Secretary of Defense to the Congress; Fiscal Year 1989* (Washington, DC: US Government Printing Office) p. 237.
21. Ibid, p. 213.
22. 'Advanced Cruise Missile – First Picture', *Jane's Defence Weekly*, 11 March 1989, p. 379.
23. *Observer*, 3 November 1985; *Guardian*, 18 December 1987 and 1 March 1988.
24. *Military Technology*, September 1988, p. 46.
25. B. F. Schemmer, *Armed Forces Journal International*, November 1982, pp. 70–2.
26. R. Simpkin, 'Countering the OMG', *Military Technology*, March 1984, p. 90.
27. Ibid, pp. 82–92.
28. B. F. Schemmer, 'Soviet Technical Parity in Europe Undermines NATO's Flexible Response Strategy', *Armed Forces International*, May 1984, pp. 80–94 (specific quote p. 87).
29. Ibid, editorial, 'Three Threats NATO's Not Addressing', pp. 86–7.
30. J. Keegan (ed.) *World Armies* (London: Brasseys, 1983, 2nd edn).
31. The Federal Year 1983, US Department of Defense Program for Research Development and Acquisition, statement by the Hon. R. D. De Lauer, Under Secretary of Defense for Research and Engineering, 97th congress, second session 1982, pp. 11–21.

32. *Report of the Secretary of Defense to the Congress: Fiscal Year 1989* (Washington, DC: US Government Printing Office) p. 105.
33. *Jane's Defence Weekly*, 26 March 1988, p. 573; *Guardian*, 17 March 1988.
34. D. Fouquet and N. Cook, 'US F-llls set for UK to fill INF gap', *Jane's Defence Weekly*, 2 July 1988, p. 1335; M. Walker, 'New US Missiles "Will Breach Pact"', *Guardian*, 17 March 1989, quoting US General Ronald Yates giving evidence before a congressional sub-committee.
35. J. Matousek, The Impact on the Social Environment of a War with "Conventional" Weapons', *Scientific World*, vol 33, no 1 pp. 14–18, 1989.
36. Private communication with Soviet and Hungarian military officers, Budapest, 1986.

Part III Towards a New Direction in Defence

1. P. R. Webber, in M. S. Kirby and S. Robson (eds) *The Militarisation of Space* (Brighton: Wheatsheaf, 1987); also W. Perry, ex-chief Pentagon scientist, reported as saying that Mr Reagan's proposed 'astrodome' system will not stand up to critical scrutiny and public debate, *Guardian*, 28 March 1988; Professor E. Salpeter (consultant to the US Defense Department for over 30 years), 'a cruel hoax on the American Public' and 'a black mark for science', *American Association for the Advancement of Science*, Boston, 12 February 1988, reported in *Guardian*, 13 February 1988.
2. R. Simkin, 'Countering the OMG', *Military Technology*, March 1984, p. 84; W. W. Kaufmann in 'Alliance Security and the No-First-Use Question', (Washington DC: Brookings, 1983); also numerous private discussions with NATO and WEU analysts and experts, 1986–9.
3. IISS, *The Military Balance 1987–88* (London: IISS, 1987) p. 229.

4 The Numbers Game

1. See Chapter 1, Note 37 (this volume); Also Lt. Col. M. G. Tweed, 'As is well known, the Warsaw Pact forces are likely to outnumber NATO forces by as much as three to one. Locally they will be able to achieve much higher levels of force superiority', *NATO's 15 Nations Special*, vol. 1, 1980, p. 136.
2. 'The Land of Hope and Gorbi', *Sunday Times*, 18 June 1989; *Newsnight*, BBC2, 12 June 1989. In West Germany, March 1987 50–60 per cent of those polled thought Gorbachev a 'trustworthy person'. By June 1989, 90 per cent trusted General Secretary Gorbachev and 58 per cent trusted President George Bush. There was a majority in favour of West German neutrality.
3. M. Gorbachev, address to UN Assembly, 7 December 1988; M. Moiseyev (Chief of General Staff and First Deputy Minister of Defence in the USSR), quoted in *Jane's Defence Weekly*, 8 April 1989, p. 611.
4. B. Starr, 'Pentagon Confusion over Soviet Tank Data', *Jane's Defence Weekly*, 20 May 1989, p. 523.

5. (GKL): K. Gottfried, H. W. Kendall and J. M. Lee, '"No First Use" of Nuclear Weapons', *Scientific American*, vol. 250 no 3, March 1984.
6. (MBFR): J. Sharp, 'Mutual Force Reduction Negotiations', Annals of Pugwash 1983, published as *The Arms Race at a Time of Decision* (London: Macmillan, 1984) pp. 148–56.
7. (UK): *Statement on the Defence Estimates, Part I, 1985*, HMSO Cmnd. 9430–I.
8. (IISS): 'Conventional Force Comparisons' in *The Military Balance*, London: IISS.
9. (NATO 84a): 'NATO and Warsaw Pact Force Comparisons', (Brussels: NATO 1110, 1984) 2nd edn.
10. (NATO 84b): 'Western Defence: The European Role in NATO', Eurogroup, 1984.
11. (NATO 88a): 'Conventional Forces in Europe: The Facts', NATO, November 1988.
12. (NATO 88b): 'Enhancing Alliance Common Security', NATO Defence Planning Committee, December 1988.
13. CFE data released January 1989.
14. (NATO 82) 'NATO and Warsaw Pact Force Comparisons', (Brussels: NATO, 1982) 1st edn.
15. 'Whence the Threat to Peace', (Moscow: Military Publishing House, 1984) 3rd edn.
16. T. Gervasi, *The Myth of Soviet Military Supremacy* (London: Harper & Row, 1986); M. Chalmers and L. Unterseher, 'Is There a Tank Gap?' Bradford School of Peace Studies Peace Research Report no 19, 1984; (also see *International Security*, Summer 1988, pp. 5–49).
17. see note 8
18. Italian White Paper on Defence, 1985.
19. J. Keegan (ed.) *World Armies*, (London: Brasseys, 1983), 2nd edn.
20. Ibid; Rear-Admiral (retd.) Gene La Rocque, quoted.
21. J. Mendelsohn and T. Halverson, *Bulletin of the Atomic Scientists*, March 1989, pp. 30–40 (quote on p. 33).
22. M. Emch, *International Defence Review*, no 2, 1985 p. 147.
23. *Red Star, Krasnaya Zvevda*, Spring, 1984.
24. US Defense Intelligence Agency data 1985; Chalmers and Unterseher, 'Is There a Tank Gap?'; D. C. Isby, 'Weapons and Tactics of the Soviet Army'. (London: Jane's 1988).
25. *Jane's Defence Weekly*, 26 March 1988, p. 573; *Guardian*, 17 March 1988.
26. As note 16.
27. V. Suvorov, *The Liberators: My life in the Soviet Army* (Berkeley: University of California Press, 1988); see also V. Suvorov *Inside the Soviet Army*, (London: Hamish Hamilton, 1982).
28. Professor J. Erickson, Centre for Defence Studies, Edinburgh University, private communication.
29. R. Simpkin, 'Countering the OMG'. *Military Technology*, March 1984, p. 84.
30. 'Warnings on Armed Forces Day', *Jane's Defence Weekly*, 25 March 1989. p. 523.

31. R. K. Betts, 'Surprise Attack: NATO's Political Vulnerability' (quoting L. Aspin). *International Security*, Spring 1981, p. 147.
32. As Note 22.
33. G. N. Thompson, *Jane's Defence Weekly*, 4 April 1987.
34. *Daily Telegraph*, 23 June 1984.
35. Col. R. C. Martin, 'Warsaw Pact Modernisation: A Closer Look', *Parameters*, vol. XV, no 2, Summer 1985.
36. Private communication from NATO source.
37. I. Murray, 'Lined up for the Scraphead'. *Times*, 12 May 1989; Major General McKenzie, 'The Counter Offensive', paper given at Senate House, London, July 1989.
38. P. E. Tyler and R. J. Smith, 'Study Finds NATO War Plans Outdated', *Washington Post*, 29 November 1989.

5 Battlefield Europe

1. A. A. Sidorenko, *The Offensive: A Soviet View* (Moscow: 1970) ch. 1.
2. Field Manual 100–5: Operations (Washington, DC: Department of the Army) 1 July 1976, p. 1–1; also IISS, *The Military Balance*, 87/88.
3. J. J. Mearsheimer, 'Why the Soviets Can't Win Quickly in Central Europe', *International Security*, Summer, 1982, pp. 3–39; also J. J. Mearsheimer, '*Conventional Deterrence*' (Cornell University Press, 1983).
4. 'NATO's Central Front', *Economist*, 30 August 1986, p. 22, 'if the NATO's conventional forces could hold out for two weeks they could hold out forever.'
5. W. W. Kaufmann in J. D. Steinbruner and L. V. Sigal (eds) *Alliance Security and the No-First-Use Question*, (Washington, DC: Brookings, 1983) pp. 66–7.
6. 'highly risky undertaking for either side', *Military Balance* (London: IISS, 1985/86, 1986/87) p. 225. In the 1988/89 *Military Balance* the IISS used the words 'high risk enterprise with unpredictable consequences', p. 235.
7. On 24 March 1985, US Military Liaison Mission officer Major Nicholson was shot dead by Soviet guards while allegedly taking pictures of a tank in a prohibited zone in Eastern Germany.
8. Major J. B. A. Bailey, 'The Case for Pre-placed Field Defenses', *International Defense Review*, no 7, 1984, pp. 887–92; and 'Pre-placed Hardened Field Defenses', *British Army Review*, no 72, August 1982.

6 Non-Nuclear Defence: Basic Principles

1. General Sir Hugh Beach (former Master-General of the Ordnance and former Deputy Commander-in-Chief of the UK Land Forces) in A. J. Pierre (ed.) *The Conventional Defense of Europe: New Technologies and New Strategies*, (New York: Council on Foreign Relations, 1986).
2. Brigadier D. M. Pontifex and Colonel E. A. Burgess, *British Army Review*, no 35, August 1970.
3. G. Brossolet, *Essai sur la non-bataille* (An essay on non-battle) (Paris: Berlin, 1975).
4. H. Afheldt, *Pour une defence non suicidaire en Europe* (Toward a

Non-suicidal Defence in Europe) (Paris: Editions la Decouverte, 1985); also *Vierteidigung und Frieden – Politik mit militarischen Mitteln* (Defence and Peace – Politics with Military Means) (Munchen und Wein: Hanser, 1976, Defensive Verteidigung (Reinbeck bei Hamburg: Rowohlt, 1983).

5. SAS (Studiengruppe Alternative Sicherheitspolitik – Study Group on Alternative Security Policy): Landstreitkrafte zur Verteidigung der Bundesrepublik Deutschland – Ein modell fur die neunziger Jahren, SAS: Strukturwandel der Verteidigung – Entwurfe fur eine konsequente Defensif: Land forces for the Defence of the Federal republic of Germany; in SAS *Outline for a Consistent Defence* (Cologne-Opladen: Westdeutscher Verlag, 1984) see also L. Unterseher, *Spider and Web: the case for a pragmatic defence alternative* (Bonn: SAS, 1989).

6. E. Boeker, 'Defence in a Peaceful Europe', *ADIU Report*, March/April 1987.

7. E. Afheldt, 'Verteidigung ohne Selbstmord, Vorschlag fur den Einsatz einer Leichten Infanterie' (Defence without Suicide, proposals relating to a mode of deployment of light infantry), in *Praxis der defensiven Verteidigung* (The Practice of Defensive Defence) ed. C. F. von Weizsäcker (Hameln: 1984); also H. Afheldt, *Pour une defence non suicidaire en Europe* (Paris: 1985) Editions la decouverte, p. 109.

8. 'On Reactive Defence Options', Institut fur Angewandte Systemforschung und Operation Research, Hochschule der Bundeswehr Munchen, Bericht Nr. S-8403, November 1984.

9. R. K. Huber and H. W. Hofmann, 'Gradual Defensivity – An Approach to a Stable Deterrent in Europe?', *Operational Research*, 1984, pp. 197–211.

10. H. W. Hofmann, R. K. Huber and K. Steiger, 'On Reactive Defence Options – A Comparative Systems Analysis of Alternatives for the Initial Defence against the First Strategic Echelon of the Warsaw Pact in Central Europe', in R. K. Huber (ed.) *Modeling [sic] and Analysis of Conventional Defense in Europe: Assessment of Improvement Options* (New York and London: Plenum, 1986), pp. 97–140. 'Conventional Defense in Europe' is the proceedings of a workshop entitled 'Long-term Development of NATO's Conventional Forward Defense' held in Bonn, 2–4 December 1984 and held by the German Strategy Forum (DSF).

11. R. D. de Lauer (former US Under Secretary of Defense for Research and Engineering) 'Emerging Technologies and their Impact on the Conventional Deterrent', in A. J. Pierre (ed.) *The Conventional Defense of Europe: New Technologies and New Strategies* (New York: Council on Foreign Relations, 1986).

12. J. Williamson, *Jane's Defence Weekly*, 11 July 1987, pp. 23–5.

13. *Report of the Secretary of Defense to the Congress: Fiscal Years 1988 and 1989* also, Freeman, Written Answer, 3 February 1988, Hansard (Cmnd 669).

7 Non-Nuclear Defence: A System for Europe

1. 'No First Use', (Cambridge, Massachusetts: Union of Concerned Scientists, 1983) p. 28.
2. Major J. B. A. Bailey, 'The Case for Pre-placed Field Defenses', *International Defense Review*, no 7, 1984, pp. 887–92; and 'Preplaced Hardened Field Defences', *British Army Review*, no 72, August 1982.
3. W. W. Kaufmann in John D. Steinbruner and Leon V. Sigal (eds) *Alliance Security: NATO and the No-First-Use Question* (Washington, DC: Brookings, 1983) p. 65.
4. An 'RAF Official Source', quoted in *Harrier V/STOL Report* (London: British Aerospace, 1984) p. 2.
5. D. Stanley, 'Hidden Defences versus Armoured Assault', *Jane's Defence Weekly*, 9 May 1987.
6. D. Gates, 'Area Defence Concepts: the West German Debate', *Survival*, July/August 1987, p. 315.
7. Ibid, p. 312.
8. Quoted in R. D. De Lauer, *The Conventional Defence of Europe: New Technologies and New Strategies* (New York: Council of Foreign Relations, 1986), ed. A. J. Pierre, p. 63; also see: 'Final Report of the Defense Science Board Summer Study on Urban Warfare' (Washington, DC: Office of the Under Secretary of Defense for Research & Engineering) January 1985.
9. D. Gates, 'Area Defence Concepts', p. 302.
10. 'NATO's Central Front', *Economist*, 30 August 1986, p. 19.
11. N. Cook, 'Sweden's Defence Budget: Expanding into the 1990s', *Jane's Defence Weekly*, 23 May 1987, p. 1019.
12. *Jane's Defence Weekly*, reporting on NATO's Defence Planning Committee, 6 June 1987.
13. UK Defence White Paper 1988 Vol 2 Defence Statistics, table 2.2, p. 9.
14. ESECS (European Security Study): 'Strengthening Conventional Defence in Europe: Proposals for the 1980s' (New York: St Martin's Press, 1983).
15. F. L. Heisbourg (Director, IISS. 1987) 'Conventional Defence: Europe's Constraints and Opportunities', in A. J. Pierre, (ed.) *The Conventional Defence of Europe* pp. 71–7 (see note 1, Ch 6).
16. D. Greenwood, 'Economic Implications: Finding the Resources for an Effective Conventional Defence', in S. Windass (ed.) *Avoiding Nuclear War* (London: Brasseys, 1985) pp. 77–86.
17. S. Canby, 'Strategy: The Impact of Technological Change', paper presented at the IISS 30th Annual Conference, September 1988.
18. *New Directions For NATO: Adapting the Atlantic Alliance to the Needs of the 1990s*, A joint report of Institute for Resource and Security Studies, and Institute for Peace and International Security, (Cambridge, Massachusetts) December 1988, pp. 34–6.
19. As note 14.
20. Ibid.

The New Defence

1. Niccolo Machiavelli, *The Prince* ('New Principalities') translated by W. W. Marriott (London: Dent, 1958) Everyman's edn, pp. 29–30.
2. D. Gates, 'Non-Offensive Defence: A Strategic Contradiction?', Institute for European Defence and Strategic Studies, occasional paper no 29, 1987: specific quote see p. 34.
3. US threats: Richard Burt, US Ambassador in Bonn, FRG emphasised the links between trade friction and US willingness to maintain US troops in Europe, Munich Defence Symposium, 2 February 1987; General Bernard Rogers, such (Labour) policies would 'cause the United States to withdraw its forces from Western Europe', speaking in Brussels on 2 March 1987, quoted in *Guardian*, 3 March 1987; Charles Price, US Ambassador to the UK, 'they [the US] simply ought to remove our troops', 2 February 1987, reported in *Guardian* newspaper.
4. As note 2.
5. J. Baylis, in K. Booth and J. Baylis, *Britain, NATO and Nuclear Weapons* (London: Macmillan, 1989) chs 8, 9 and 10.
6. Material released under the US Freedom of Information Act: *Observer*, 22 February 1987, and *Guardian*, 23 February 1987.
7. 'compensate': NATO High Level Group meeting, Norway, 14–15 May; Monterey, California, November, 1987. See also note 19, ch. 3.
8. 'modernise': Final Statement of the NATO Summit 2–4 March 1988; 'buttress': General John Galvin SACEUR, speech at the Centre for European Policy Studies Brussels 30 July 1987.
9. Chancellor Kohl, quoted in *Jane's Defence Weekly*, 12 March 1988 p. 446.
10. 'arm twisting': debate between George Bush and Al Haig, Huston Conference Center, BBC1 Six o'Clock News, 29 October 1987.
11. *Guardian*, 25 February 1987.
12. *Guardian*, 22 January 1988, 'France to Sign Defence Pact with Germans'; 14 January 1988 'Hands Across the Rhine'.
13. Marplan Poll conducted in UK, France, West Germany, Italy, 16 February 1987, and reported in *Guardian* newspaper; 'General Report on the Alliance and Public Opinion', North Atlantic Assembly Civilian Affairs Committee, rapporteur Mr G. Astori, September 1987, NAA International Secretariat, Brussels; See also report of same title published October 1989, rapporteur Mr J. Genton.
14. G. Zhukov, Marshal of the Soviet Union, in *Reminiscences and reflections*, vol. 2 (Moscow: Progress Publishers, 1985) pp. 158–210.
15. Warsaw Pact Budapest Declaration of July 1986; S. Shenfield, 'In Quest of Sufficient Defense', *Détente*, vol. 11 1988, pp. 26–9; L. V. Sigal, 'Conventional Forces in Europe: Signs of a Soviet Shift', *Bulletin of the Atomic Scientists*, December 1987, pp. 16–20; D. Senghaas, 'Conventional Forces in Europe: Dismantle Offense, Strengthen Defense', *Bulletin of the Atomic Scientists*, December 1987 pp. 9–11.
16. M. Gorbachev, Address to 43rd session of the United Nations General Assembly, 7 December 1988.
17. Ibid.

18. '50% of UK Budget Going on Excess Costs', *Jane's Defence Weekly*, 19 March 1988, p. 493.
19. P. Kennedy, *The Rise and Fall of Great Powers*, (London: Collins, 1988); M. Oden in *Bulletin of Municipal Foreign Policy* (Irvine, California Autumn 1988), pp. 10–15.
20. *State of the World: 1988*, Worldwatch Institute (New York: Norton & Co, 1988). See also: *New Directions For NATO: Adapting the Atlantic Alliance to the Needs of the 1990s*, A joint report of Institute for Resource and Security Studies, and Institute for Peace and International Security, (Cambridge, Massachusetts, USA) December 1988, pp. 50–3.

Index